I0586437

Frederick James Crowest

The Story of British Music

From the earliest time to the Tudor period

Frederick James Crowest

The Story of British Music
From the earliest time to the Tudor period

ISBN/EAN: 9783337036454

Printed in Europe, USA, Canada, Australia, Japan

Cover: Foto ©ninafisch / pixelio.de

More available books at **www.hansebooks.com**

THE STORY

OF

BRITISH MUSIC

*(FROM THE EARLIEST TIMES TO THE
TUDOR PERIOD)*

BY

FREDERICK J. CROWEST

AUTHOR OF
'THE GREAT TONE POETS,' 'MUSICAL ANECDOTES,'
ETC

LONDON
RICHARD BENTLEY AND SON
Publishers in Ordinary to Her Majesty
1896

[All rights reserved]

PREFACE.

THIS is an attempt to tell the story of British music. Wide and comprehensive as the scope of English literature undoubtedly is, we have hitherto been without a book dealing specifically with the birth and growth of English music. Histories of music almost rival the planets in number, but they are for the most part singularly unlike the heavenly bodies in the light they throw upon that aspect of the divine art concerning which every Briton would naturally desire information—namely, the history of the music of his own country. I know of no work which deals at all adequately with the rise and progress of the art as found and practised in England, the nearest attempt at anything of the kind being the late Sir Frederick A. Gore Ouseley's brief, and necessary, additions to Naumann's 'History of Music.' Yet the subject of England's music deserves ample treatment.

To remedy such a state of things, I several years back devoted my attention to the present work, the first instalment of which is now given to the public. I have not attempted a learned book, but one which will, I hope, possess interest not alone for the many thousands of students and workers who are musical, but also for that far larger section of general readers who profess to know nothing of music. My aim throughout has been to tell a connected, simple story, free from technicalities, so that all who will may read and learn something concerning the glorious past, and the excellent present status and promise, of musical England.

I must, I fear, confess that the ground covered by the present volume, while being the most sterile in material and facts, is also—and I am fully sensible of it—the least interesting period over which my narrative will extend. But better things are in store, and the good wine will be kept until the last. My next volume will take us into that genial region, the Elizabethan period, wherein native musical art burst into its fullest glory. Then comes the Victorian era, during which so much has been accomplished for music in this country by our gracious Sovereign and her Royal Consort, the late Prince Albert, as well as by other members of the Royal Family. All this must be told ere our story is complete ; and I shall be glad to receive any suggestions and information from those interested in this national matter which will tend in any way to the better interest or telling of the narrative.

THE AUTHOR.

24, AMPTHILL SQUARE,
LONDON, N.W.,
December, 1895.

CONTENTS

STORY OF BRITISH MUSIC

INTRODUCTION.

BRITAIN'S first musical breathings! Dear must such be to all who love Old England; for in these earliest **Pre-** artistic symptoms lie the germs of much of **historic.** that happiness that pervades every home, whether palace or cot, in the land to-day, where cultivated music is a factor in the round of daily life. And what circle is now without its music?

The story of musical England cannot be soon told; nor for a while can it pretend to be a narrative of facts, since so much that we should all like to know has become lost in the mist and haze of the past. It is not until we reach the thirteenth, fourteenth, and fifteenth centuries that we become possessed of data concerning music and musicians which can be positively proved, and therefore depended upon. Even then the information is frequently most scanty. It will be easily understood, consequently, how difficult

I

it is to provide a thoroughly connected narrative until that period is reached. The reader should be informed, too, at the outset, that it will be to sacred rather than to secular sources that we must have recourse for much of our story at first. At times he will seem to be reading merely an account of Church music in England ; but he must not be discouraged. It is to the Church that we are bound to go for the first regular and systematic employment of the art in this country. The religious services often kept the art alive when everything relating to secular matters was in a condition of disturbance which must have made men despair. Occasionally we get glimpses of secular art and practice ; but on the whole, it was sacred rather than secular music that rarely waned, and which furnished the backbone of the art in its far-off infancy which we have to trace.

For the first melody and the earliest harmony which sprang from the soil on which the future homesteads of our fair land were to stand, we must look back through the ages to that period when Europe was peopled only here and there, to a time long and long before that when St. Paul is said to have looked into the very eyes of Linus and Claudia, the children of Caractacus, the British chief. Then Albion shared the conditions of other isolated spots in the slowly-waking Western world, when men beat at the doors of Nature with sharp flints. The Stone and Flint Age produced means, no doubt, of making sounds from objects of stone; but it is remarkable that scarcely a single article of this kind exists.

The fragment here illustrated was found among some flint implements at Reading, and may have been used as a whistle. It is a small oval stone, not manufactured, but more probably a sponge petrifaction; and, the centre of the sponge being absent, a clean hole is left which emits a loud whistle on being blown into, as into the hole of a key.

FLINT WHISTLE.

At this earliest stage the music of our country was the carollings of birds, the monotone of bees, the fluttering of the leaves, and the chirpings from the night insects. Sometimes it was the rush, at others, the ripple, of waters that have since swollen into our pleasant rivers. Then the groan of the wild ox and the wolf's cry clave the air; while here and there rose the human voice of gifted savages, vehement with the emotions of the giant frames which emitted it. We can but surmise how such aborigines would proceed—musically. Like all primitive beings, they would clap with the hands, shout and wail, whistle with hands and mouth, imitate the sounds of beasts and birds, construct, and then amuse themselves with instruments of percussion of the coarsest kind, invent a reed or pipe with a blowing hole, turn the cattle-horns into signal trumpets, perchance make something approaching a drum, flourish a stick of bits of metal, and otherwise satisfy their cravings after varied sounds and many jinglings. For centuries such music rose in early Albion. It seems to have been all swept away in the tremendous deluge which overtook the country before the historic period, when men and animals were drowned out, never to be succeeded here by the like again, in that great convulsion before which beautiful spots like Wells and Glastonbury were being washed by the sea-surf.

With the spreading westwards of the races which were to be the forefathers of the Celt, Teuton, and Cymry, a faint musical clue seems to present itself. These wanderers were from the East, and came pushing in a north-westerly direction, fated to leaven musically, as well as socially, the Western continent and this land of ours. Their home was Persia, India, and Arabia. They might leave their native plains and hills behind them, but the songs of their youth and the lays of their land would cling to them with irresistible force wherever they pitched their camp. These germs of Oriental art drifted into Europe, and no doubt influenced the music of the inhabitants of Albion. The native's drum, the rude pipe, and the coarse vocal soundings which may have been here, commingled with whatever musical elements the Aryan emigrants brought with them. The lyre was an introduction. It was invented ages and ages ago in the art nursery of Central Asia. The Tartars, the troubadours of the East, brought it westward. In the lapse of years it reached this country, and became an instrument for the ancient Britons, and the parent of subsequent instruments struck by a hammer. Another Eastern-world instrument was the lute—the forerunner of instruments whose strings are plucked by the fingers, which, in its turn, grew into the harp. This also found its way into Britain—when, no one really knows. Bardic traditions say it was taken into Ireland by Heber and Heremon, the first princes of the Milesian race in Ireland, about the year 1000 B.C. The most early specimens of ancient British harps that have been found, of which we give some drawings, were strung with brass, with the exception of some of the extreme upper notes, which were of metal, like pianoforte wires. The number of these strings varied from

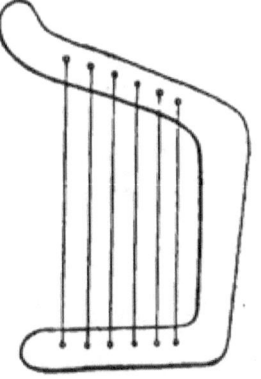

MOST ANCIENT FORM OF IRISH HARP.

THE CRUIT (IRISH).

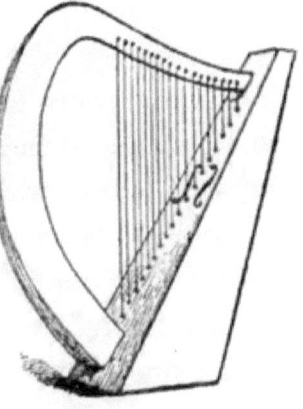

THE CLAIRSEACH (IRISH).

fifty-four to sixty, but a few cords probably sufficed for the earliest instruments.

Antiquaries and collectors occasionally find a fragment which seems to throw light upon these far-off periods to which we would fain trace our musical genesis; but the evidence is always slender. Ibero-musical proofs are scanty indeed. The accompanying

CELTIC WHISTLE.

sketch represents what would seem to be a Celtic whistle. It is made of bone, and is stored in the Dorset County Museum, near which it was found.

Reaching the Bronze Period, we meet with horns of brass, such as are to be seen in the British Museum and other collections. These horns are of semicircular shape, moulded after the fashion of the horns of oxen and other animals. Covered as Britain was with woods and forests, the goat and ox horn would be plentiful enough. It could be turned into a variety of uses, indoors and out. Thus, there were banquet-horns, horns for the chase (which could be used for both sounding and drinking purposes), and war-horns. These latter gave out the note of alarm, or summoned the tribes together against the common enemy. The animal's horn was undoubtedly among the earliest instrumental possessions of primeval Britain. Its telling tone would render it singularly valuable as a 'call'; and, doubtless, it was an instrument common to the tribes of our country. The lost huntsman in the forest could indicate his whereabouts by its sound; while it would be serviceable indeed to the chief, erect before his height-fires, rallying his followers around him.

Druids, and Druidism their teaching (a modified form of the Iberian religion which preceded it in Britain), constituted the first national schoolmaster, **The** and much that was cultured and elevating **Druids.** had its origin in this source. Caius, the historian, believed that the order originated in Britain as early as 1013 B.C., continuing till 179 A.D. Belonging to it were priests, bards, and ovates, robed in white, blue, and green respectively. Amid the ritual of the Druidical service, plaints and chants— familiar probably to the whole body of assembled worshippers—blended with the sacrificial fires and aromas as these lifted to the sun and moon, or to such gods as Ofydd, Mapon, Camulus, Ludd, and Brigantia, which deities the Britons worshipped. Tradition for the most part pictures the religious assemblies of the Druids, with the chiefs and tribes supporting them, as gatherings of magnitude and rude splendour. The excited women, dressed in black, with long loose hair, and brandishing torches, were a startling feature. We can imagine the vocal outpourings to have been grand and solemn melodies, teeming with intensity and variety of acute intonation

peculiar to the melodies born of the natural ear,
and satisfying its requirements, as the British tunes
did. If the great storehouse of the past could but
reveal its treasures, we might expect these sacrificial songs which our progenitors sang to their
'unknown god' to be Laments, not unlike such
plaints as the Maneros (which the Egyptians performed at their funerals), the Linos of the Greeks,
or the ancient Chinese melody in praise of the dead,
limited to a compass to suit men and women, old

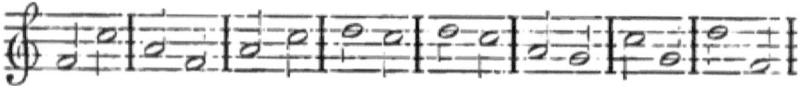

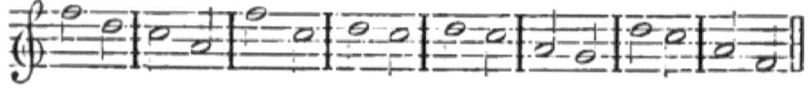

CHINESE TUNE SUNG IN PRAISE OF THE DEAD,

*With F, the Chinese patriarch of all tunes, forming the beginning, middle,
and end of the melody.*

and young alike. Whatever may have been the
antiquity of the Druids, it was through them and
their bardic orders that the musical continuity of
this country was maintained.

 That there was a native music here—probably to
the extent of being an established system—long
before the invasion of Julius Cæsar, is certain.
The land itself (Britain), some lovingly say, takes
its name from Prydain, son of Aedd Mawr, one of

the most distinguished characters of whom bardic memorials are preserved.

Prydain's son was Dyfnwal, in whose day recognition was made of three primeval bards of Britain. These were Plennyd, Alawn, and Gwron, called, in one copy of the Triads, the three Primitive Institutional bards. Plennyd enjoys the reputation of being bard—*i.e.*, singer or narratory chanter—to King Brutus, who is said to have obtained sovereignty of Britain as far back as 1149 B.C.

Wace, the author of 'Le Brut d'Angleterre,' a metrical account of Brutus, the pretended founder of the British nation, represents Gabbet, one of the kings, as the most able musician of his time—one who

> 'Every instrument could play,
>   And in sweetest manner sing,
> Chanting forth each kind of lay
>   To the sound of harp and string.'

The skill of the British monarch as an instrumental performer is set out in the following strain:

> 'He to psaltry, viol, rote,
>   Chorus, harp, and lyre could sing;
> And so sweet was ev'ry note
>   When he touch'd the trembling string,
> That, with love and zeal inflam'd,
>   All who joined the list'ning throng,
> Him with ecstasy proclaim'd
>   God of minstrels, God of song.'

So must we end this brief review of the remotest period in old Albion's musical life, dating from that

far-off era when lions and tigers, with the wild
elephant and rhinoceros, roamed the forests of our
now well-trimmed land. The survey has taken us
back under the dark shroud of thousands of years in
our country's existence, a time covering not only the
Neolithic or New Stone Period, but also the still older
Stone Age, when Palæolithic humanity, unnamed and
unstoried, trod our precious soil. Much, very much,
has been effaced in the long past relating to Britain's
artistic life ; but, happily, there is still testimony of
her great musical position long before the age of
books and written documents.

CHAPTER I.

EARLY BRITISH AND ROMAN MUSIC.

The First light thrown upon musical England — British life according to Pytheas—Roman Influence—Idris—The Crwth — Helen — British children musically instructed — Social uses for Music—A British musical System—Character of British Music—The Melodies most authentic—Welsh Music allied to the original British—Musical gifts of the Welsh— Music indigenous to Britain—Britain's earliest Sacred Music — Before the Saxon Invasion—Tertullian—St. Alban— Character of First British Ecclesiastical Music — Gildas's references to Dress and Fashions — Baptisms and Confirmations—St. Patrick—British Bishops in Conference at 'Augustin's Oak'—Characteristic British Melodies.

PYTHEAS, the Greek navigator and Marseilles merchant, who was contemporary with Alexander the Great and Aristotle (384-322 B.C.), visited Britain, and throws the first light upon the musical and artistic tendencies of the natives.

Pytheas.

They, according to him, were capable of enjoying social pursuits and pleasures of some refinement. Landing in Kent, he saw houses of wood and thatch, and witnessed the method of threshing corn in barns, and the storing thereof afterwards in pits. He met here a hospitable people—not a foreign settlement, but sons of the soil—whose manners had been polished by contact with visitors from the outer world. At the western extremity of the land he found the Cornish tin-mines, with their shafts and galleries being worked much as they are to-day. The people drank their curmi, a liquor fermented from barley. The horn, Pytheas adds, was a common accompaniment to the person, and in war the onslaughts of the British hosts were preceded by loud cries and the blowings of these horns.

In the year 55-54 B.C., the Roman trumpet-call arrested the ear of the brave Briton, yet, beyond a few references in their literature, the first or subse-
Roman Influence. quent visits of the invaders of Britain scarcely aided music here. Save the harp, lyre, and cithar, the tuba and buccina, the valorous Romans had nought but martial instru-

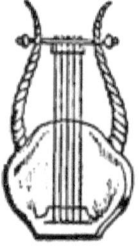  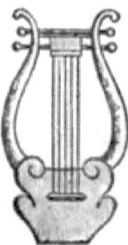

ROMAN LYRES AND CITHARS.

ments, and no vocal music beyond profane songs ; so that, although they came and went for three centuries, they did not seriously influence the music of Britain. The natives refused association with their conquerors, and every tribe retained its old tastes and customs, musical and otherwise.

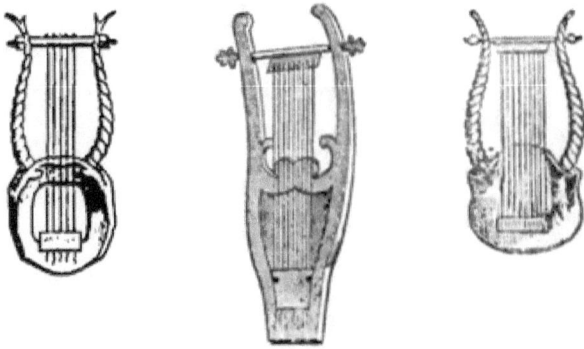

ROMAN LYRES AND CITHARS.

Pending the Roman scourge (54 B.C. to 450 A.D.) the natives, especially those of South Britain, devoted such time as could be spared from the constantly-recurring periods of war to musical exercise. The art, as has been said, retained its old British warmth and sympathetic character, untainted by any influence of the conquerors, and every century is bright with the name of some musician, kingly or lowly-born, whose skill in music exalted him in

A ROMAN TRUMPETER.

the estimation of the people. For generations the groves of Britain resounded to the praises of Idris,*

* Idris is, of course, a figure only in Welsh tradition, whose history cannot be traced with certainty. He is supposed to have been at once a giant, a prince, and an astronomer. On the summit of Cader Idris in Merionethshire may be seen his rock-

the most ancient chieftain and lord of the borders of Idris Mountain.   His home was the highest peak

A ROMAN BUCCINATOR.

in Merionethshire, and he boasted a genealogy from Cadwaladr, Meirion, and more. The harp, which the Italian poet Venantius Fortunatus* (565 A.D.) wrote was, with the crwth, the instrument of the 'barbarians,' or Britons, is said to have been invented by Idris. It is more probable that he improved some existing instrument, or the cognomen of 'inventor' may have been won through sheer proficiency as a player.   Writing about the year 609 A.D. to Loup, Duke of Champagne, this same author mentions the *crotta*, the Latinized name for the cruth, or crwth :

> ' Romanus lyrà, plaudit tibi, barbarus harpâ
> Græchus Achilliaca, *Crotta Brittanus* canit.'
> VENANT. FORT., Carm. VIII., lib. vii.

In shape the crwth was an oblong body, with a

hewn chair, and an ancient tradition says that any Welsh bard who should pass the night upon it would be found next morning either dead, mad, or endowed with supernatural poetic inspiration. This tradition forms the subject of a fine poem by Mrs. Hemans ; the gigantic size of the chair is alluded to in Tennyson's 'Geraint and Enid.'

* Bishop of Poictiers.

neck and finger-board, as here illustrated. It had six strings, four over the finger-board and two open

The Crwth. strings beyond it. Consequent upon the flat bridge, the strings when sounded must have given off harmony, since they were not tuned to the same note, but as follows :

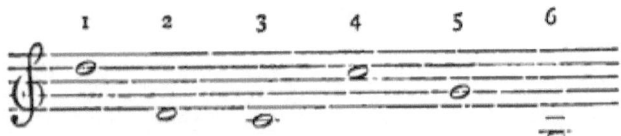

five and six being the open strings.

It is this peculiar construction of the crwth, and the mode of tuning it, which furnishes proof of the early addiction of the Welsh and British to harmony. In any case, this ancient violin is one of the very earliest-known instruments played with a bow.

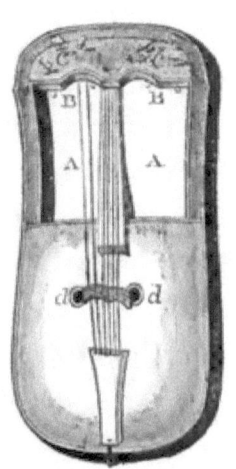

THE CRWTH.

AA, *the apertures for the hand ;*
BB, *the strings conducted under the endboard ;*
cc, *the pegs ;*
dd, *the sound-holes.*

The word 'crwth' is pronounced in English 'crowth,' and corruptly 'crowd'; a player on the crwth was called a crowther, or crowder, and so also is a common fiddler to this day; and hence, undoubtedly, crowther, or crowder, a common surname.

Butler, with his usual humour, has characterized a common fiddler, and given him

the name of Crowdero, in the following passage of
the ' Hudibras ':*

> ' I' th' head of all this warlike rabble,
> Crowdero march'd, expert and able.
> Instead of trumpet and of drum,
> That makes the warrior's stomach come,
> Whose noise whets valour sharp, like beer
> By thunder turned to vinegar.'

Of fairer mould was another most skilful in music.
She was Helen (250-330 A.D.), the only daughter of
Coel Godbebog, King of Britain in the third century. She was esteemed the loveliest woman of her
time, and the accounts say that the Britons named
her Helen Luyddawe, or Helen with the Great Army,
which she led out to Jerusalem, where, tradition
says, she found the cross of Christ.

At the call to arms, at the banquet board, and at
the orgies, the accompaniment of music was ever
present with our early ancestors. Sometimes the
voice and harp were attuned to the warrior's requiem;
at other times the victories, prowess and virtues of
notable chieftains formed the lays of the singers.
King, chief, and dependent strove to excel in vocal
or instrumental music, and very commonly were proficient in both. Never was an art held in higher
honour than was music among the ancient Britons.
Occasionally it led to high promotion in the land,
and, in special instances, deft performers and chosen

* Part I., canto ii., v. 155.

singers, from the lower orders, were elevated to the dignities even of princes — ruling dominions and **British Musical Customs.** having privileges, rewards, and honours bestowed upon them solely for their musical worth and talent.* At every turn there was a call for music among the natives here.

British children were accustomed from their infancy to sing the glorious actions of their ancestors. It was the paramount duty of the proficient in song or instrument to impart this knowledge to the young, and they in their turn were required to hand on the teaching which they had received. This responsibility became sacred. Well, too ; for without it much of the tradition concerning the country which was carried through centuries. until writing became known, would have been lost. The Welsh melodies, handed down in this way, and which appeal to the feelings with almost irresistible force as they break the deep night air in the remote villages of the Principality, are to-day alive with tones and intervals of themes which centuries ago burst forth from most heroic Britons. In the south-west extremity of England smoulder the remains of many an early British theme, religious and profane. The folk-song, or song of the soil, the origin of which dates back to a time of which

---

* For many years this practice prevailed in Britain ; and, to cite a notable case, was it not this same spirit and custom which led King Richard II. (1366-1399), many years afterwards, to convey to Geoffrey Chaucer the manor of Neweline in Oxford-shire, in reward for his poems ?

man knoweth not, is, now and then, the unex-
tinguished fire of British ancients, which untold
centuries of future usage will barely efface. So with
the carol.   Many an example of this beautiful musical
form hails from some outlying district where its
origin is unknown. We cannot divine the authorship of the tune, and although the carol itself generally has the sacred Bethlehem scene for its subject,
so unlike is the music to any earliest Church music,
that very often the tune would appear to be older
even than the Holy Manger story which it clothes.
Traditional, we say of such tunes ; and it is not unlikely that among them are remnants of ancient
sacrificial chants and melodies, understood of the
people long before Christianity was introduced into
Britain ; tunes which have passed from breast to
breast ; tunes so affecting, so deep-reaching, that
they can never be obliterated, but remain as good
to-day as they were when sounded amid the heathen
temple-worship of Britain 2,000 years ago, or when,
perchance, they fell upon the ears of a kingly
Caractacus or Togodumnus.

In their homes the Britons used music to lull the
children to sleep much as we do now. Here is a
Uses for lullaby, that was played to soothe to sleep
Music. the Princess Gwenllian, or 'fair beauty,'
daughter of Prince Rhys ab Griffith, who died in
the year 1190. The tune, however, is probably of
much more ancient date :

ORDDIGAN HÛN GWENLLIAN.

(The Harmony of Gwenllian's Repose.)

At the British funerals, especially, music was a feature. From the Ossianic poems we learn that the most important of all the rites of sepulture among the ancient Britons was the funeral-song containing the praises of the deceased, sung by a number of bards to the music of their harps when the body was deposited in the grave :

> 'Then about the mound
> The warriors rode, and raised a mournful song
> For their dead king, exalted his brave deeds,
> Holding it fit men honour their liege lord,
> Praise him and love him when his soul is fled.'
>
> BEOWULF (Fourth Century).

To want a funeral-song was esteemed the greatest misfortune and disgrace, as the belief prevailed that without it the spirits of the dead would enjoy neither rest nor happiness in the world to come. The Britons even introduced the art into their ornament, as the pavement at Brading shows. When the Romans had taught them the art, the British worked wondrous tessellated pavements, and often incorporated a representation of Orpheus with a lyre. At Woodchester, in Gloucestershire, a splendid pavement of musical design has been traced.

To the laudable spirit concerning the handing down of the art may be attributed that growth and influence of music in the island during several centuries, when appalling trouble and disaster might easily have tempted the people to unstring and hang up their harps for ever.

It was to these eminently practical uses that music was put in early Britain, besides which it served not less prominently as a favourite amusement. It was all this also which the Roman legions, with steel gladius, pilum, and short double-edged sword, sought to obliterate ; but the soldiers could not penetrate the caves and fastnesses of armed Albion, to which the British harper and singer escaped when hunted for his life.

Whether the British possessed any actual musical system is unknown. Most likely they did. A well-ordered people like the Britons probably had means **Method** for delineating and disseminating their **or System.** musical knowledge. Such an arrangement would be obvious, especially for the purpose—so important with the Briton—of teaching the art to the young. Nothing exists pointing to a method. Every remnant of even a most perfect system would easily have become effaced and destroyed, however, during the centuries of devastation which the country passed through under the rule and visitations of the Saxons and Danes. The Irish, it is tolerably certain, had a system of musical notation of their own, long before Guido's invention of the staff and musical characters. 'The very earliest Welsh records,' wrote the late Sir Frederick A. Gore Ouseley, Oxford University Professor of Music, 'seem to prove the existence of harmony in Wales. Doubtless it was of the rudest kind ; but it was far in advance of the miserable attempts at harmony (if we may call it so) which we find in the works of the early writers on musical theory.'*

Every ancient Briton carried music in his breast, however, and the soul of harmony ne'er was stilled till death laid him low.   Then came the outpourings of great grief moulded into incantation, funeral chant, and lamentation—plaints which these big-hearted ancestors of ours sang with strong resemblance to the manner of the Hebrews.   Here and there in an early manuscript an ancient sepulchral verse has been preserved, and may well be cherished if we would commemorate the deeds of valiant Britons who were our forefathers.

Fortunately, we are not without a clue to the style of British music.   Its striking feature was its indisputably indigenous character.   Hospitality and warm affection were esteemed a virtue among the Britons, and this quality reflected itself in the native music, stamping it as a home production.   When visitors —even strangers—arrived at a house, this genial and good-natured spirit diffused itself over the whole place, and music from the harps resounded on all sides.   The art was a growth, swelling with that warm affection and naturalness out of which our scientific musical system has grown.   So that the traditional tunes, even as they have come down to us, may well be believed

British Music. Character.

* 'History of Music' (Naumann-Ouseley), vol. i., p. 395.

in ; for they carry with them the flavour of sterling antiquity, and a thorough genuineness. Some have reached us we know not how, others in written characters ; while many have been noted down by more recent enthusiastic collectors as they were sung from the lips of the old people who best remembered them, and who had received them from their ancestors. Here are two further specimens of these old time tunes :

Y BRYTHON.

(*The Britons.*)

Plaintively.

YR HÊN ERDDIGAN.

(*The Ancient Harmony.*)

With dignity.

Tenderly.

Our attention is chiefly directed to the melodies, since these are necessarily the more genuine portion. The basses and harmonies supplied to them are, for the most part, the creations of comparatively recent 'improvers' and adapters with a craze for investing all old relics with their personality, and as such should be received with caution. The tunes themselves, however, breathe the genuine lyrical spirit, and have the true ring of originality. This is not surprising, for they were spontaneous outbursts, prompted by the very scenes and occasions which they picture. All are strongly marked and charac-

terized by wild flight and imagination — features
which become the more noticeable the further we
trace back for such tunes :

> ' Britain, whose genius is in song exprest,
> Bold and sublime, but negligently drest.'

That which we know as Welsh music, most closely
resembles the original British music. As Sir
Frederick Gore Ouseley has said, ' Probably no race
of men has preserved so much, unaltered, from the
great storehouse of the past as these Cambro-
Britons ; and it is, therefore, not unreasonable to
conclude that in their oldest tunes we may have
the remains of what was anciently the music of this
country long before the Roman invasion under Julius
Cæsar.'*

In many cases the melodies sound like the actual
tunes themselves, brought down to us through the
ages with scarcely a flaw or a missing tone—so
strongly-linked was the first workmanship. Here
and there, however, a tune has become slightly
altered and modernized in the process of handing
down from generation to generation ; but the old
structure remains, and though the ' improvers ' may,
as they do, soften and spoil its sturdy character,
they cannot get rid of the grand original theme, which
has braved the ravages of time and fashion while
borne along down the ages. We still recognize the

* ' History of Music,' Naumann, p. 395.

same plaintive mood in these ancient vocal relics,
their peculiarly sympathetic reach, and the pent-up
earnestness which are alike properties of our oldest
Irish, Welsh, and Scottish airs, as well as of that
music of the East which, with other characteristics
of the great Aryan family, affected the artistic tendencies of Britain and other parts of Europe where
this Celtic off-shoot originally settled.

To this day the old British spirit permeates the
Welsh more than other musical people. We all
know how musically-gifted they are, and what fine
musical perception is theirs. It needs but a glance,
too, at musical life around us, whether in the home
or in the concert-room, to see how our best singers
and choirs may be traced to those outlying districts
where the conditions of Britain's earliest inhabitants
and their descendants have been least affected by
the march of time and fashion. That the art of
song should also be the direction in which the
Welsh show a predilection—just as Britain's earliest
musicians did—would seem to warrant the theory
that those germs of our musical life of to-day which
burst from the soil when Britain was emerging from
a state of paganism, have not only always been
indigenous, but have come down to us with something of their grand old force and affecting properties.

Nor was Britain's music, long and long prior to
the Saxon invasion, confined to the secular kind

alone. Sacred music had been slowly but surely spreading its benign influence in Britain, in services dedicated to the true God, two or three centuries

Earliest Sacred Music. before the time of Augustine, who, as we shall see, first set foot on English soil in the year 597 A.D. Historians have conclusively proved the existence of a regular church in Britain some 150 years and more preceding the Saxon period. 'As early as 203 A.D.,' says Tertullian, 'there were Christians in Britain.' Origen, writing about 240 A.D., says that in his day the religion of Christianity was established in Britain; and one Amphibalus, a native clergyman, is singled out. Who does not know the story of St. Alban, the proto-martyr of Britain, who gave up his life for the Cross? History places beyond dispute, too, the fact that British Bishops of York, London, and Usk, in 314 A.D., attended the Council of Arles, etc. All these holy men preached Christianity, which first reached Britain, it may be, from St. Joseph of Arimathea—

'From our old books I know
That Joseph came of old to Glastonbury'*—

or other eye-witnesses of the incidents in that awful drama of the Crucifixion.

The first musical element in the services of the new faith in Britain must have been slender indeed —consisting probably of an early Christian chant,

* Tennyson : 'The Holy Grail.'

sung antiphonally, after the manner in which the Hebrews sang—thus forecasting the beautiful double choir, or decani and cantoris, effects of later ecclesiastical music. Probably it was restricted to vocal music, for although the Christians of Alexandria (180 A.D.) set the example of using a flute during the singing of the Last Supper chant, orchestral accompaniments in religious services might only have attracted and incensed the more the enemies of the new religion in Britain. In the second century the minds of holy men thought of such a service-music as could be adopted generally in Christian churches. Britain particularly shared in this, and as the churches were built on a larger scale, the simple unaffected music of early times probably gave way to more advanced singing by trained voices. Indeed, it is known that in 367 A.D. the Laodicean Council issued a canon prescribing that only those duly appointed should sing in the churches. ' None but the canons and the choir who sing out of the parchment books should presume to sing in the church '—so ran the order.

Nowhere did early sacred music find more scope than in Britain. The people in several districts had become cultivated, and grown wealthy. There is not sufficient evidence to prove that the Church service-music partook of other than the original character of a simple chant and hymn which the Bishops and clergy could sanction by ecclesiastical

precedent.   Yet it is hard to believe that the Britons,
so fond of music, and enraptured with the Christian
faith, would content themselves with anything short
of a hearty service of song, if not of instrumental
music.   There is little reason to doubt that the

**The
Church
Services.**

Church services became of an elaborate
and gorgeous character, anticipating not
unfavourably the vocal part of the Roman
ritual as rendered now.   In such a case music would
necessarily be a feature, and one which the harmonious tendencies of the tribes would render quite
practicable.   A people with distinct musical talent
and aspirations—who made the practice of the art a
part of their daily life, who used music in so many
secular ways—would be all disposed towards giving
of their best when their art took the shape of music
of the sanctuary.   There could easily have been
a united effort in choral song, consisting largely,
perhaps, of unisonal singing, varied by outbursts
of harmony.   Such a polyphonous art would have
been as possible then as now.   If only of an im-
pulsive and intuitive order, it was yet pure British
harmony, and would prove grand indeed, coming
spontaneously from the lips of men and women full
and fresh with ecstatic enthusiasm for the new
Christianity, and as pre-eminently gifted in and
sensitive to song, as the native Britons unquestionably ever were.

It would not have been impossible even for an

ecclesiastical music system to have existed.   In
civilized districts of Britain, like the south - east,
much social refinement had been obtained.   According to Gildas (516-570 A.D.), there were some twenty-
eight principal cities in the time of the old Britons,
where were the homes of nobles whose costly apparel
included garments dyed in gorgeous colours and
embroidered with gold, chains of gold about the
neck, finger-rings and gold armlets.   The ladies
were adorned with gold bracelets, brooches, corselets
of silver and gold, with necklets of amber and gold
intermixed.   Then even was London 'crowded
with merchants.'

We may assume that the ceremonials in which
such an aristocracy engaged would be conducted
with corresponding splendour, and, since the churches
would be the scenes of important gatherings, we
may conclude that the music and ritual employed
were on a scale of some grandeur.   Could there
have been a function, for instance, like the baptism
to Christianity of such important personages as the
Kings of Dublin and Munster (which ceremony St.
Patrick himself performed) without the aid of
praise and thanksgiving ?   Nor is it conceivable
that music would fail to be a feature at the regular
services, and especially at the confirmations, one of
which is historically famous on account of Carotick,
Prince of Wales, attacking the congregation and
pursuing it before the eyes of St. Patrick.

Historical records furnish collateral evidence ·respecting early sacred music resources. The Roman Breviary tells us that St. Patrick, Bishop of Ireland (420-492 A.D.), was accustomed to perform daily 'the whole Psalter, together with the canticles and hymns,' which were, of course, the forms of song and praise used in his day throughout the Irish churches. Now St. Patrick, it is maintained, knew nothing of Papal authority, and as he was ordained in Scotland, and afterwards devoted his life to the work of converting the Irish,* who were all idolaters, it is fair to claim that the music of his Church was of distinct parentage from that which Augustine the missionary subsequently brought with him.

After Augustine had landed here, we read of the seven British Bishops, who with Dinoth, Abbot of Bangor, met Augustine and his followers at a conference at a spot in Worcestershire, since cherished as Augustine's Oak. Here it was, probably, that the great Apostle to the Saxons made his appeal to the British clergy to join with him in combating the paganism of the country, especially the idolatry of that pre-eminently destructive people, the heathen English. Our forefathers built the British churches, and we may be sure as religiously provided some

---

* A MS. 'Hymnus S. Patrii Magistri Scotorum,' originally in the library of St. Columbanus at Bobbio, and now in the Ambrosian Library at Milan, is worth examination.

kind of music for the services ; but just as scarcely a fragment survives of the ecclesiastical architecture of Christian Britain, so also every musical remnant, whether note or record, has vanished in that complete destruction of everything British which the Saxon pagans wrought. One thing is tolerably certain : The ancient British Church before the Conquest must have been a greater, grander reality than any historian has ever painted it.

There is no reason whatever—despite the persistent foreign neglect of us as a musical nation—why we should not continue the cherished belief that from time immemorial music has been a decided characteristic of the inhabitants of this country ; also that a deep-seated passion for vocal and instrumental harmony—strong and distinctive enough to outlive all untoward processes of time, calamity, and fashion —has filled the breast of the British subject since the remotest ages. It ever was unquestionably and distinctly British, and to-day it still lives in the melodies of England and Wales, Scotland and Ireland. If the music of this country should, happily, be ever re-invested with its own legitimate character, it would probably derive more distinctive quality from the Welsh, Scotch, and Irish melodic germs than from the English, which is less marked in character than either of its neighbours, as a comparison of the following melodies will show :

3

Ruder, of course, than the above melodies were the first British tunes; but the peculiar character—the plaintive pathos—distinguishing the quotations will have been even more strongly marked in

Britain's earliest music. Each century softens that original musical distinctiveness ; and, easy as it is to detect the splendid Celtic quality, this cannot be expected to grow more prominent as Time rolls on. That this true native flavour will ever cling to our national music, admits of little doubt. It is a property which marks all our past music, and belongs exclusively to Britain. No other country's tunes are tinctured with the same strange influences as are the tunes of Ireland, Scotland, and Wales particularly. The older the tunes the better are all their qualities. They are at once grand and pathetic. Even the perversity of interval and modulation which characterize the tunes of Scotland and Ireland— ascribed, it is said, to imperfect transcription at some time—cannot rob them of their lasting beauty. How symmetrical in form, and lovely in their stately evenness, too, are the Welsh melodies — almost without an exception.

PRINCIPAL AUTHORITIES.

'The Bardic Museum' - - -	Jones.
'*De Excidio Britanniæ*' - - -	Gildas.
'Celtic Heathendom' - - -	Rhys.
'*De Bello Gallico*' - - -	Cæsar.
'Origin of English History' - -	Elton.
'Ancient British Church' - -	Pryce.
'Early English Church History' -	Bright.
'Life of St. Patrick' - - -	Todd.
'History of Music' - - -	Naumann.
'The National Music of the World'	Chorley.
'History of Music' - - -	Burney.

CHAPTER II.

SAXON MUSICAL INFLUENCE.

Saxon Visitors—Their National Characteristics—Destructiveness
of the Saxons—Gallican Church Assistance—Germanus and
the 'Alleluia' Victory—Ambrose and the Ambrosian Chant
—Its Effect on Bishop Augustine—Battling with Saxon
Paganism—Success of the English Clergy—Columba—
Aidan—Beowulf—Anglo-Saxon Festal Hall—Gleemen or
'Gladdeners' of the Hall—Cædmon—Cædmon's Musical
Vision — Light from Northumbria — Benedict Biscop—
Foundation of Jarrow and Wearmouth Monasteries—Bede
—Bede's Writings and his Work in the Monastery—Papal
Singing-masters for Jarrow and Wearmouth—Music Schools—
Death of Bede—Alcuin—Giraldus Cambrensis on Singing in
England—An Anglo-Saxon Concert—Part-singing—Descant
—William of Malmesbury and the Ballad—A Mixed Art-
Foundation.

THE ruthless Roman all but extinguished the fire of
early British music. A few embers of sacred and
secular art still glowed in impenetrable spots known
Saxon to the natives, and it was these remnants of
Music. the national musical instinct and practice—
an art which had cheered the island for more than
four hundred years past—which again were to be at
the mercy of an obliterating conqueror—the Saxon
(420-870 A.D.).

With the advent of the fifth century Britain received something of an English, as distinct from the original British, musical character from that branch of the Teuton family that occupied the district of Schleswig, and which, with clans of Jutes and Frisians, settled here from the marshy coasts of Low Germany. All were maritime marauders, lofty of stature, inured to hardships, ferocious and aggressive beyond measure—Goths, say some, who would slit the nostrils of a horse, sew up its ears to destroy its hearing, and dedicate it to their god of war. What could their musical sympathies be? One characteristic that marked them all was their jovial, boisterous nature. Whether Jute, Saxon, or Angle, all were alike in their fearless, adventurous disposition. They came first on plunder bent, and soon proved 'barbarians' indeed. Clambering into osier and skin vessels, which held a hundred or so, they ploughed the ocean and channel by day and night, armed with brown shining swords, long-handled spears, and battle-axes, which dealt destruction to every obstacle. Then arose the coarse song and drunken chorus, the drift of which was invariably death and confusion to their enemies. Chieftain, freeman, and serf, each had his song, a chorus to which was not infrequently tinged with the howl and oath. Now it was a boisterous sea-song which these sea-pirates poured forth in tempestuous tones from sturdy surf-hardened throats,

for these visitors were for the most part genuine
buccaneers and maritime robbers — not the industrious population of the German district that was
to change the name of Britain to that of England.
If it was not a sea-song which they bellowed forth,
it was an effusion having a theme to the praise of
women, the virtues of wine, or hatred for enemies.
Tune and words alike were worse than worthless to
all who heard them.

Such was the species of music, if it can be called
music, which constituted the first foreign influencing
element in our national music ; and that this phase of
German art did not favourably impress the Briton is
not surprising. For a long period, therefore, British
music, or such of it as had survived the Roman
ordeals, was yet cherished and practised by the
natives—just as it had been in the past.

Neither Britain's men nor manners were proof,
however, against the steady inroads of the enemy
waging a terrible war - scourge. Worshippers of
Tiw, Woden and Thor, they were inspired with
fearful rage against the religion of Christ. What
says an Anglo-Saxon Chronicle ? ' Ælla and Cissa
besieged Andreds-cester, and slew all that dwelt
therein, so that not a single Briton was there left.'
Out of the skulls of their foes they hoped to drink
ale in the hall of Woden,* and in this frenzy hosts

* Our Saxon ancestors being addicted to the barbarous practice
of quaffing their ale and mead on festive occasions out of the

of them flew to the altars of the British churches,
murdering the priests, slaughtering the congregations, defiling the sanctuaries, and with fire and
axe razing the buildings to the ground.   Not a
church, not a priest or worshipper was spared, so
thorough was the destruction wherever it was
directed.   Thus, what was beautiful in the first
Christian churches in Britain was mercilessly effaced
by the English. No wonder that later bards lamented
such doings with regret and reproach.

> 'Ye sapient Druids,
>   Sing praises to Arthur,'

sang Taliesin, in lauding the son of Uther for his
prowess at the battle of Goddan ; nor can we be
surprised that, when nearly two centuries afterwards
Augustine called upon the remnants of the British
clergy to help him in the work of conversion, they
pointed to the terrible struggles and exterminating
processes of the past, and were tardy in promising
peace or pardon to a race which had torn down their
churches and violated holy things.   No ordinary
power was needed to reconcile Briton and Saxon ;
only the precious influence of the new Faith could

---

skulls of their enemies, Rowena, the fair daughter of Hengist,
obtains the credit of having converted the Prince Vortigern from
the custom by presenting to him a wine-bowl with the salutation,
'Wass-heil,' to which the Prince not only responded by a counter-
sign of 'Drinc-heil,' but, smitten with her great beauty, forthwith
married her.

avail. This blessing, happily, was hovering over
the island, and like a dove was soon to settle with
the olive branch of peace for all. The work of the
Church was destined to break out again in Brito-
England ; sacred musical art would exert its power
over the hearts and minds of heathen oppressors
alike with the natives who, through toils of un-
successful warfare, had degenerated and fallen from
the Faith.

The new help came from Gaul, and the aid and
guidance which the British clergy received from the
Gallican Church materially forwarded the cause of
Gallican Church music among the Saxons. Brought
Church originally from Ephesus, the Gallican
Music. Liturgy included the Apostles' Creed,
Baptism, Confirmation, and Burial services. Little
is known of its style of music, yet as hymns, psalms,
and a Mass were used, a species of monotone with
inflexions was probably employed. This was the
ecclesiastical music which preceded the Cantus
Romanus of Gregory, which Augustine brought
two hundred years later. Sturdy prelates were
these bishops from France, and the names of two—
Germanus, Bishop of Auxerre, and Lupus, Bishop
of Troyes—have fitly been preserved. Germanus
(380-448 A.D.), Bishop of Sodor and Man, and
Lupus (383-479 A.D.), his co-bishop—true soldiers
of the Cross — served not only at the altar, but
were required to lead their British flocks against

their foes, sometimes Saxons, at others Picts and Scots. A memorable encounter was in the Dee Valley (429 A.D.), when, by a strategic shout of an 'Alleluia,' which made the hills reverberate, the affrighted Picts flew before Germanus and his hosts, and a bloodless victory— since famous among the conquests of the Cross—was gained at Maes Garmon.

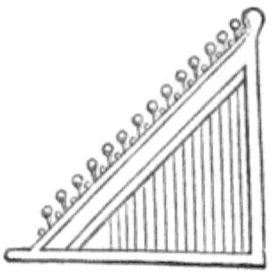

TRIANGULAR SAXON HARP
OF THE NINTH CENTURY.

Our British ancestors were indebted to Germanus for the introduction of the Gallican Church chant many years prior to the coming of Augustine. It is well to remember the condition of ecclesiastical music in England before it received the stimulating example and influence of the Gregorian method which Augustine introduced. The old British Church music had all but gone, and the Church music here of which we have the first historical information, if no specimens, was undoubtedly the Gallican chant—*id est*, the music of the Church in Gaul. It was the chant adopted, probably, in all the Christian churches of Europe immediately preceding the introduction of the Gregorian chant, and since the British bishops were then frequently consecrated in France, they would naturally bring that service-music with them to England to displace the heathen temple tunes which were still obtaining under the

Druids, and to cement together such fragments as remained of the old British Church music. When Restitutus, Bishop of London, with Eborius, Bishop of York, and Adelphius, Bishop of Caerleon-on-Usk, attended the Church Council at Arles (314 A.D.), they would hear this Gallican chant, and, approving of it, use it in their churches. It, or the native British Church music, constituted the sole musical means in the Church until the Roman chant came to displace and carry all before it.

In the year 374 A.D. the music school of Milan, presided over by Ambrose (333-398 A.D.), was opened. Its first music principles were derived from **Ambrose and the Ambrosian Chant.** the Eastern Church, but the then known ecclesiastical chanting having fallen into much confusion, this prelate introduced into Milan Cathedral a form and style in which Divine service should be sung, which he named the *Cantus Ambrosianus*, or Ambrosian Chant. It was based on the following four modes or scales, bearing the names of four 'Authentic' Greek modes, not identical with them, but probably founded by Ambrose on the same principle :

AMBROSE'S AUTHENTIC MODES.

First Tone: Dorian.

Second Tone : Phrygian.

Third Tone : Lydian.

Fourth Tone : Mixo-Lydian.

AMBROSIAN CHANTS.

Scarcely a vestige of this music can be traced for certain, despite the researches of Burney, Choron, and other authorities who examined the missals and listened to the singing at the cathedral of Milan without observing any marked difference between it and the Gregorian music, into which the Ambrosian chant would seem to have merged. Its character, however, has been fairly estimated, as the few bars from the following *Te Deum,* as set in the 'Choir Directory of Plain Song,' indicate :

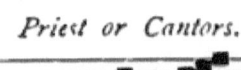

Priest or Cantors.   *Full.*   *Unison.*

We praise Thee,   O God :   we ac-knowledge Thee to be   the   Lord.

All the earth doth wor   .   ship Thee : the Father ev-er-last   .   ing.

Trebles.   Unison.

To Thee all An-gels cry a-loud : the Hea-vens, and all the Pow'rs therein.

To Thee Che-ru-bin and Se   .   ra-phin : con-tin-u-al-ly   .   do cry,

Men.   *Full.   Unison.*

Ho · ly,   Holy, Lord God of Sabaoth :

Ho · · · ly,

The style of sacred chanting ordered by Ambrose had the great merit of being at once simple and grand. Its soul - stirring effects may be judged, indeed, from the exclamation of Bishop Augustine (354-430 A.D.) when he first heard the Ambrosian chant at Milan : 'O God, how I wept over Thy hymns of praise. The sound poured into mine ears, and Thy truth entered my heart.' It would prove a priceless treasure could we trace some of this music ; as it is, we can only conjecture what was its character, and that of the hymns which the saintly Hilary (367 A.D.) composed for the British churches.

A dark and terrible reality did the paganism of the Angles and Saxons prove, and it was generations after their arrival in Britain ere they ceased to fall down to Woden and Thor. In the midst of paganism and barbarism the British clergy continued their work. When the Saxons poured in from the south and east coasts, and the Picts and Scots from the north and west, it was the Church only that was not lost in dismay. The services of prayer and praise held the British together, but the impression upon the Saxons was slight indeed, despite the splendid efforts of valiant preachers. In the four Saxon kingdoms the ancient British or Irish-Scoto clergy had sustained the Christian religion in those provinces including Mercia, the Midland counties, Norfolk, Cornwall, Devonshire, Somerset, Wilts, Hants and Berks ; Aidan, Bishop of the Scots, had similarly

laboured in Northumberland, Durham, York, Lanca-
shire, Westmoreland and the South of Scotland ;
while Essex and Middlesex were cared for by the
British prelate Cedd (654 A.D.), and all this religious
enthusiasm went hand-in-hand with the wondrous
sway of sacred tone and cadence.

What were the feelings of the clergy, battling
against the ruthlessness of the Saxons through so
many years, can readily be conjectured. Happily, they
did not despair, and in God's time there were signs,
here and there, which encouraged them. A severe
blow was struck at the pagan religion in Britain, for
instance, when Coiffi, declaring himself a convert to
Christianity, called for a horse and rode off to spear
the walls of the neighbouring temple of Godmunding-
ham ; when, with no avenging fires descending from
heaven, as were predicted by the crowds that looked
on, he set to and burnt the fane and the idols contained within it, which had been so long venerated
and feared. Yet how opposite was the demeanour of
the chief Maglocune, surnamed the ' Dragon of the
Island,' who, a chronicle says, ' preferred poets' pæans
and satires to God's lauds sung by Christ's soldiers !'
To Patrick (*circa* 410-492 A.D.), the Apostle to
Ireland, we have already referred ; but in the century
next following the Gospel labours were continued by
Columba (521-597 A.D.), who, crossing the seas in
a wicker-work skiff covered with hides, carried the
first tidings of Christianity to the North of Ireland,

Iona, and the south-west portion of Scotland. It was an old bard, Gemmain by name, who trained Columba, the Apostle of Caledonia, with the traditions, and no doubt the songs and music, of Ireland. The bardic gift of song thus acquired, and afterwards exercised by Columba, won the hearts and ears of the Irish people—not less than did his preaching—for they loved much to listen to his singing.

Another great North of England missionary was Aidan (*circa* 600-651 A.D.), originally a monk of Iona, and later Bishop of Northumbria. He built his monastery at Lindisfarne, where King Oswald granted him lands, and there he restored the services and carried on the good work begun by Paulinus (597-644 A.D.), Apostle of Yorkshire. So that all through these troublous times between the Britons and Saxons, the English Church carried on its work fearlessly, and by its teachings and methods—among which was sacred music—it led the people on to that light and learning which conduced not only to their subsequent settlement, but to the great intellectual advances of the country in future generations. Without the Church, music as an art might have been irretrievably lost at this period.

England was now, after several generations of warfare and conquest, more musically Saxon than British, and it was only in the remote districts where the original music of the Briton could be heard—districts where remains of it smoulder to this day.

In considering this later Anglo-Saxon art, we are no longer upon traditional ground, since several contemporary writers can be quoted who repeatedly allude to it.

Our first authority is that most ancient fragment of Teutonic literature—the Epic bearing Beowulf's name. The date of this poem is about 520 A.D. It **Saxon** furnishes a glowing picture of the musical **Glee Hall.** habit and usage of the period, proving conclusively that music was assiduously practised and encouraged by these ancestors of ours. There was the great festal hall, wherein drinking and the gleeman's song went on. It was two hundred feet long by forty feet wide, with a high roof and curved gables. It had a nave and narrow side-aisles, and pillars dividing the aisles from the nave supported the central roof. Thus, it was not unlike a modern church interior. The nave, or centre, formed the hall, and down the middle of its floor ran a stone hearth, upon which the logs blazed and crackled. At the upper end was the raised seat, or daïs, of the chief, with a crossbench, where his wife and some familiar thanes privileged to sit beside him filled the cups of the guests. On each side of the long stone hearth ran lines of tables flanked with benches and stools, whereat sat the chief's hearth-sharers. At the end, opposite the daïs, was the table for the drinking-cups, while the liquor itself was stored in gilded vats, which stood in side-spaces. Into these vats the cup-bearers dipped their pails. Sleeping benches were provided at the sides of the aisles, and altogether the arrangements seem to have been designed for comfort and enjoyment. In such halls the gleemen chanted to their harps. Now it was one tune and story, now another, as call was made for this or that favourite incident. ' The glee-wood was touched, and Hrothgar's gleemen, "gladdeners" of the hall, told of the works of Fin's offspring, the tale of Fin Folcwalding, of Hnaef and Hengest, and the sons of Hildeburh, burnt by their mother at Hnaef's pile. The lay was sung, the gleeman sang, games were begun again, the noise was loud, the cup-bearers gave wine from wondrous cups.' So sings Beowulf in his romantic poem. Another rendering puts it : ' There was song joined with the sound of music, the glee-wood was welcomed, the song frequent, when Hrothgar's scóp, the joy of the hall, told after the sitting at mead of Fin's offspring seized by sudden danger when Healfdene's hero, Hnaef of the Scyldings, fell in Friesland.'*

Cædmon is our next witness to first English music and custom. He was a secular monk of Whitby, and the author of poems on the Creation and other Bible subjects. He died about 680 A.D. In his **Cædmon.** day the Anglo-Saxon youths were much given to music, and it was considered derogatory to their social position to be without a knowledge of the

* Beowulf.

art, either vocal or instrumental. Cædmon laboured under this disadvantage: Inspired he was with poetic grace and choice metre, but he had made no acquaintance with the art of music—a disadvantage which he often deplored. 'Cædmon continued in a worldly state [*in habitu sæculari*],' says Bede, 'until he arrived at an advanced age without learning any song, and thus frequently, when at a banquet it was for merriment's sake determined that every one in his turn should sing, accompanying himself on the harp, when Cædmon saw the harp approaching him, he would arise from the table in confusion and quit the house.' The full story of Cædmon's musical disabilities, and of his great poetic talent, is one of the happiest pictures in Bede's panorama of history, and may well be produced here in a translation which conveys not a little of the quaint vein of the original :

'In the Monasterie of the Abbesse Hilda (614-680),* at Whitby, there was a certaine brother endewed with the speciall grace of God, which was wont to make songes and meters fitt for religion and for godly meditation, in so much that what so ever he learned of the holy Scriptures by other men's expounding, he turned and made the same anon

---

* Abbess of Whitby, and daughter of Hereric, nephew of Edwin, King of Northumbria. Under her the monastery at Whitby became famous, and five of the monks became bishops. She was called the 'Mother.'

after with poeticall and musicall wordes, set together
with wonderfull swetenesse and melodie in his own
mother tonge. With whose verses and songes the
mindes of many men were often inflamed to the
contempt and despysing of the world, and desire of
the everlasting life of heaven. After whome diverse
other among the English men assayed to make
godly and devowt meters, but noman cowlede matche
his connyng therein. For he learned this arte of
singing and making, not towght of men, nor by any
man's helpe, but he receaved the gyfte thereof freely
by the only ayde and grace of God. And therefore he cowld never make any fond or vayne balade,
but such things as belonged to religion and godly
meditation were only mete to come out of his
religious and godly mouth. For as long as he was
a secular man, which was till he was well stricken
in age, he never had learned any such matter of
singinge. In so much that sometimes at the table,
when the company was set to be merry, and agreed
for the nonse, that eche man showld syng in order at
his course ; he, when he sawe the harpe to com nere
him, rose up at myde of supper, and gat him owt
of dorres home to his owne howse. And as he
so dyd on a certaine time, getting him owt of the
place where they were drinking and making mery
together, to the stable among the beastes which he
had appoynted him to kepe and look to that nighte,
and when the houre of slepe came, was gone his way

quietly to bed, as he laye, he dreamed that a certaine man stoode by him, and bad him God spede, and calling him by his name say'd to him Cædmon,

I pray thee, singe me a songe. Whereto he mayde awnswere and say'd, I can not synge. For that is the matter why I came owt from the table to this place here, because I cowld not singe. But yet, quothe he againe that spake with him, thow hast somewhat to sing to me. What shall I sing? quoth he. Sing, quoth the other, the begynning of all

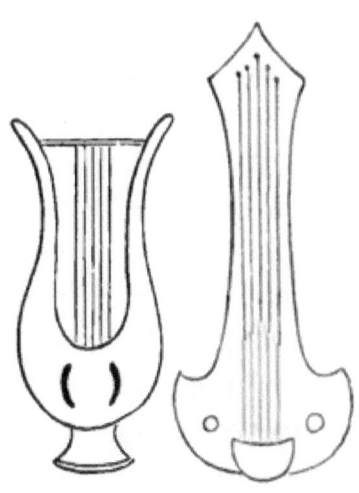

SAXON MUSICAL INSTRUMENTS.
(*From the Cædmon MS., Oxford.*)

creatures. At which answere he began by and by to singe in the lawde and prayse of God the creatour, verses which he had never heard before, of which the sense and meaning is thys :—*Nowe must we prayse the maker of the heavenly kingdome, the power of the creatour, his counsell and devyse, the workes and actes of the father of glorie Howe he being God eternell was the maker and author of all miracles, which first unto the children of men created heaven for the top of their dwelling place, and after the omnipotent keeper of mankinde created the earthe for the flowre thereof.* This is the meaning, but not the order of the wordes which he sange in his

sleepe. Now when he awoke and rose up, he
remembred still by harte all the thinges that he had
songe in his slepe, and dyd straight way joyne
thereto more wordes in the same maner and forme
of meter, and mayde up a song fitte to be songe and
applyed to God. And on the morrow he came to
the farmer or baylie under whom he was, and told
him of the gifte that he had receaved, and being
browght to the Abbesse he was commaunded in the
presence of many learned men to tell his dreame
and rehearse the song, that it might by the judgment of them all be examyned and tryed what or
whence the thing was which he reported. And it
seemed to them all that some heavenly grace and
gifte was graunted him of our Lorde. For more
triall whereof they recited unto him the processe of
some holy storie or example, willing him, if he
cowld, to tourne the same into meter and verse.
Which he took upon him to doo and went his way ;
and on the morowe after came againe and brought
the same made in very good meter which they had
willed him to doo. Whereupon straightway the
Abbesse acknowledging and embracing this grace
and gifte of God in the man, instructed and exhorted
him to forsake the world and to take the monasticall
lyfe and profession upon him. Which he did, and
was therefore by the commandement of the Abbesse
placed in the company of the bretherne.'

This house was one of the first double monasteries

which multiplied so much in England for many years afterwards. They were composed of nuns and monks, so that vocal resources for excellent singing were always at hand. From this fact, therefore, we may conclude that the Church services and singing were on a much grander scale than is commonly imagined. One especial feature of the religious practices was the *Laus Perennis*, or Service of Perpetual Praise, kept up by seven choirs of nuns, who relieved each other in succession. Nor were the doings of such ministering singers forgotten. The Liturgy contained a special clause for them : 'Ora pro populo, interveni pro clero, intercede *pro devote femineo sexu.*'

Now was a bright light to burst forth from the gloom of the far North of England. Suddenly we are face to face with a noble figure in Early English ecclesiastical history, one whose life and example in Northumbria in those dark days are fittingly remembered and honoured in ours, especially as he was the instructor of the beloved Bede. This was **Benedict Biscop.** Benedict Biscop (628 - 690 A.D.), a rich Anglo-Saxon nobleman, and one of the Anglo-Saxon Benedictines who fostered the growth of the Gregorian chant in England. Biscop, in obedience to the custom of the times for the clergy to go to Rome for studying and acquiring music, had visited that city no less than five times, and was highly regarded by Pope Agatho for his perfect

knowledge of Church music.   In 678 A.D. we find
him sending to Rome for singers versed in the
Cantus Romanus for York Cathedral.   Bede wrote
the Life of Benedict Biscop, and does not forget to
add the tribute that it was owing mainly to his exertions that the Roman chant became so well known,
and firmly rooted, in the monasteries of Durham,
Gerwy, and Wearmouth.   In a neighbourhood
where at an old temple of Apollo the people were
worshipping the heathen Sun-god, he built the
monasteries of Bishop Wearmouth and Jarrow, and
beautified them with relics, paintings, stained-glass,
illuminated Bibles, and Service-books which he
brought from Rome.   Biscop was himself head of
the Jarrow House, where Bede succeeded him.

Bede stands out prominently among the first
English authors who have borne testimony in
their writings to Anglo-Saxon musical methods.
Bede. The 'Father' of English Church historians,
familiarly known as the 'Venerable' Bede
(672-735 A.D.), was born just before Cædmon died.
The educational system of the period was divided into
four divisions, of which music formed one, and Bede
was among the recipients of this liberal education.
He wrote a musical treatise in two parts—'Musica
Theoretica' and 'Musica Pratica.'   The former
treated of the division of the octave, consonant and
dissonant intervals, etc., the latter of notation and
measure, as these existed before the inventions of

Guido and Franco. Bede, broad-minded and sweetly disposed as he was, takes a lofty and beautiful estimate of the art. According to the Venerable Presbyter, 'Music is the most worthy, courteous, pleasant, joyous and lovely of all knowledge; it makes a man gentlemanly in his demeanour, pleasant, courteous, joyous, lovely, for it acts upon his feelings. . . . Music encourages us to bear the heaviest afflictions, administers consolation in every difficulty, refreshes the broken spirit, removes headache and sorrow, expels foul spirits, and cures crossness and melancholy.'

Venerable Bede

Priest and monk, he was an indefatigable worker for the Cross, never wearying whether in the schools, his study, or in the performance of daily religious ministrations. Anxious to secure sound musical training for the scholars at Jarrow, to which monastery he had been appointed by his preceptor, Benedict Biscop, Bede not only devoted his personal energies to this end, but sought outside aid. Acquiescing, no doubt, in such earnest representations, Pope Agatho despatched John, Precentor of St. Peter's at Rome, to teach singing to the monks of Wearmouth and Jarrow, an opportunity for improvement of which the music-masters in the North diligently availed themselves. The decision of the Synod of Whitby, held in 664 A.D., in favour of the Roman Liturgy, necessarily benefited the Roman music, and Celtic Church music is afterwards heard of but little. John arrived in England in the year 680 A.D., from which time the knowledge of sacred music rapidly increased in the North. The monks recognised in him a skilful teacher, so much so that the Abbots of Wearmouth and Jarrow prevailed upon him to open music-schools in the various districts of Northumbria.* Another Papal singing-master who came here later was Paul the Deacon (*circa* 720-800 A.D.). Yet another singing-master in Northumbria, whose name has come down to us, was

* This singing-master wrote Pope Gregory's Life, 'Vita S. Gregorii,' in which he warmly rates the Germans and French, whom he had met probably at the Court of Charlemagne, for being unable to properly sing the Gregorian chant. 'Wholly unable to express its sweetness,' writes the aggrieved voice-trainer, 'they injure it by barbarous changes, suggested either by their natural ferocity or inconstancy of disposition. Their figures were gigantic, and, when they sang, it was rather thunder than musical tones. Their rude throats, instead of the inflexions of pleasing melody, formed such rough sounds as resembled the noise of a cart jolting down a pair of stairs.' As there is no blame attached to the English singers, we may fairly assume that they secured good results from their singing.

The following are two specimens of the Gregorian chant harmonized: the one is from the solemn *Miserere*, which is chanted in the Roman Catholic service during the Holy Week; the other is the beginning of the Easter Hymn, which is of a more lively character :—

Edde, surnamed Stephen, who was sent thither out of Kent by Wilfred the Primate, 709 A.D.

Thus, the Roman service method, and the manner of rendering the Gregorian music, came from the fountain-head, thanks to the wisdom and foresight of Benedict and Bede. Productive of so much good, too, was this step, that the example was followed by the missionaries in other parts of the island. As Augustine and his successors proceeded in their work, churches were built, and the need for clergy increased accordingly. This demand was met by a steady flowing in of prelates and other Churchmen from Rome, who being all more or less familiar with Gregorian music, also steadily advanced the cause of Church music throughout England. Wherever a

THE MISERERE.

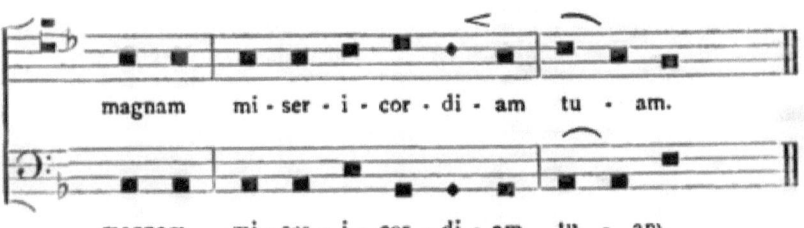

monastery was founded—and pious souls of the
time reared them with almost prodigal splendour—
a music-school was attached with conveniences for

THE EASTER HYMN.

housing as well as for training the singers in the
proper rendering of the Mass and evensong music.
An obstacle, however, was the difficulty of finding
competent teachers outside Rome, which was not
overcome until the first musical training-school was
opened at Canterbury.

Every good work is hindered, and a day came
when a dark cloud spread over Jarrow. A higher
call awaited the saintly servant—the last scene of
Death whose life furnishes a pattern day for all
of Bede. earnest workers, and serves also as an index
to the regular life within the monastery when Bede
was its head. It was Ascension Day (May 26, 735),
when, distressed and exhausted with asthma, Bede
had all but concluded his translation of St. John's
Gospel for the use of the people. ' In the evening his
boy-scribe (Cuthbert) said to him : " One sentence,
dear master, is left unfinished." He bade him write
quickly. Soon the boy announced that it was
finished. " True," the dying man said, " it is finished.
Take mine head between thy hands and raise me.
Full fain would I sit with my face to my holy
oratory, where I was ever wont to pray, that sitting
so I may call on my Father." And so he sat on the
floor of his cell, and chanted, " Glory be to the
Father, and to the Son, and to the Holy Ghost."
And as he breathed the words " the Holy Ghost " he
died.' Thus passed to the eternal habitations this
priest-teacher, who had spent nearly the whole of

his life in the monastery at Jarrow 'observing the monastic rule and the daily ministry of singing in the church ' :

> 'O Venerable Bede !
> The saint, the scholar, from a circle freed
> Of toil stupendous.'
> WORDSWORTH.

The Church having spread her loving hands over the land, men, large in mind like the Venerable Bede, were to rise up to carry on her work in England.

Alcuin. Alcuin (735-804 A.D.), born in the year of Bede's death, became a leading musical writer and ecclesiastic. He followed in Bede's footsteps. As a boy he entered St. Mary's Abbey, York, and studied under Egbert, Archbishop of York, who gave him a tonsure and ordained him deacon. He became well versed in music and other liberal learning—so much so that, after succeeding Egbert at York, the Emperor Charlemagne begged him to accept a permanent appointment as head of the Palatine schools, one great object that Charlemagne had being to disseminate Gregory's system of music throughout the churches and schools of France and Germany. Alcuin's labours have been well set out in the words of a German poet, who, after recounting Britain's indebtedness to her son, turns aside to sing :

> ' Nor smaller tokens of esteem from France
> Alcuinas claims who durst himself advance
> Single against whole troops of ignorance.

'Twas he transported Britain's richest ware,
Language and arts, and kindly taught them here.
With him, his master Bede shall ever live,
And all the learning he engross'd survive.'

We are informed by Bede that in the beginning of the eighth century the custom of the Saxons here was to indulge in social and domestic singing in **Saxon Part-sing-ing.** their own language, accompanying their singing with the harp. Many years later we meet with another musical authority, Giraldus Cambrensis (born 1147, died 1220). He was Archdeacon and afterwards Bishop of St. David's, and although not altogether to be depended upon in literary matters, remains nevertheless a valuable chronicler concerning an age when writers upon contemporary social life were scarce indeed. He wrote and addressed his 'Gemma Ecclesiastica,' or 'Jewel of the Church,' to the Welsh clergy; and in this book occurs an anecdote which shows that even in those days the catchy vein of a popular song was apt to obtrude itself at not always the right time or place. Gerald opposing the popular custom of dancing and singing profane songs in the churchyards on saints' days—a form of amusement which had grown into a nuisance — says that a priest of Worcester, who had been hearing the refrain of a song all night in such dances in the churchyard, when he stood next morning at the altar, in full canonicals, instead of proceeding with

the *Dominus Vobiscum*, chanted in a loud voice, to
the scandal of the congregation, the refrain of the
song that had haunted him :

'Swete lamman dhin are.'

William of Norhall, the Bishop, hearing of this,
publicly anathematized that song by synod and
chapter, and forbade it ever to be sung in his diocese.
How excellent a thing if not a few of the popular
airs of the present day could be publicly accursed in
the same way! Naturally, both the professional and
amateur musician are chiefly interested in Giraldus
for the musical information he affords them. In
praise of his native country this early English antiquary and scholar says: 'Britain, although divided
from the rest of the world, has always been partial to
bards, among the most celebrated of whom are to
be reckoned Plennydd, Oron and Gildas,' names
which have already come under our notice. Giraldus
refers especially to an Anglo-Saxon concert, and
describes the mode of singing—a style which had
obtained, probably, among the British long before
that time. 'In their musical concerts,' he says,
'they do not all sing in unison, as is the custom of
other nations, *but in different parts*, so that as many
as you see individuals, so many melodies and various
parts you hear, all ultimately smoothly uniting under
the softness of B flat into consonance and organic
melody [*i.e.*, in harmony]. And moreover, in the
northern parts of Britain, beyond the Humber, in

the neighbourhood of York, the Angles in singing
employ a similar kind of symphonious harmony, using,
however, only two parts, one deeply murmuring in
the bass, the other delightfully warbling in the
treble.   Nor is this an acquired custom among the
nations, but by long usage is, as it were, converted
into their nature ; and has now taken such root in
the constituent prejudices of both peoples, that
neither among the former, where the custom of
singing in several parts prevails, nor among the
latter, where they sing in two parts, can a simple
melody be well performed.   What, moreover, is more
remarkable, children from their earliest years observe
the same custom.   Since, however, among the
Angles this method is not universally observed, but
only by the more northern inhabitants, I conceive
that they have borrowed their method of singing, as
well as speaking, from the Danes and Norwegians,
who were more frequently accustomed to occupy as
well as longer to retain possession of those parts of
the island.'

'This,' to quote no less an authority than that
learned antiquary, the late Mr. William Chappell,
'may fairly be taken as evidence that part-singing
was common in Wales, or that at least they made
descant to their tunes, in the same way that singers
did to the plain-song or *canto fermo* of the Church
at the same period ; also that singing in two parts
was common in the North of England, and that

children tried to imitate it. Burney and Hawkins think that what Giraldus says of the singing of the people in Northumberland, in two parts, is reconcilable to probability, because of the schools established there in the time of Bede ; but Burney doubts his account of the Welsh singing in many parts, and makes this "turbâ canentium "[*] to be *of the common people*, adding, " we can have no exalted idea of the harmony of an *untaught* crowd." These, however, are his own inferences. Giraldus does not say that the singers were untaught, or that they were of the common people. As he is describing what was the custom in his own time, not what had taken place a century before, there seems no sufficient ground for disbelieving his statement, and least of all should they who are of the opinion that all musical knowledge was derived from the monasteries call it in question, since, as already shown, part-music had then existed in the Church, in the form of descant, for three centuries.'[†]

This Descant—the forerunner of counterpoint and prick-song, or written music—it may be well to add,

Descant. was the first ecclesiastical harmony, and consisted originally of extemporaneous singing by the more skilled musicians in fourths, fifths, and octaves, above and below the plain-song melody, or tune of the Church ; and although in its

[*] Bede's Latin.
[†] ' Popular Music of the Olden Time ' (Chappell).

original sense it implied only singing in two parts,
it had more considerable advances in the ninth
century, towards the end of which we find specimens
still existing, of harmony in three and four parts.

SPECIMENS OF DESCANT.

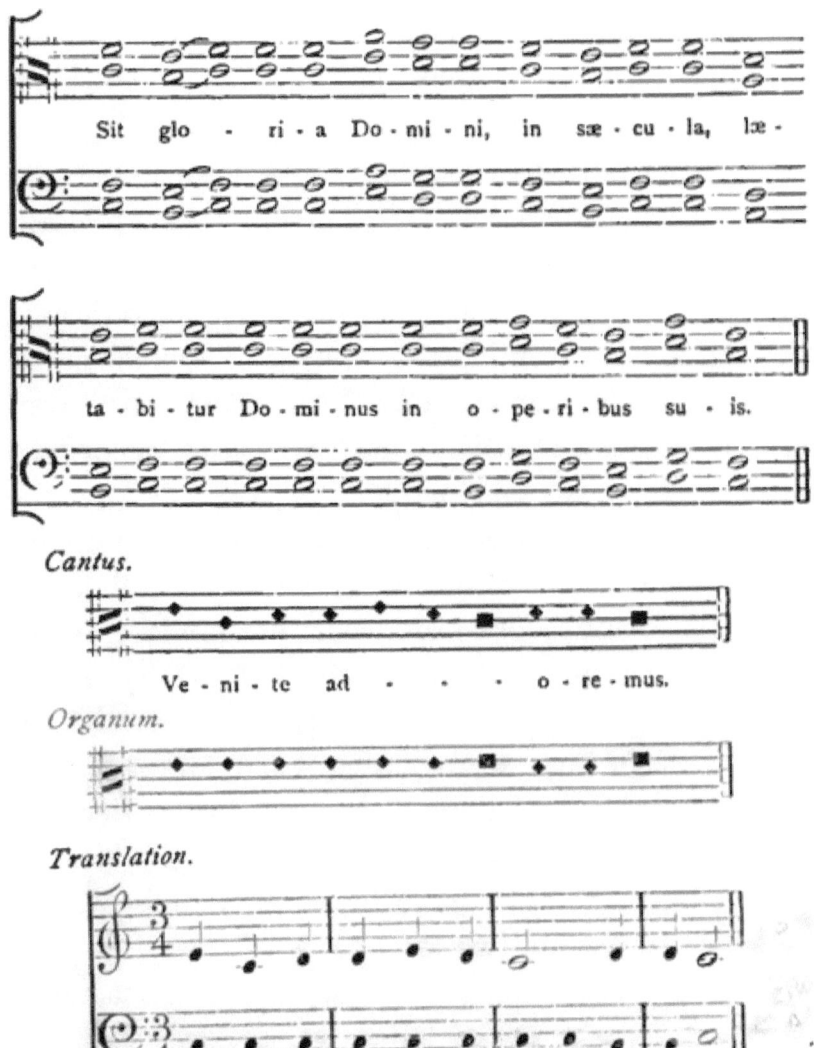

Sit glo - ri - a Do - mi - ni, in sæ - cu - la, læ -

ta - bi - tur Do - mi - nus in o - pe - ri - bus su - is.

Cantus.

Ve - ni - te ad - - - o - re - mus.

Organum.

Translation.

It would be difficult to determine when such a natural art as that of adding another vocal part to one that was already known did not exist in this **An Unwritten Art.** country. Man is a harmonious creature, who must have been endued from the beginning with the faculty of forming harmony with his voice — just as the merest children to-day can add what they term 'seconds' to a tune—albeit he was far removed from the age when musical thoughts could find literal expression through signs which could be understood not only by their creator, but also by all to come after him. Thus, little reliance can be placed upon deductions concerning the extent to which music was, or was not, practised in this country when conclusions are based solely upon what can be proved by actual manuscript evidence. That before the age when writing became known and was practised, there existed here a species of natural vocal music of a truly harmonious order, part-music more extensive and complete than is reflected in any manuscript for several centuries after, is, to our mind, as reasonable a matter for acceptance and belief as would be the proposition that at that period the winds were blowing and the trees growing. Having an existence, then, it is of little moment by whom or where it was cultivated.

We are indebted, doubtless, to the monasteries for all that we possess relating to our earliest music

but that for several centuries there was a great unwritten art growth which has been forgotten or
neglected by the first musical writers and theorists
can scarcely be refuted. Secular music must have
been much more varied and extensive than any documents of the period suggest, since it was the art of
writing and musical notation which were so little advanced, not the native enthusiasm for music. The
inventions of Guido and Franco had hardly become
felt, and for long after this time musical notation was
in such an imperfect state that it used to take nine
or ten years to acquire a fair knowledge of it. The
capacity of our ancestors, the Briton and Saxon, to
provide musical enjoyment for themselves and those
around them would be considerably more than is
indicated by any musical data of the time, for the
first writings show only the state of music as it was
growing into a science, capable of being expressed
by a notation. Notation long afterwards represented
almost solely the music of the cloister, for secular
music found little favour in the eyes of the clergy
and those who occupied the monasteries.

We must not fall into the error, then, of supposing that only such music obtained during the early
centuries as is represented by specimens to hand.
These refer entirely to the scientific art of our
country, not to the natural, innate, harmonious
expression of our forefathers, which no musically-
learned one has transmitted to us, and of which we

should have known nothing, save for such fortunate
digressions in the current annals as are afforded
here and there in the strains of the bards and scóps,
and in the writing of such chroniclers as Bede,
Giraldus, and others.

The ballad, for instance, was a favourite musical
form with the people at this time. The English have
always been a ballad-loving people, and even the

Saxon Ballad. present-day tendency towards this class of
music does not exceed the passion displayed
for it eight hundred years ago. In them was preserved much of the country's history and glory.
William of Malmesbury (1095-1143), who wrote 'De
Gestis Regum Anglorum,' and had access to English
historical materials now lost, remarks : 'Thus far I
have written from trustworthy testimony. That
which follows I have learnt more from old ballads,
popular through succeeding times, than from books
written expressly for the information of posterity.
I have subjoined them not to defend their veracity,
but to put the reader in possession of all I know.'

Concerning the music which accompanied the
Anglo-Saxon ballad, little is definitely known. No
threads of such secular music exist, and all that
authorities can do is to point to remnants of the
Church music of such early times, which afford the
only clue to the probable melody of the ballad or
narratory story. In this sacred music, consisting
chiefly of hymns with Latin words, regulated tune is

definable—all pointing to the existence of, and an acquaintanceship with, a systematic scale. So that at the period which we are considering there were at least three musical elements at work in this England of ours, namely : (α) the old British spirit, which still lingered in the extreme parts of England, and especially of Wales, Scotland, and Ireland ; (β) the home tastes and musical fashions of the Saxons or English, which were to be replaced eventually by (γ) the musical means and modes of the new generations of Englishmen. These were the parts out of which the important musical fabric of British art of to-day were to spring. One more powerful factor— Norman art and influence—was presently to step in, and the solid, if mixed, foundation of our country's musical life and practice was permanently provided.

PRINCIPAL AUTHORITIES.

'Anglo-Saxon Chronicle.'
'Popular Music of the Olden Time'   Chappell.
'History of England'   -   -   -   Lingard.
'History of Music' -   -   -   -   Burney.
'English Writers'   -   -   -   Morley.
'English Songs'   -   -   -   Ritson.
'History of the Anglo-Saxons' -   -   Sharon Turner.
'History of Wales' -   -   -   -   Williams.
'Reliques of Ancient English Poetry'   Percy.
'Music of the Anglo-Saxons'   -   -   Wackerbarth.
'Saxons in England'   -   -   -   Kemble.
'*Historia Ecclesiastica*'   -   -   -   Bede.
'Constitutional History' -   -   -   Stubbs.

CHAPTER III.

BARDS, BARDISM AND SCALDS.

Cæsar's References to Music—Bardic Triads—The Eisteddfod, or
Session of Bards—Famous British Bards—Bardism and the
British Administration—Electing the Bards—Vortigern's
Example—Arthur and other Bards—The Scóp—Widsith—
Specimens of his Songs—Deor—Scalds—Their Origin and
Relative Orders—Taliesin—A Musical Competition at Con-
way—The *Leges Wallicæ*, or Welsh Laws and the Bards—
Howel—Privileges and Rank of the Bards—Secular Music
in Alfred's Reign—The Saxon Harp—Its Manufacture—Poet
and Musician sundered in England.

CÆSAR mentions British music here and there in his
'Commentaries.' There appear to have been three
musical officers, or privileged bards, attached to the
British King's palace, and enjoying the
favour and confidence of the ruler. They
were the Harp Bard of the King, whose duty it was
to communicate every new song to the Sovereign ;
the Crwth, or Poetic Bard ; and the Ensign Bard,
who recounted the genealogical tables and deeds of
Britain's famous sons. They stood the judges of the
country, and administered the law. At some even

Cæsar.

earlier time they must have been held in really high esteem, since an ancient Triad singles them out :

> ' Three men there are of same regard :
> A king, a harper, and a bard.'

Tacitus—and his Britons are not the savages of Cæsar's narrative (205-276 A.D.)—relates that the ancient Britons stored their history and annals in verse, sung to the music of the harp. As authentic records of early facts, customs, etc., these bardic songs and poems, then, are invaluable, for the laws strictly forbade the bards to introduce fable, or to pervert the truth in their narrations, under penalty of fine, imprisonment, loss of dignity, and even death.

The Bardic Triads—fragments of written evidence which are treasured in museums and libraries—record the names of the principal among these ancient bards, and their characteristics. These memorials are in the Welsh language, some of them as early as the tenth, eleventh, and twelfth centuries, and were originally oral traditions, which anciently were sung by generations of bards at their gatherings :

> ' But heed, ye bards, that for the sign of onset
> Ye sound the ancientest of all your rhymes,
> Whose birth tradition notes not, nor who fram'd
> Its lofty strains.'*

The Welsh national meeting, entitled Eisteddfod, or session of bards, had its origin in these remote

* ' Caractacus ' (Mason).

times, when the bardic or Druidical institution prevailed in this island in its primitive purity. The
most ancient notices on this subject now extant

The Eis- occur in the Triads of Dyvnwal Moclmud,
teddfod. a British lawgiver, who is thought to
have lived about three or four centuries before the
Christian era. In these early records the meeting
in question is minutely described, under the name of

REMAINS OF DRUIDS' TEMPLE, STONEHENGE.

Gorsedd y Beirdd, or Congress of the Bards, and is
numbered among the national privileged assemblies
of the Cymry. The Gorsedd was not originally
confined to the cultivation of music and poetry, but
had an ulterior and more important aim in the
preservation of bardic traditions, the commemoration
of illustrious and praiseworthy deeds, and a general
promotion of religious, moral, and scientific instruc-

tion. Among the places in this island which were selected for the occasion, Salisbury Plain is conspicuous, as the stupendous Druidical remains, still to be found there, abundantly testify. Other probable localities were the island of Bardsey, the Hebrides, *i.e.*, Æbudæ, or Ovates Islands, from the class of Druids called Eubates or Ovates, who sang the sacred and prophetic hymns.

How long the Gorsedd continued to retain its original constitution and purpose cannot be ascertained with any degree of precision. The wars and intestine feuds, consequent on the successive invasions of the Romans and Saxons, were fatal to the exercise of a practice that was peculiarly founded on principles of national peace and tranquillity. For some centuries, therefore, we are without any particular records of these musical meetings. However, as the ancient Welsh poets have frequent allusions to them, and as the important privileges of the bards are recognised as well by the Saxon writer Bede as by the laws of Howel, or Hywel, compiled two centuries later, we may conclude that the right of holding these harmonious congresses was in these times frequently exercised.

Alawn's fame was long preserved in the locality of Alawr Beirdd in Anglesey, named after him. Concerning Gwron there is scanty account. These 'Fundamental' bards, as they have also been called, are specially honoured, because they secured official recognition for their order long before the idea was revived in the minstrelsy age. There had been bards like Tydain—Father of the Muse—who first established British vocal tradition into system and order, but hitherto no privilege or distinction was accorded to musicians. Once under the ægis of the government, however, they became a recognised and legally protected body, as did their successors the minstrels.

Little wonder that for several centuries the singer and harpist won the hearts and ears of the natives in all parts of early Britain. Their theme was **British Bards.** stirring in its note and drift. It told of Tydain, whose tomb was the summit of Bryn Aren in Merionydd ; of Gwyddon Guabebon, 'the first in the world to make vocal song '—as their tremendous faith had it ; of Hû, surnamed the Mighty, whose fame spread over the island of Iona, and was not forgotten as long afterwards as the time of St. Columba, Apostle of the Picts, in the sixth century —all illustrious Cambrians, 'ministers of song,' and conservators of traditions as loved of the natives as the true soil on which they stood erect.

The warriors of the island, too, had their deeds sung thus early. There was Gwrgan Varvdrwch— the Bushy-bearded Songster—not less renowned in music than in war, a reputed British king, who flourished some 375 years B.C., and is credited to have founded the city of Cambridge, where he and his son Gwythelin set up their regal seat ; also

Cubelyn, twenty-third King of Britain (348 B.C.),
whose skill in music Caius celebrated; Blegywryd,
King of Britain 190 years B.C., who excelled all that
lived before him both as a singer and musical performer; Eidiol Gleddyfeud, or Ruddy Sword—
another warrior bard and arch-druid, whose nick-
name, ' Ruddy Sword,' refers probably to his duties
at the sacrifices offered to the gods; the Emperor
Manogan, 120 B.C., called also the Man of Joy, or
Musician; Beli the Great, and several more—
desperate foemen when disputing an inch of soil,
albeit peaceful enough in unmolested enjoyment of
their home pursuits. Among these music stood out
beyond all else.

In many directions there was a call for music—
not a too refined art, perhaps, but one born of
splendid barbarism—among these sharers of grand
heroic days and ages which history recounteth not.
The pathetic nature of such earliest native music
may be gauged by the following melodies which
tradition ascribes to the ancient British:

MWYNEN GWYNEDD.

(The Sweet Melody of North Wales.)

It is difficult to fix the date of the following tune, but it is believed to allude to the departure of King Cadwaladr when a plague and famine raged in his dominion.   He sailed to Britany to his cousin Alan about the year 665 A.D.   It possesses all the character, however, of the early British music :

YMDAWI AD Y BRENHIN.

(The Departure of the King.)

Sorrowfully.

There was much for bardic song-men to do in an
age when men depended upon the memory for the
preservation of fact. Pedigrees and items of genealogy had to be told by the bards, who accompanied
on the harp all that they narrated : the division of
lands required to be known and confirmed ; the

praises of benefactors were to be sung ; national
matters needed to be reduced to an almanack form ;
the herald of the palace was expected to inform his
King and chiefs of events of note, past and present,
while ovates had to divine and augur.   All this fell
to the share of these poet-musicians, who sang their
records, and accompanied them on an instrument.

We know that the order of the bards was a
prominent feature in the British administrative
system.   Such a natural element, together with the
enduring vitality of an art-growth which had been
begotten of Britons themselves, which was, in fact,
born of the very soil of Britain, will easily account
for the hold which the native music continued to
have on the Britons long after the inroads of the
Saxons and the introduction of their barbarous
music—such as the first sample undoubtedly was.
The Briton clung to his own tune, preferring its
pathetic tone and interval—the independent style
and beauty of which have been mentioned—to anything the foreigners brought with them.   He scorned
the music of the intruder as disdainfully as he did
his intrepidity and daring.

Prominent among the oft-mentioned British bards
in the period we are considering is Aneurin, son of
Câw.   Chief of the Gododinians, he was surnamed
King of the Bards, and flourished about 510 A.D.
He also was one of the three Golden Torque
bards, whose necks were adorned with gold chains

—symbols of honour, and denoting high proficiency in the art. Two others who enjoyed this proud distinction were Prince Llywarch Hen—ruler of Cumbria (580 A.D.)—and Brenin Penbeirdd. Brenin the natives surnamed King Supreme of the Bards, for he was the most renowned player on the harp then known. At about this same time appears Gwrhir, who was bard to Teilaw, Bishop of Llandaff 514 A.D.

With Brenin Penbeirdd we get a glimpse of bardic usage. In his time the custom was to sit under the oak and decide relatively the bards of **Bardic** every degree. This took place annually. **Usage.** Three orders of singers and musicians were adjudged to be preferable, and of an exalted class. These were the harper, because he praised God on a stringed instrument; the ode bard, because he praised God in vocal songs; and the heraldic bard, who praised the Deity and preserved in song and verse the memorable actions of warriors, and all excellencies, personal and national, worthy of commendation for the good of the world. The establishment of Prince Vortigern—Prince of the Demetæ tribe in the middle of the fifth century—included a retinue of twelve principal bards. On a certain occasion he found it necessary to consult them and to gather information which they should have supplied. Subsequently the King found out that he had been deceived by his bards, whereupon he had them put

to death, either to satisfy his personal vexation, or
to exact the penalty of the law, which forbade the
bards from subverting the truth in whatever they
sang or related.

At times the King himself was a bard, so highly
was music long regarded in our country. One such
was Talhairn Tad Awen (540 A.D.), of Llanvair
Talhairn in Denbighshire. Owain, Prince of Reged
in the sixth century, and whose tomb at Llan-Morvael
the 'memorials' say was 'girt with four stones,' was
another. Then there was Arthur, of Round Table
renown, crowned Emperor of Britain by Archbishop
Dubritius at Caerleon-on-Usk.

'Emperor and leader of the toil of war,'

Llywarch Hen sings, when recounting his prowess
and the daring of Geraint ab Erbin, Admiral of the
British fleet, who, with King Arthur, drove the
King Saxons from our shores (530 A.D.). Arthur
Arthur. could tune the harp with cunning hand, and
through his hall the strains of music favoured many
a knight and chief. Under the system of the Druids
there were three musicians who, it appears, filled
the high office of 'imperial performers on the harp.'
King Arthur was one of these, the others contemporary with him being one Crella, and Glewlwyd
Gavaelvawr, or 'Brave Gray with Powerful Grasp,'
who was Master of the Ceremonies in King Arthur's
palace, and one of his knights. With one more

enumeration from the long list of famous British bards, and this of a period as far off as 640 A.D., we are made acquainted with the 'three bloody-speared bards of Britain,' though why they should rejoice under such a distinction is not recorded. Their names were Taliesin, head of the bards ; Avan Verddig, bard to King Cadwallon, the son of Cadvan, King of North Wales ; and Aneurin— perchance a descendant of that Aneurin already mentioned, who was styled the King of the Bards.

Such were the men who sang and wept over the departing ancient song and harmony of Britain. Eye-witnesses of goodlier times, memory and tradition alike revived in their breasts story and tone which made them hate their new enemies even more bitterly than they did the Romans. They were not likely to be willingly affected by the manners and customs of the invaders, rapidly as these were thrusting them-selves upon the country by reason of the constant ingress of Saxons. This exclusiveness was purposely studied, and to it must be attributed the slow decay of British music ; for we must remember that the early music and native harmonious methods remained long after the arrival of Saxons, Danes, and Normans.

Very similar to the British bards in their habits and occupation were the Saxon scóps or scalds. In England the scóp became the Anglo-Saxon scald —a word which denotes a smoother or polisher of language.

The origin of the art of the scóp or scald was
attributed to Odin or Wodin, the father of the
Saxon gods, and the professors of it, like the
Saxon ancient British bards, were held by the
Scalds. Saxons in the highest esteem. Their skill
was considered as something divine; their persons
were accounted sacred; their companionship was
required by kings; while they were everywhere
loaded with honours and rewards.

When the Saxons turned from the forests of
Angle-land it was not, as we have seen, to leave all
their social habits and customs behind. Many were
brought with them into England, and contributed to
make musical Britain what it now is. The scóp
and gleeman, for instance, made the minstrel of
Norman and later times, and of the minstrel was
eventually begotten the ballad-singer and concert-
room vocalist of the past and to-day. The scóp
invented and often also recited; the gleeman recited
and otherwise provided entertainment as musician,
and rope-dancer.

Widsith was a scóp of the fourth century, attached
to the Court of Queen Ealhhild, among the Myr-
gings by the Elbe. He, like most scóps, could sing
loudly in praise of his benefactors, and still more
loudly concerning his own virtues and talents:

> 'Therefore I can sing
> And tell a tale, recount in the Mead Hall
> How men of high race gave rich gifts to me.'

' A circlet given to me by Guthhere,
A welcome treasure for reward of song.
That was no tardy king.'

                        ' And I was
With Eormanric, and all the while the King
Of Goths was good to me.   Chief in his burgh,
A collar of six hundred sceats of gold—
Beaten gold—counted in coin, he gave me.'

' When I and Skilling for our conquering lord
With clear voice raised the song, loud to the harp,
The sound was music ; many a stately man,
Who well knew what was right, then said in words
That never had they heard a happier song.'

The success of the scóp depended wholly upon
his power to please.   He struck the glee-beam, as
the rude harp was called, in the halls of the great
chiefs, whose deeds were shaped into triumphant
song, wherein enemies figured as monsters, while
the chiefs were praised as little else than gods.
Sometimes the scóp's own genius failed him—perhaps in composing, playing, or singing.   Then, to
hold his ground, he would associate himself with a
comrade who supplied the deficiency, for it was a
disgrace to be supplanted in the favour of a chief.

The scóp Deor was so displaced, and his ' Lament '
shows him a miserable wanderer—though not altogether without hope : ' I had a good following, a
faithful lord, for many winters ; until that now
Heorrenda, a song-crafty man, has obtained the
landright, which the refuge of warriors gave to me
before.'

Whether called scóp or scald, they were generally poets and musicians combined, whose main employment was to celebrate the deeds of the brave and great in heroic poems, sung to the accompaniment of the harp or lyre, just as did the British bard. Each rich and powerful chief brought with him his native bard, whose duty was to transmit history and to shape the lay or ballad recounting the valorous deeds dear to the ears of the noble. The Teuton bard was indeed little inferior to the Celtic. The people respected and welcomed him wherever he went, just as the British did their bards, for they loved to hear such narratives as the scalds told, and the recounting of deeds of courage and daring incited them to heights of great ambition and valorous desire. The King and Prince even constituted the Bard the eighth officer in dignity at his Court.

Their order, divided into four classes, consisted of the most distinguished musicians, outside which was a lesser order of itinerant musicians and performers, from which probably later musical oddmen and merry-makers sprung. Among so jovial a race, it is not surprising that amusement-makers multiplied apace. Itinerant performers, musicians of all kinds, and buffoons, increased amazingly, and for many subsequent generations they plied their calling at all early English fairs and gatherings, where music, song, and dance would be sure to please.

One such wandering musician was Cynewulf (720-

800), especially famed in Northumbria. The songs and music of these Saxon musicians were extremely affecting, and productive frequently of great good in quelling quarrels and preventing bloodshed. At times when the armies of rival princes were about to engage in furious combat, the bards rushed in between them, and engaged in playing subdued strains. Then the contending forces, with their fury softened by the music, and respecting the bards, desisted and submitted to be dispersed without loss of honour.

Taliesin was a Welsh bard, who flourished about 550 A.D. He sang in the time of King **Taliesin.** Maelgwn Gwynedd, but he was originally patronized by Elphin, son of Urien.

An interesting story has come down of this King Maelgwn, showing something of the struggle for supremacy in musical contests even in those far-off days. Maelgwn (or, as others say, his father Casswallon) went to judge between the poets and the musicians, and caused the poets and harpers to swim the river Conway. The harpers and crwthers' instruments were spoiled, whereby the poets, whose tools could not be destroyed, won the competition. There was some humour here, probably. Music and poetry were often ranked as separate professions, and at the public contests of skill the musicians invariably carried off the prize. Maelgwn, by way of encouraging the poets, adopted the ruse, so that the poets, who had some ground to recover, might get on a level with the estimate entertained of the musicians. Taliesin, with other British bards, kept the old national musical spirit alive during the troublous Saxon period in which he lived. His vocal song was framed upon five, out of some twenty-four, metres which the native bards used, and these were denominated the five pillars or canons of poetry. Among his odes is 'Cunobline's Incantation,' wherein occur repeated and appreciative references to music, remarks which show clearly that it was only necessary to remind the people of their musical traditions and excellence to inspire them with all the fire and enthusiasm which the art could provoke.

> ' The king of the land of harmony,
> Mine is the lot to lament him.'

Such is the prevailing note of Taliesin's productions, and probably of all those bardic compositions which have become lost. Their object was to insure success to the heroes in their day of battle, and the recitation of the odes was held to be productive of a protective charm—a mystic efficacy from the Gorchanan—to the body :

> ' The guardian spell of Cynvelyn,
> On the plains of Gododin,
> Shall it not prevail over Odyn ?'

The tone of this expression shows that the spirit of enmity against the Saxon was far from crushed in

the Briton as he was met in Taliesin. Another
extract from a poem* of a battle supposed to have
been fought in the Vale of Garant, is suggestive of
music being employed in Taliesin's day in much the
same way as it is used in modern warfare.

> 'The sons of slaughter the reeking plain will leave,
> When the string of harmony resounds.'

Taliesin mentions, too, the hunting-horns, which
were the common accompaniment to the person.
This occurs in 'The Salutation' poem, wherein
Taliesin is welcoming Ugnach, a celebrated bard :

> 'Thou knight that goest towards the city,
> With white dogs and large hunting-horns.'

The *Leges Wallicæ*, or Welsh Laws, throw much
light on Saxon habits and customs, especially concerning the bards. The laws were framed by Howel
Leges Wallicæ, or Welsh Bardic Laws. Dha, or Howel the Good, King of the
Welsh (915-948 A.D.), one who, as a
chronicler says, 'was greatly loved by
every Welshman, and by the wise among
the Saxons.' Besides his qualities of ability and
learning he was a devoted lover of music. At his
Court every wandering bard found a home as long
as it pleased him to remain, while a talented musician
was permanently attached to the palace. Another

---

* The original Welsh of this British relic is found in one of the
oldest Welsh manuscripts—the Black Book of Caermarthen
(Y Llyfe dû o Gaerfyrddin)—in the eighth century handwriting,
on goat-skin.

musical Prince Howel, son of Prince Owain
Gwynedd, one of the ancient British Bardic Kings,
is recorded. The latter is supposed to have flourished
about 1140, having for a contemporary Owain Cy-
veilliog, Prince of Powis, also a British Bardic King.

From these Welsh Laws we gather much interesting information relating to musical procedure of the
Saxon period. The *Bardd Teulu*, or Bard of the
Palace, was, in rank, the eighth officer of the King's
household ; he was also one of the royal guests, and
sat at his table, next to the Heir Apparent. On
his appointment the bard received a harp from the
King and a golden ring from the Queen. He won
his claim to pre-eminence by his superior merit in
the science of music and poetry at one of the British
Olympics. The King found him his woollen apparel
and a horse, and the Queen gave him his linen
apparel. His lodging was in the house of the Heir
Apparent (who was the controller of the household),
and on three great festivals in the year it was the
office of the prince to deliver the harp into the
hands of the bard when about to perform, for which
service he was entitled to a song (or a tune) from
the bard whenever he chose. When the royal
family desired a song in the great hall, the *Bardd-
Cadeiriawg*, or Chaired Bard, had first to sing a
hymn in praise of God, and another in honour of the
King, and of the most worthy of his ancestors and
their exploits. When these were over the bard of

the palace was to sing next upon some other subject, in the lower part of the hall ; and if the Queen
desired to have music after she returned from the
table to her apartment, he was then to perform three
tender and eloquent songs or pathetic tunes, different
from those which he had played in the hall. The
bard accompanied the army when it marched on a
warlike expedition into an enemy's country ; and
when the soldiers were preparing for battle he
recited and performed to them the animating song
called ' Unbeniaerth Prydain,' or, the ' Monarchy of
Britain,' to remind them of their ancient right, in
praise of their brave ancestors, and to inspire them
to heroism. For this service he was rewarded with
one of the most valuable things of the plunder. If
he went with other bards upon a musical peregrina-
tion he was entitled to a double portion for his
share. He held his land free. If the bard desired
any favour of the King, he was to perform to him
one of his own compositions ; if of a nobleman, he
was to perform to him three ; and if of a plebeian
he was to set him to sleep. Whoever slightly injured the bard was fined six cows, and a hundred and
twenty pence ; and whoever slew a bard was fined
a hundred and twenty-six cows. Five bards formed
part of the King's retinue when he rode in state.

The *Pencerdd*, or *Cadeir-fardd*, the Head of
Song or Chaired Bard, was one who had gained
pre-eminence in a musical and poetical contest, in an

Eisteddfod, or Session of the Bards, held triennially
in the royal palace or in the hall of the lord. This
solemnity was decided by the venerable judge of
the palace, and as a reward he received from the
victorious bard a bugle-horn, a gold ring, and a
cushion for his chair of dignity. This Chaired
Bard, according to Howel's Laws, was the bard of a
district, or county, and chief president of music and
poetry within that precinct, and in him was vested
the control of all the other bards within that jurisdic-
tion. He was also a bardic teacher, and at stated
periods he prepared students to take their degrees,
which were ratified by the Sessions of the Bards
every third year ; and he also regulated and assigned
to each of the other bards their *clera* circuits within
his district. This *Pencerdd Gwlad*, or head bard of
the district, had his lands free ; his perquisites arose
from his scholars, and he was also entitled to a fee
from every bride, and the *Amobr*, or marriage fine
of the daughters of all the inferior bards within his
district. He sat in the tenth place in the royal hall.
His privilege of protection lasted from the beginning
of his first song in the hall of the palace to the conclusion of the last. Every *Pencerdd*, or chief bard,
to whom the lord assigned privileges was supplied
with musical instruments—that is, a harp to one, a
crwth to another, and pipes to the third ; and when
the bards died such instruments reverted to the lord
or his successor.

Secular music, apart from the art of the bard, begins to stand out as an item of polite education with King Alfred's reign. The harp is constantly

Secular Music in King Alfred's Reign. being noticed as an adjunct to all secular music ; indeed, it was the national instrument—taking precedence among the Saxons over the psaltry, fithele, and the ' pip,' or pipe—just as it was with the Britons, who styled it, however, the crwth, or teglin. It was one of the three things that were necessary to constitute a gentleman or freeman, and none could pretend to

that character who had not one of these favourite instruments, and could, besides, play upon it. To prevent slaves from pretending to be gentlemen it was expressly forbidden to teach, or to permit them to play upon the harp ; and none but the King, the King's musicians, and gentlemen, were allowed to have harps in their possession. A gentleman's harp was

HARP OF THE NINTH CENTURY.

(*From MS. of St. Blaise.*)

not liable to be seized for debt, because the want of it would have degraded him from his rank, and reduced him to that of a slave.* That it was an

---

* Distinction is made of three orders of harps—the harp of the King, the harp of the chief bard or laureate, and the harp of a gentleman.

instrument common also among the Saxons before their settlement here, however, may be seen in the Anglo-Saxon words *hearpe* and *hearpa*, which are not derived from the British nor any Celtic language, but are the genuine Gothic originals. The word 'glee,' Anglo-Saxon *gligg*, it may be added, is another instance of a Saxon radix from which a variety of musical terms and phrases spring, thus affording strong evidence that the Saxons were a people who brought musical materials into this country.

Alfred in one of his translations furnishes us with a clue to the mode of playing the harp, *i.e.*, whether with the naked finger or a plectrum—a rather moot point. Burney instances the matter. 'Alfred,' says the historian, 'translates the Latin word *plectrum* into *hearp-nægel* (Saxon), by which it would seem that the harp, in the time of this royal musician, was played, like the ancient lyre, with a *plectrum*. Nægel is likewise Saxon for a nail of the finger or toe.'

No writers of the period make reference to the manufacture of these harps among other instruments —matters of this nature having altogether slipped their attention—and whether it was a separate calling, or whether the harper, Briton, Saxon or Scandinavian, constructed his own instrument, does not transpire. It is probable that he did, since all the materials were close at hand, and his skill as a harper would guide him in making exactly the class and style of instrument that he required. There were no imports of musical instruments in such early times, and Celt and Teuton were thrown much upon their own resources in such matters, leaving it quite feasible, as has been explained, for even the ancient Britons to have possessed much more in the way of instrumental material than is commonly credited to them. At the same time there is, it must be admitted, something incongruous in the performer having first to construct his instrument, especially if we reflect upon what the possible consequences would be if present-day violin, harp and pianoforte *virtuosi* had to go through such an experience before getting anything to play upon !

PERFORMER ON THREE-STRINGED CROUT.

But whether under the name of scóp, gleeman, or scald, the ancient musician or bard, as he existed among the pagan northmen, declined in time, and with the sweeping changes in England, especially at the Norman Conquest, gave place to a new musician.

When the Saxons had thoroughly settled here as Englishmen, the old poet-musician of their German home became two persons, viz., poet and musician. The former was a man of letters—a poet as we understand the term now. The latter was one who gained his livelihood by singing verses to the harp, principally at the houses of the great, whereat he and his companions were welcomed and hospitably treated, just as the scóps or scalds had been before them.

Principal Authorities.

'Anglo-Saxon Chronicle.'
'History of the Anglo-Saxons' - - Sharon Turner.
'Music of the Anglo-Saxons' - - Wackerbarth.
'History of England' - - - Lingard.
'English Writers' - - - - Morley.
'Dictionary of Music and Musicians' Grove.
'History of Music' - - - - Burney.
'Popular Music of the Olden Time' - Chappell.
'Reliques of Ancient English Poetry' Percy.
'Beowulf' - - - - -
'Chronicles' - - - - - Ingulph.
'*Historia Ecclesiastica*' - - - Bede.
'Early English Church History' - Bright.
'Essays on English Church Music' - Mason.

CHAPTER IV.

AUGUSTINE AND HIS MUSICAL WORK.

The Coming of Augustine—Scene at Thanet—Ambrosian *versus* Gregorian Church Music—Gregory—Instruments in the early Church Services—Repairing the Churches—Notable Abbeys—Monastic Musical Establishments—A Magnificent Dedication Service—Saxon Musical Instruments—The Cotton MSS. References to Instruments—String and Percussion—The Organ—The Psaltery—The Viola—Drums and Cymbals—The *Sambuca-Canticum*—Aldhelm and the Trumpet—Tuning in Chords.

HERE we reach a great situation—one no less momentous than the introduction of the Roman Church service and teaching into England. The event, as we all know, was to prove pregnant with tremendous issues in the future social, political, and religious history of our country.

The upraising of Christ's Cross in England by Augustine (died 605 A.D.)—an event which has been hinted at in the previous chapter—was **The Coming of Augustine.** the signal for a fresh outburst of sincere musical emotion. The old British Church services had all but died out in the distractions of years of war and bloodshed with pagans, so that there were few altars left whereat sacred music was poured forth. Withal there was to be a glorious revival. At the spot where the Roman missionary and his band landed with their Gospel of Peace, and wherever they went, there arose for the first time in this country the glorious strains of chants and melodies of the Roman Church which are to be heard in so many of the churches of Great Britain to-day where Gregorian music is used.

Pope Gregory (c. 550-604 A.D.), moved to extend Christianity into England, charged Augustine, a Roman Abbot, with the mission. He selected forty missionaries, and one day took his departure from the Benedictine monastery of St. Andrew's on the Cœlian Hill. The journey from Rome to England in those days was a serious undertaking, but after surmounting many difficulties these Gospel messengers reached the favourable coast of Kent. Augustine chose this as his landing-place, conscious, no doubt, that Ethelbert, the King, though himself a worshipper of Odin, had not long before married a French Princess who was a Christian. The flat and marshy coast of Thanet afforded a good landing-stage, and, what was more, was nigh to Canterbury, the city for which they were bound. From this place the Primate of All England has since taken his title, while in its Cathedral a service of prayer and praise has daily ascended

for hundreds of years with scarcely a single inter-
ruption.

A safe landing being effected (597), saintly Augustine, a man of great stature, at the head of his band
of faithful monks marched to the meeting-place,
heralded by a procession bearing a silver cross, with
a picture of the crucified Christ, and singing a
Litany and a jubilant Alleluia. That solemn Litany
was the precursor of many a glorious pæan of sacred
harmony which has rung in our church roofs for
these centuries after.

Every detail befitted the occasion. The canopy
of heaven afforded roof to the actors in this historical
scene. Ethelbert, King of the Jutes in Kent,
seated under an oak, was surrounded by his chiefs
and body-guard; and the spectacle must, indeed,
have been an impressive one, as the Christian
missionary, with his train of monks, paced the green-
sward to take the 'yea' or 'nay' of the regal pagan.

The sacred music—probably a special Canticle or
Psalm, since we learn that it was sung antiphonally
to a Gregorian Tone—touched the heart of the King,
who gave permission that Christianity might be
preached in his dominions. The answer was received joyfully. A Benediction was given, the procession turned, and with sure step, to the accompaniment of holy songs, these messengers of peace
were soon treading the dust of the quiet city of
Canterbury.

Here good Queen Bertha had provided for the missionaries a house adjoining the Church of St. Martin, on the hill to the east of the city, where anciently had been a British church, and where a Christian altar stood. To this church Augustine

CHURCH OF ST. MARTIN, ON THE HILL.

'dayly went to syng service, say Masses, pray, preache and christen.'

Thus was Pope Gregory's wish, as he beheld the British slave-children in the Roman market-place, consummated :

> 'Subjects of Saxon *Ælla*, they shall sing,
>   Glad *Halle*lujahs to the eternal King.'
>   WORDSWORTH.

Few are unfamiliar with that beautiful story and Gregory's resolve on meeting the golden-haired children from Deira. 'What is the name of the kinge of that province?' asked Gregory. 'When it was answered that his name was Ælla, "Alleluia," sayde he, "must be *sounge* in that Prince's dominions to the prayse of Almightie God his Creator."'* Gregory, it will be noticed, used the word 'sung' and not 'said.'

Thus the coming of Augustine marked a new era in Church music—an awakening, as it were, into the early morning light of a glorious new-born day.

The style of chanting ordered by Ambrose (340-397 A.D.) for use in the churches had, in the course of years, lost its stately simplicity, and was neglected

Ambrosian Church Music. for an ecclesiastical music of a more gay and florid style—produced by an amalgamation of pagan theatrical music with the Ambrosian chant. This deteriorated art-form had found its way into England, and was adopted in the few scattered churches where the old British services were continued during the Saxon invasions; but, unhappily, at this period a greater evil existed in the almost total neglect of the Christian worship throughout the land. So, practically, before Augustine there lay the work of re-conversion, and in this task sacred music was to prove a sure and powerful agent.

* Bede (Thomas Stapleton's translation).

Born about the year 550 A.D., Gregory, whose
system Augustine adopted, had done much for
music at Rome, establishing there a singing-school,

Gregory. whereat Church music could be taught,
which flourished for full three hundred
years after his death (A.D. 604).

It would appear that the juvenile choristers were
little better behaved then than they frequently are
now, for the harmonious rudiments had betimes to
be instilled with the aid of a mild corrective ; and
long after Gregory's time visitors used to be shown
the whip for the choristers, and the couch on which
Gregory reposed when staying at the school. His
reformed system of Church music included only
such chants and melodies as the first Fathers of the
Church had approved. While Ambrose, as we have
seen, used four scales, called the ' Authentic ' modes,
Gregory introduced four more, known as ' Plagal '
or relative scales, thus increasing the Ecclesiastical
Modes to eight.

GREGORY'S PLAGAL MODES.

First Tone: Hypo-Dorian or Æolian.

Second Tone: Hypo-Phrygian.

Third Tone : Hypo-Lydian or Ionian.

Fourth Tone : Hypo-Mixo-Lydian.

The latter he constructed by prefacing each original scale with its last four tones—*e.g.*, in the first scale (D—D) the four final tones are A, B, C, D ; these he placed an octave lower, at the same time putting them before the initial note of the scale, viz., D. The new scale thus formed ranged from A to A, and the whole eight scales, *i.e.*, the four Authentic and the four Plagal, were then called Church Modes. Written in present-day notation they are as follows :

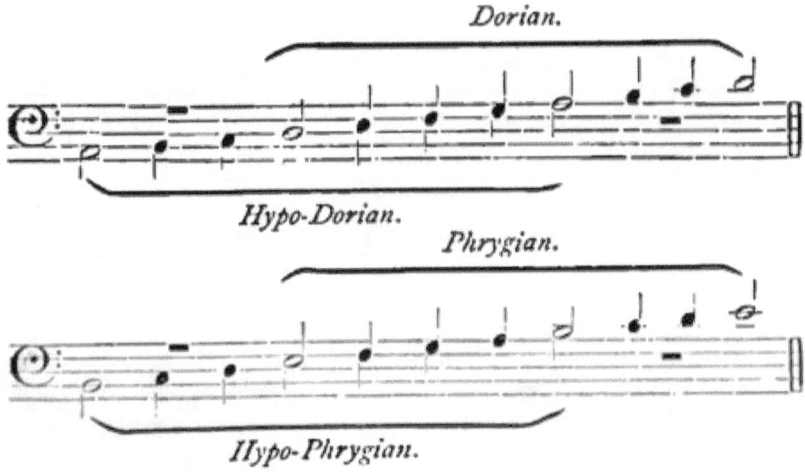

It will be noticed that the initial note of the Authentic scale becomes the fourth note of the Plagal scale. Upon these Gregory built the melodies or 'tones' which have ever since been associated with his name.

THE EIGHT GREGORIAN TONES.

First Tone.

Dixit Dominus Domino me - o, Se-de a dextris me - is.

Second Tone.

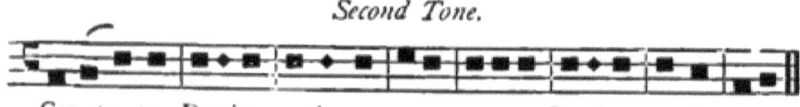

Can - ta - te Domino canticum novum, cantate Domino omnis terra.

Third Tone.

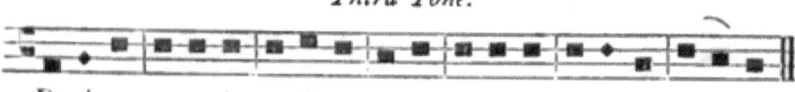

Dominus regnavit ex-ul-tet terra, lætentur in - su-læ mul - tæ.

Fourth Tone.

Qui confidunt in Domino sicut mons Sion, non commovebitur in e·ternum.

Fifth Tone.

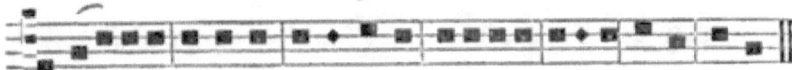

E·ruc·ta·vit cor meum verbum bonum, di·co e·go o·pe·ra me·a re·gi.

Sixth Tone.

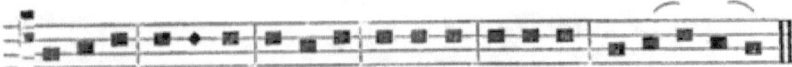

Laudate Dominum de cœ·lis, lau·da·te e·um in ex·cel·sis.

Seventh Tone.

Le·va·vi oculos meos in monte, unde ve·ni·et aux·i·li·um mi·hi.

Eighth Tone.

In ex·i·tu Is·ra·el de Egypto, domus Jacob de po·pu·lo bar·ba·ro.

These tones, arranged to the hymns, canticles, psalms, and other parts of the Liturgy, Augustine brought with him to England; and from that day to this they have been used more or less in English churches, whether under Roman or Protestant rule. All had to sing the *canto fermo*, or fixed melody, and improvisings in the shape of harmonial adornments were strictly forbidden. This was to distinguish Gregorian from that florid style of music which had crept into the religious services. The square and lozenge-shaped notes, familiar in present-day Gregorian music, if not actually invented by this Church musician, were at an early period applied to his chants, and came to England through Augustine. The Gregorian era, therefore, may be regarded as a distinctly second epoch in English Church music history.

That instrumental music soon followed upon Augustine's exertions in the cause of Church music in England—if, indeed, such accompaniments to **Instruments in the Church.** singing were not in use much earlier in the British Church services—is by no means unlikely. With the example of David and the Temple musical system before them, the Fathers of the Church encouraged instruments as well as

CITHARA.

singing in the services. 'If you accompany your voices with the lyre or cithara,' said Clemens Alexandrinus, in the second century, 'you will incur no censure.' Augustine urged the 'singing of the psalms to the accompaniment of the lyre or psaltery,' from which it is evident that boisterous instruments like cymbals and dulcimers were eschewed for the sweeter and more chaste accompaniments of the lyre and harp. No testimony can be adduced, however, proving the use of instruments, suitable or otherwise, at this early stage of ecclesiastical music in England, when, the glories of the ancient British Church having departed, the missionaries from Rome may well have contented themselves with such variety as was afforded by the plain, simple singing of the chants in unison by choir and congregation alternately.

What the old Britons and Anglo-Saxons thought of the first Roman Church music is unrecorded, but that it was received with favour may be easily imagined if we consider its rapid spread over the island, as new churches took the places of those destroyed by the Saxons. The ravages of the Teuton had proved disastrous indeed to the ancient British Church, and so fierce was the enmity between Briton and Saxon, that advances from the British clergy towards a reconciliation availed but little. What with the paganism of the invaders and the native inclination towards the Druidical teachings in all remote parts of the island, the Christian clergy were sore put to it. It was to heal the breach between the natives and their invaders, and to preach Christianity to these Saxons, that Augustine was sent from Rome :

> ' For Christe's love and His Apostles twelve
> He taught, but first he followed it him selve.'
>
> CHAUCER.

Wherever Augustine or his followers had founded churches—and they sprang up with rapidity—there was the Gregorian chant and model Roman service

adopted. It may be that the people longed for
some such sustaining art as the Roman missionaries

**Spread of
Gregorian
Music.** brought with them. The old Church
music had been all but annihilated, cast
to the winds, stamped out. Successive
periods of fire and sword visitations had consumed
every remnant of the past British Church service,
whatever its form. Little wonder, then, that native
and Saxon eventually alike drained eagerly at the
new fount which Pope Gregory's messengers brought
with them. Rude ears, if not others, would listen
attentively to that which was chanted by the monks
with much dramatic energy.

After all the destruction and burning, slaughter
and bloodshed attending the Teuton invasion of
Britain, there came a lull. The havoc had been
awful and complete ; but as the ravenous wolf lifts
its teeth from its prey to pant awhile, so the ferocity
of the Saxon at length slackened. He cast his eyes
to heaven from sheer satiety of despoil, yet to him
it was nought but a bewildering blank, and his faith
in the gods of his country was beginning to falter.
It is terrible to contemplate what the native Church
and the clergy must have passed through during the
slow but certain occupation by the Saxons ; but it is
a relief to reflect over the quiet yet successful work
that went on. While conquering, the invaders were
being conquered, so that a wonderful change was ere
long to come over the land. The predatory Saxons,

who for generations had been fighting their way into England, were no sooner safely located here than they dropped their profession of sea piracy and became permanently at home. It is surprising how they took to the soil, cultivating it, and erecting dwellings after the fashion of the peoples and lands which they had renounced. Every favourable season also brought fresh bands of these English—each generation better than its predecessor, and fully ready for such a beneficial and grateful aid as music, whether sacred or secular.

Now did both Britons and Saxons consort to repair the devastation of the past. The churches were the first to receive attention—and many were built of both wood and stone—for from the clergy the training of the people in religious and secular teachings could alone come. With marvellous industry, stately minsters and abbeys were here and there erected on old church sites, and matin bell and sacred choral chant once more lent themselves to the efforts of the clergy in dispelling the heathen darkness inherent in the Saxons, and the majority also of the Britons. At this period churches were erected at Winchester, Lindisfarne and Ely. Bangor, Croyland and Sherborne, Axminster, Huntingdon, Repton, Wareham and Coldingham, also had churches, many of which, unhappily, were to suffer subsequently from the scourge of the Danes and Scandinavians. Much

Repairing the Churches.

attention was bestowed once again upon music employed in the religious services, secular music being
left to the minds and imaginations of those who
could snatch opportunity to practise it. That there
was not a little secular music remaining in the country
among the descendants and families of bards would
be only natural, although its cultivation and practice
does not appear to have been enjoined upon the
people by the clergy, probably because of the pernicious results which had followed from much of the
music which the Saxons had introduced. The real
musical teachings, therefore, sprang wholly from the
Church, and to it we owe indisputably whatever
advance our country made in musical art during the
stormy Saxon period.

We need not detail the services, arrangements and
working of these monastic musical establishments,
for such, indeed, they largely were ; but that they

Monastic Musical Houses. flourished often on a large and splendid
scale is certain. When Edilfrid (616 A.D.),
King of Deira, for example, fought against
Cadvan, King of North Wales, at Chester, he espied
on the summit of a neighbouring hill a vast unarmed
crowd praying. These were the monks of Bangor.
'If they pray,' exclaimed the pagan, 'they fight
against us.' He then ordered them to be put to the
sword. It suggests something of the ecclesiastical
condition and promise of the country, too, when we
find such grand spectacles surrounding the cere-

mony of church dedications as that at the opening
of Winchelcomb Church, of which we have historical
data. Cenwulf (796-819 A.D.), King of Mercia, had
built this edifice with royal magnificence, and upon
the occasion of its consecration there were present
two Kings, thirteen Bishops, ten Ealdermen, and
an 'immense concourse of people.' The musical
features in this dedicatory service have not come
down to us, and whether it consisted of the Gallican
or Roman Church music is uncertain—most likely
it was the Roman, for Augustine's labours had borne
much fruit already ; but that music in a large degree
was present only the most sceptical will doubt. Such
an assembly could scarcely have participated in that
spectacle and have remained dumb. An entirely
spoken service, too, can hardly be thought of on an
auspicious occasion when the church was thronged
with worshippers, the chancel with monks, and a
long retinue of officiating Prelates and clergy, which
the Roman ritual permitted.

The information we have respecting musical
instruments of this period affords a clue to the
possibility of something of an orchestrally accom-
Saxon panied service, it being probable that the
Musical fullest and best vocal and instrumental
Instru-
ments. resources would be employed in the religious services. It is to Bede that we are indebted
for much evidence relating to musical instruments
in use here during the Saxon period. He is careful

to draw a distinction between the greatest of all instruments—the human voice—and other sound-giving agents. Thus, in contradistinction to the voice he styles them 'artificial' instruments. These included the organ, the psaltery, the viol, drums and cymbals, the canticum, the triangular harp—not

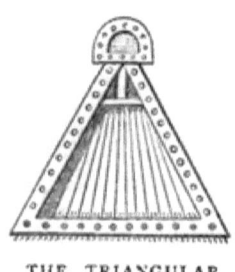

THE TRIANGULAR PSALTERY.

unlike the nablium of the Phœni-cians—etc., about the existence and use of some of which, how-ever, there has grown up much difference of opinion. The organ is often called into question, both as to its introduction into England and its construction. The former point we shall treat of in the next chapter. As to their make, some writers assert that all early organs had keys some inches wide, and were played upon, like carillons, with a blow of the fist.* Others state that the Anglo-Saxon organ had not only a register of stops, but that it was furnished with the semitones.

* Hence, perhaps, the term 'organ-blower,' as Purcell is most discordantly styled in the records kept by the Dean and Chapter of Westminster. The same term is also used in the vestry-books of St. Andrew's Church, Holborn. A Greek enigmatical epigram, in which the riddle to be solved is the organ, and commencing, Ἀλλοιην ὁρόω 'δονάκων φίσιν ἦτου ἀπ' ἄλλης, attributed to the Emperor Julian, suggests that as early as the middle of the fourth century the organ was played with the fingers; so that it would not have been impossible for a finger organ to have been among the possessions of the Saxons before and after their settlement in Britain.

The psalterium or psaltery—a sort of harp-lute—belonged apparently to the Anglo-Saxons. The Cotton MSS. in the British Museum contain much valuable matter respecting Anglo-Saxon music, among which is a Latin-Saxon Psalter, with a picture representing David performing on a psaltery, an eleven-stringed instrument. According to Bede, the harp, or cithara, was contrary to the psaltery, since the harp had in its lower part that hollow portion which the psaltery had above. This remark seems to suggest that whereas the psaltery had a belly and sound-board in its upper part, parallel to the strings, like those of the lute or viol, the hollow sound-board of the harp was in its lower limb, at right angles with the plane of the strings. The Anglo-Saxons

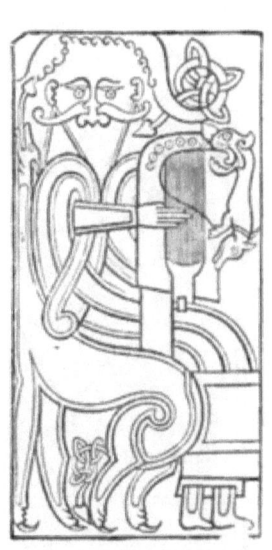

KING DAVID PLAYING
UPON THE HARP.
*(From an Irish Miniature
of the Eighth Century.)*

had two harps—a large instrument standing four feet in height, which was played with the right hand in the treble, and the left hand in the bass; also a smaller instrument held in the left hand, and manipulated with the right. This smaller instrument was of different varieties, such as the nabulum, pennola, corus, etc. They had three or four strings, and were without neck or peg arrangements, to raise or lower the pitch of the strings, and since they were carried, and were used chiefly for convivial music, no great art results were probably expected from them. Another stringed instrument was the viol—not unlike our violin, since it had four strings, and was held and played with a bow, just as a fiddle is nowadays. That playing upon this instrument had

reached any perfection among the Anglo-Saxons is extremely improbable, for as recently as Purcell's day (1658-1695) the wonderful properties of the violin had not been fully ascertained. They were all plucked either with the fingers or a plectrum formed of quill or bone.

PERFORMER ON A SQUARE PSALTERY OF THE NINTH CENTURY.

Instruments of percussion were the drum (tympanum), which Bede describes as 'a tense leather stretched on two cones joined at the acute ends, which resounds on being stricken.' Thus, it was not unlike the present-day drum, having two resounding surfaces; but the modern tonic and dominant tunings were no doubt unknown to the Saxons, who probably disregarded the tones of their drums. 'Anglo-Saxon cymbals [cymbala],' says Bede, 'are small vessels composed of mixed metal, which, when stricken together on the concave side,

in skilful time, produce by their delightful collision a
very sharp note.' The modern cymbals do no more
than this, so that in this detail we are not more
advanced than were our far-off ancestors.

The Cotton MSS., so full of interesting early
musical data, give particulars of another curious
Anglo - Saxon instrument called the sambuca-
canticum. It appears to have been a wind and
string instrument combined, of long triangular shape,
with seven strings in its lower
part, and three pipes in the
upper end. Possibly the seven
strings were attuned to the
tones of the natural scale—our
diatonic scale. The pipes have
sound-holes bored at their sides,
but whether they emitted sounds,
or were blown into with the
lips, can only be matters of conjecture. The instrument, at any

PLECTRA.

(a, *From a Greek vase in the
British Museum;* b, *from
a wall-painting at Pom-
pcii.*)

rate, testifies to the pertinacity with which our progenitors applied themselves in their quest after
music.

Aldhelm, Abbot of Malmesbury, and subsequently
Bishop of Sherborne (*circa* 650, died 709), credits
the Saxons with the trumpet, referring to it in one
of his eight-lined epigrams as a warlike instrument ;
and he could scarcely be confounding it with the
hunting-horn—a sort of trumpet—since that was as

old as the country itself. Instruments of the flute and reed tribes seem to have been unknown.

That they possessed bells also seems clear from the accounts we have of the death of Æthelwald, King of England (*circa* 850-905), at whose burial we read 'bells were rung, and Masses sung.' The earliest notice we have of a belfry and a ring of bells is contained in the following : ' Egelric, Abbot of Croyland (died 984) in the time of King Edgar, caused a peal of bells to be made for his abbey, to each of which he gave names. His predecessor, Turketal, had previously led the way in this respect.'* The celebrated *Benedictional* of St. Æthelwold, in the library of the Duke of Devonshire, furnishes us with an early instance of a belfry with four bells. The illumination, showing the belfry and bells surmounted by chanticleer, appears in the MS. executed at Hyde Abbey about the year 980 A.D.

The Anglo-Saxons were also, it would appear, acquainted with chords long before the tenth century, for, according to Bede, 'a deft harper, in drawing up the cords of his instrument, tunes them to such pitches that the higher may agree in harmony with the lower, some differing by a semitone, a tone, or two tones ; others yielding the consonance of the diatessaron, diapente, or diapason '—*i.e.*, the fourth, fifth, and octave.

In the face of all this evidence, it is difficult to think

* 'Ecclesiastical History' (Collier), vol. i., p. 198.

of our English or Saxon forefathers other than as a distinctly musical race provided with appurtenances for a fair musical performance. The absence of wind instruments would leave a hiatus between their string and percussion instruments, which could, however, have been appreciably lessened by the interposition of vocal music. Whether singing was so employed is not known. Some early light has been thrown upon Anglo-Saxon musical performances by writers other than Bede, but these must be left to another chapter.

Principal Authorities.

'Bede'	Stapleton.
Historia Ecclesiastica	Bede.
'Chronicles'	Ingulph.
'History of the Anglo-Saxons'	Turner.
'Early English Church History'	Bright.
'Saxons in England'	Kemble.
'Music and the Anglo-Saxons'	Wackerbarth.
'English Writers'	Morley.
'Social England'	Cassell.
'Ecclesiastical History'	Collier.

CHAPTER V.

SAXON MUSICAL ECCLESIASTICS TO THE IN-VENTION OF NOTATION.

Dunstan—Abbot of Glastonbury and Bishop of London—Encourages the Use of Organs—A Mysterious Harp—Dunstan a Composer—The Introduction of the Organ—Aldhelm and Bede's References to Organs—Wulfstan on the Winchester Organ—Ælfheah—Representations of Early English Organs—Influence of the Organ—Wulfstan on Orchestral Resources in Church—Ecclesiastical Music Schools—Canterbury—Influence of Religious Music—An Antidote to Profane Music—Duplicating the Service Books—*Neume* Characters—Invention of Notation—Guido d'Arezzo—Franco of Cologne—John Cotton—Effect of Sacred Music upon the National Saxon Character.

BETTER remembered, inasmuch as many churches have been dedicated in his honour throughout our land, is the Prelate Dunstan (925-975 A.D.). The **Dunstan.** name of Dunstan stands out in early English musical annals, as well as in Church history, for no man was more honoured by the generation in which he lived, and by many generations that followed, than was this great ecclesiastical statesman and man of culture. Not alone was he an excellent musician, who composed a Kyrie, which is said to be an excellent sample of early music, but he fostered and encouraged the art in others to the extent of giving personal tuition to the monks and clergy. He conceived a love for the art when as a diminutive fair boy he loitered about the hall of his father's house at Glastonbury. His chief pleasure was the singing of the Church chants and traditional songs of the country. This passionate love of music grew, and in later years, when he became a scholar and teacher, he always carried his harp with him, whether on journey or visit. He even suffered some contumely for music's cause. Born of aristocratic parents, he was brought up for and made great advance in the Church, being constituted Abbot of Glastonbury at the early age of eighteen years. This great church he restored to considerable splendour. At the age of thirty-four he was appointed Bishop of London. His musical talent lay especially in the direction of the organ. In common, too, with the ecclesiastics of the day, he could sing his part in the Mass music of the services. The organ was now coming into use, especially as an instrumental support to the singing. No one was more zealous than Dunstan in encouraging the use of the organ. To this end he provided several English churches and monasteries with instruments, in order that the service music might be the better rendered.

In those days music was the highway to ecclesiastical preferment, and Dunstan—soon to be the twenty-third Archbishop of Canterbury—with the monks, spared no pains to obtain for the art all the recognition which it deserved. Unhappily, such ability in music at that time did not escape the attention of calumniators, who regarded his talent in the light of a crime. Dunstan was accused of magic, and it was urged against him that he had constructed, with the assistance of the devil, a harp

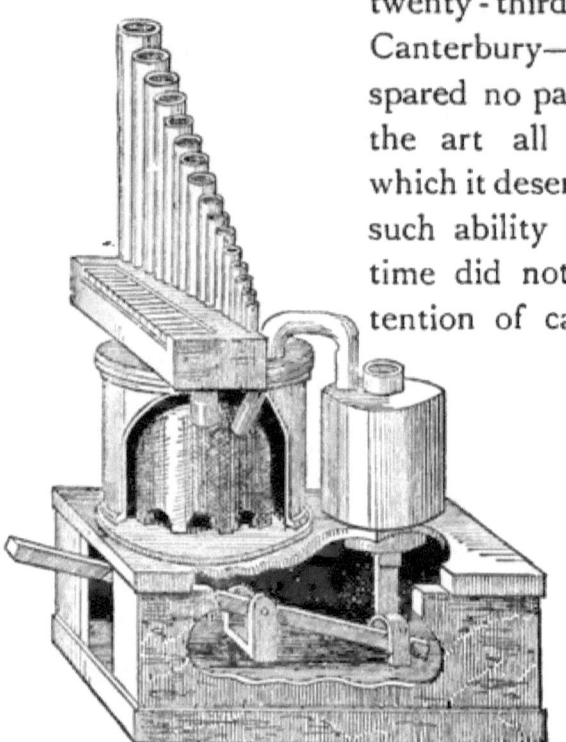

PRIMITIVE ORGAN (HYDRAULIC).*

which not only moved of itself, but played without human help. What he merely did was to invent a

* The Saxon name for a bellows was *bilig*, or *blast-belg ;* but the organ-blower was rather a treader of the bellows than a blower by muscular arm-power—the general method nowadays. The bellows-treader, or *balgentreter*, took his stand on the furthermost end or mouth of the bellows, and literally pressed them down by the weight of his body—thus forcing wind into the pipes. This plan superseded the ancient water or hydraulic organ system, and even as recently as the last century the St. Paul's Cathedral organ was

sort of Æolian harp, which he hung against a crevice in the wall, so that the wind passing the opening vibrated the strings. The soft and gentle sounds thus emitted by an instrument untouched by human hand so greatly astonished and awed the ignorant people that they accused Dunstan of sorcery.

Another story runs that when he was one day instructing a lady of high rank in the design of a robe that she was embroidering—he appears to have been frequently consulted for his taste and talent in ornament and design—his harp, as it hung upon the wall, suddenly, and without mortal touch, gave off heavenly music, which melody and harmony the worker-maiden framed into a joyous anthem.

Dunstan is also said to have been a composer, a Kyrie written in Neume characters in tenth-century MSS. being attributed to him. A story attaches to the composition. On a certain day when King Edgar, who was still alive, was going a-hunting, he asked Dunstan to delay Mass until his return. Towards the third hour the man of God assumed the sacred vestments, and, awaiting the King, knelt before the altar absorbed in tears and prayer. And behold, suddenly, overcome by sleep, he was taken up to heaven, and in the company of the angels he heard them sing to the Trinity with tuneful voices, *Kyrie eleyson, Christe eleyson, Kyrie eleyson.* Coming

blown by treading or walking upon the bellows. The larger the organ the greater was the number of men required for the business.

to himself, he inquired if the King had returned. The answer was 'No.' Again, therefore, he fell to prayer, and being again taken up to heaven, he there heard said in a loud voice : *Ite Missa est.* But when *Deo Gratias* should have been responded, the clerks came in haste saying that the King had arrived. He replied to them that he had already heard Mass, and that he should neither hear nor celebrate another that day. On being asked wherefore, he recounted his vision, and, taking it for his text, forbade the King's hunting any more on the Lord's Day. The *Kyrie eleyson* which he heard in heaven he taught his clerks. Its melody is contained in that trope so popular with the English, *Kyrie rex splendens.*

MISSA—REX SPLENDENS.

Kyrie Eleison.

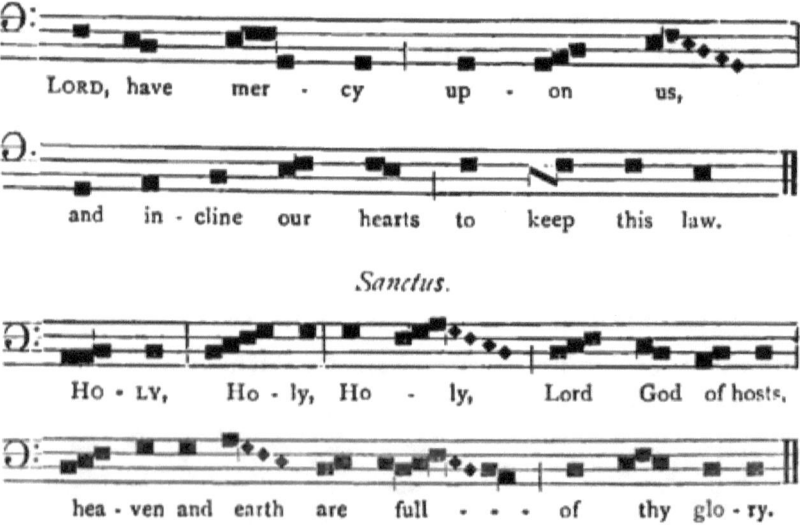

LORD, have mer - cy up - on us,

and in - cline our hearts to keep this law.

Sanctus.

Ho - LY, Ho - ly, Ho - ly, Lord God of hosts,

hea - ven and earth are full · · · of thy glo - ry.

Benedictus.

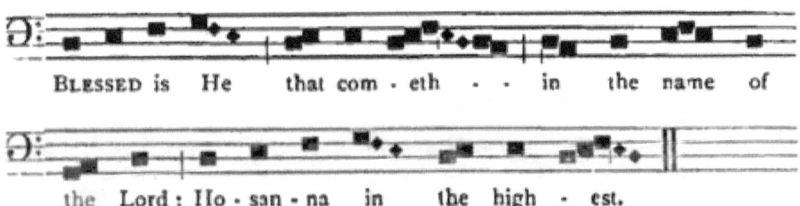

BLESSED is He that com - eth - - in the name of
the Lord : Ho - san - na in the high - est.

Agnus Dei.

O LAMB of God, that ta - kest a - way the sins
of the world, have mer - cy up - on us.

Gloria in Excelsis.

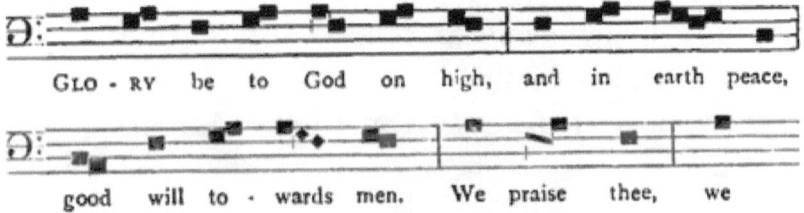

GLO - RY be to God on high, and in earth peace,
good will to - wards men. We praise thee, we

Credo.

I be-lieve in one God the Father Almighty, Maker of heaven and earth,

The introduction of the organ into England—of which more anon—constituted quite a landmark in our national musical history. Not only was the

instrument destined to play a chief and really valuable
part in the church services for many generations, but
it was to grow into a musical body of truly wonderful

**Introduc-
tion of the
Organ.**

power and workmanship—such as its first
constructors would scarcely, perhaps, have
believed.   In time, too, gradual processes
of improvement and development ensued, and in
these the English workmen were always to the
front, until eventually the best organs that were to
be obtained in Europe were constructed solely by
English firms.   To-day the building of organs,
whether for church, concert-hall, or chamber, has
become one of the leading trades of this country ;
and if the British workman will only cling to the
best traditions of his trade, there is no reason why
any foreign element should supplant him in this art
for very many years to come.   But he must build
lovingly and honestly.

The musical tastes of the monks and those who
attended the regular services of Matins and Evensong could not fail to be quickened by the advent of
an instrument like the organ, primitive as its condition was.   From the outset it possessed one quality
that lifted it above every other instrument, namely,
its 'sustaining' character—a property which proved
of great service in the Church establishments where
the singing of the monks had no other support than
was afforded by the occasional introduction of a flute
or harp, such as the canons of the Church then per-

mitted. It is improbable that the adoption of the organ was either speedy or general, chiefly because of the cost of manufacture, the time occupied in constructing instruments, and the difficulty of learning the art of organ-playing; although, judging by the earliest known instruments, the first organists were scarcely required to be very dexterous at the keyboard.

Some doubt exists concerning the first use of organs in England. An old manuscript known

First Use of Organs. as the 'Utrecht Psalter,' generally supposed to be of the fifth or sixth century, indicates their existence here long before the Conquest, and as early, indeed, as the time of Augustine. This is improbable, however, since it was only introduced into the Romish Church by Pope Vitalian I. about the year 666 A.D., although the instrument had been known and recognized on the Continent as a valuable adjunct to congregational singing long before that time. Vitalian's missionaries, Theodore and Adrian, are

PNEUMATIC ORGANS OF THE FOURTH CENTURY, SHOWING THE METHOD OF BLOWING.

reputed to have brought the art of organ-playing to England, and they were also charged to lead the singing at the Church services, and to instruct others so to do. Cassiodorus (*circa* 481-577 A.D.), Consul of Rome under King Vitigas the Goth in 514 A.D., thus describes the organ of his day: 'It is composed of divers pipes, formed into a kind of tower, which, by means of bellows, is made to produce a loud sound, and, in order to express agreeable melodies, there are in the inside movements made of wood that are pressed down by the fingers of the player, and produce the most pleasing and brilliant tones.'

Bishop Aldhelm (died 709 A.D.), sometime Abbot of Malmesbury and subsequently Bishop of Sherborne, is credited with introducing an organ into England—'a mighty instrument with innumerable tones, blown with bellows, and enclosed in a gilded case'; but it is more difficult to substantiate such a record than that which states that Dunstan in his musical zeal furnished numerous churches and convents with organs. Faithful Aldhelm! In order to ingratiate himself with the lower orders of the Saxons, and to induce them to listen to his preaching, he was in the daily habit of dressing himself like a minstrel, and taking his stand on the bridges and highroads, first singing to his listeners some of their national songs.

When Dunstan restored the monasteries of Ely,

Peterborough, Tewkesbury, Glastonbury, Evesham, and many others, an organ—the latest addition to ecclesiastical adornments—would scarcely have been forgotten by the musical enthusiast and liberal-minded Prelate. William of Malmesbury (1095-1143) chronicles one such gift which Dunstan provided for the Abbey of Malmesbury in King Edgar's reign (942-974). This instrument is important, since it appears to have been entirely made by English organ-workers, who had become such skilled craftsmen that they had already inaugurated 'improvements' in the shape of copper pipe in lieu of lead. In this particular instrument the pipes were of brass, probably for the purpose of obtaining a more brilliant tone, and it appears to have been fabricated on the Abbey premises, probably under the direction of Dunstan himself, who, to his other attainments, added that of an expert artificer in metals. Dunstan gave an organ to Abingdon Abbey also. In this same century Earl Elwin presented an organ to the convent at Ramsay. On this instrument he is said to have expended the then large sum of £30 in copper pipes, which 'resting with their openings in thick order, on the spiral winding in the inside, and being struck on feast days with a strong blast of bellows, emitted a sweet melody and a far-resounding peal.'

Although we are not without details relative to these first English organs, their exact character can

scarcely be ascertained from the fragmentary information which early historians have left; while
the manner of playing upon them, and the situation

Character of First English Organs. of the organist, or organists—for there would often appear to be more than one —constitute real problems, the solution of

which would seem to have departed with the original
organists.   That they were instruments blown with
bellows is certain.   Bede describes the organ of his
day as 'a tower built up of many pipes, from which
by the blast of bellows a most copious sound is
obtained, and that the same may be composed
of fit melody, it is furnished on the inside with
wooden tongues, which, being skilfully depressed by
the master's fingers, produce grand and very sweet
music.'   Aldhelm mentions an instrument with 'a
thousand pipes,' the external ones of which were
gilded—a common feature of Anglo-Saxon organs.
Thus :

> ' Maxima millenis auscultans organa flabris
> Mulceat auditum ventosis follibus iste,
> Quamlibet auratis fulgescant cœtera capsis.'

Some further insight into the style of construction
of these early organs is gleaned from the account

Winchester Cathedral Organ. which Wulfstan, or Wulstan, has left re-specting the organ erected in Winchester Cathedral, and which must have been,

from all accounts, the musical wonder of the age.
Ælfheah, surnamed Elphegus Calvus, was Bishop

of Winchester in 935-951 A.D., and provided, among other adornments, an organ the like of which had not been seen or heard. Wulfstan, cantor and Benedictine monk of Winchester (*circa* 900-963),* has preserved the fame of this organ in a poem which is printed in the 'Acts of the Order of St. Benedict.' Extravagant as the poet is, it is improbable that his enthusiasm affects his accuracy, since the details are clear enough. We learn that this organ was built with two

Diaphdigs and Calcantes. so ya bit ani bty berfeiben Orael an rancht morben.

ORGAN BELLOWS AND BLOWERS, SHOWING THE OLD METHOD OF ORGAN BLOWING.†

sound-boards. It was erected in honour of St. Peter, to whom the cathedral was dedicated, and

---

* ' Acta Sanctorum Ordinis Benedict.'

† An essential condition in modern organ-playing is a sustained supply of wind uniformly distributed. Several expedients, involving water-power, gas-engines, etc., have been resorted to in order to secure the desired pressure for all pipes in the instruments. The present hand system of blowing is not satisfactory, but the jerky results from pressing the wind in with the feet must have been infinitely worse.

had twelve bellows ranged in a row, and fourteen
more below. These were worked by seventy strong
men, who, covered with perspiration, laboured with
their arms so industriously that an immense quantity
of wind was supplied in alternate blasts by these
bellows.

The poem goes on to relate that each blower
excited his companions to drive the wind up with
all his strength, so that the 'full-bottomed box,'
with its four hundred pipes, might speak worthily.
Details are given of the organist's method. The
whole four hundred pipes he pressed
with his hands. Some pipes when
closed he opened, others when
opened he closed, according to the
nature of the varied sounds required. Two monks of concordant
spirit presided at the instrument,

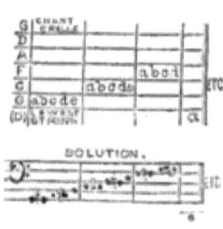

MUSICAL TABLATURE.

each managing his own alphabet or musical tablature.
Concerning the power of the instrument the poem
translates forcibly : ' Like thunder the iron tones
batter the ear, so that it may receive no sound but
that alone. To such an amount does it reverberate,
echoing in every direction, that everyone stops with
his hand his gaping ears, being in no wise able to
draw near and bear the sound which so many various
combinations produce. The music is heard throughout the town, and the flying fame thereof is gone
out over the whole country.'

'Twelve pairs of bellows, ranged in stated row,
Are join'd above, and fourteen more below;
These the full force of seventy men require,
Who ceaseless toil, and plenteously perspire;
Each aiding each, till all the wind be prest
In the close confines of th' incumbent chest,
On which four hundred pipes in order rise
To bellow forth the blast that chest supplies.'

MASON : *Essays on English Church Music.*

This organ was intended to be heard all over
Winchester, and probably was, since the city then
was but a small and quiet settlement of learning and
piety. In modern times there is no such ambition,
which is well, since the prospect of all the organs,
say in London, proving as persistent as the church
bells would be too alarming.

An instrument possessing forty keys, among
which were the semitones of the chromatic scale,
and the compass of which has been estimated to
have been three and a half octaves, that is, from

to —*i.e.*, CC to E—would

permit of much that might have proved of musical
value, provided the 'two monks of concordant spirit'
worked in harmony; otherwise the consequences
could easily have proved disastrous musically and
physically.*

---

* Wulfstan turned his fellow-pupil Lantfred's 'Posthumous
Miracles of St. Swithun' into Latin verse. Of Wulfstan's verse

The representations of early English organs which
have reached us cannot, it is to be feared, be wholly
trusted. The illuminations in MSS. and missals
are not always faithful pictures of existing instruments, but a curious illustration of an organ of about
this date, and apparently a faithful delineation, is
given in a MS. Psalter of Eadwine preserved in the
library of Trinity College, Cambridge. The pipes
are placed within a frame, and the surface of the
organ is represented as being perforated to receive
a second set of pipes, though the draughtsman
appears to have sketched one hole too many. The
two organists, whose duties seem for the moment to
have been brought to an end by the inattention of
the blowers, are intent on admonishing their four
assistants, who are striving to get up the wind
supply, which their neglect has apparently allowed

only a few fragments remain, but there is a dedication of many
distichs to his Bishop, Ælfheah. The Bishop is praised for the
spirit with which he carried on the building works at Winchester
Cathedral, for the labyrinth of secret crypts, for the great organ
(on which he expatiates), and for the great tower with five
windows, surmounted by a gilt cock with a sceptre in its claws.
Wulfstan celebrates the stately consecration of the church in which
eight bishops were engaged ; he instances also the holy men there
buried, Swithun and Ethelwold, with whom Ælfheah, who so well
follows in their steps, will hereafter be joined. This MS. is in the
British Museum Collection. William of Malmesbury states that
Wulfstan wrote a practical work entitled ' De Tonorum Harmonia '
(On the Harmony of Tones), and describes it as a ' very useful '
book. As a fact, it remained a standard work for two hundred
years.

to run out. The bellows are blown in a manner which we here meet with for the first time, namely, through the intervention of handles instead of directly by the hands ; and as in so small an organ there could not have been room for four persons to compress the wind by standing upon the bellows, as had hitherto been the custom, we may infer that they were loaded with weights in the manner that

ANCIENT ENGLISH CHURCH ORGAN, WITH BELLOWS AND DOUBLE KEYBOARD.

(*Eadwine Psalter, Cambridge MS.*)

has generally been supposed not to have been introduced until some centuries later.

The influence which the introduction of the organ actually had upon the services seems to have escaped the notice of early writers. That it proved a great boon in the rendering of the services, we have previously suggested. Those monks of old who chanted the Gregorian Liturgy must have had strong throats indeed, and have sung

Influence of the Organ.

lustily to have made themselves heard amidst the
solid brick and stonework of the more important of
the Saxon churches, without the aid of such support
to the voice as only the organ could supply. The
question of pitch, too, would be important. Given
an accurate starting-note, which the more gifted of
the singing monks would be able to secure readily,
there would still be the inevitable sinking in pitch
which always follows unaccompanied singing, especially when the congregation takes its share therein.
This would be more present in hymn-singing than
in the restricted range of the Gregorian tones ; but
in either case it is easy to conceive a gradual and
imperceptible depression, ending eventually in the
complete disappearance of the original tune.

Here would seem to be some small additional
reason, therefore, for supposing that instruments of
some kind were an adjunct in both the British and
Anglo-Saxon Church services long before the introduction of the organ, since the art of congregational
singing had scarcely reached its present-day perfection, when here and there congregations numbering
thousands are capable of producing profound effects
from plain, unaccompanied singing. This would seem
to be borne out by Wulfstan, according to whom the
instruments employed in the church services were
not restricted to organs. He writes : ' When the
choral brethren unite, each chants your prayers by
the peculiar art whereof he is master ; the sound of

instruments of pulsation is mixed with the sharp voices of reeds, and by various apparatus the concert proceeds sweetly,' from which we may fairly infer that the Anglo-Saxons resorted to all their orchestral resources in order to enhance the effect of the Church service. That there were resources in every choir-stall, from which the monks could, if needs be, pitch their intoning notes, and which would aid their singing if occasion required, would be only natural, albeit such details have not reached us. It was not because it supplanted such musical appliances, however, nor on account of its valuable properties as an eminently suitable foundation for singing, that the introduction of the organ into English churches stands out as an important matter. Its advent meant a vast stride in the progress of the art, and a mighty step in theoretical music. Organists began to invent, or descant, upon the organ, by which the plain chant, or *canto fermo*, had another part as an accompanying melody added to it. Here was the first step in the opening up of the vast field of contrapuntal science and possibility in which the organ, and, later, British organists, were destined to play a prominent and most excellent part.

Thus, the music of the Church firmly established once more, and this time among the Anglo-Saxons, continued to grow for very many years, exercising a vast influence for good upon the minds and dispositions of the inhabitants of the country, and gradually

but surely, moulding our national musical style and
manner. View the matter as we may, we should
be ungrateful indeed did we fail to acknowledge our
indebtedness to those prelates and churchmen from
Rome who introduced their Christian musical art
into England, and not only took pains to impart a
knowledge of it in their wanderings and settlements
in our island, but even helped in the building of
the music-schools in which they were afterwards to
serve as masters and instructors.

The first of these ecclesiastical music-schools was
inaugurated at Canterbury, thanks to the efforts of
Gregory, Augustine—his missionary—and their
successors. Hitherto, as we have seen,
Music-Schools in it was the custom for the clergy to travel
England. to Rome for improvement in music, and
frequent requests had to be made to the Holy
College for teachers, who could impart the Church
service music here. With the Canterbury seminary
once provided with teachers, all this was at an end,
and for many years afterwards pupils were taught to
become instructors, and were then despatched to
such parts of the island as owned obedience to the
Roman see. The exact date of the founding of this
music-school is unknown, but it was probably subsequent to Bede's appeal to Pope Agatho for Church
singing-masters for the Northumbrian diocese. With
the increasing need of singers, as the new churches
sprang up, the expense and delay of sending to

Rome for instructors would naturally suggest to
Augustine the desirableness of such a home school.
We may conclude, therefore, that whatever the
British clergy had formerly possessed in the shape
of musical training-schools, this one at Canterbury,
associated with Augustine's name, was the first
school of its kind which the Roman clergy built.
Here we may be sure the Gregorian chant, as used
in the different parts of the service, was thoroughly
taught by qualified Roman masters ; and this with
such success that every vestige of early British
music, and the subsequent Gallican chant, ultimately
disappeared before the rapid progress of Gregorian
Tones in every part of the island.

The effect of this new wave of religious music can
be imagined. As it spread over the land it did a
threefold work : it made its power felt as a beautiful
and fitting aid to the worship of Almighty God in
the precincts and courts of His sanctuary ; it materially shaped and moulded the musical aspirations of
the then existing, and successive, generations of
Englishmen ; and it went to the hearts of the rugged
Saxon races, softening the characteristic asperities,
and preparing all who came within its power for the
better reception of the Gospel message, all of which
was propitious, since for the news of Christ which
the British clergy had taken to the heathen Germans
they in return brought much that was bad into
Britain. One form of this was the amorous songs

and romantic effusions, little calculated to improve the minds of either those who sang or those who heard them.   These songs reached such a pitch of lewdness and indecency that their suppression became imperative, and in the work of cleansing and stamping out this pernicious element the monks engaged with laudable rigour and results.   Sacred music was the antidote employed, and its elevating power proved as beneficial as it ever has proved to all who have been brought under its benign influence. Music—purest of all arts, and an innocent and beautiful employment for mind and body when shaped in its best secular forms

DANCE OF THE NINTH CENTURY, WITH LYRE AND DOUBLE FLUTE.
(*From the Cotton MSS.*)

—ever becomes, indeed, a potent agent for good when it reaches philosopher or savage in the form of sacred music.

'O secret music! sacred tongue of God!
I hear thee calling to me, and I come!'
LELAND: *The Music Lesson of Confucius.*

In the religious houses it was as a blessing, since it proved well fitted to fill the periods of leisure and relaxation which followed upon the meditations and offices in the lives of saintly ones vowed to celibacy and monastic life. Thus, in the convents and monasteries music was always present, beautifying the lives and minds of those within the cloister walls ; while to the outside world its practice was constantly recommended as a remedy and alternative for idle hours and unprofitable pursuits.

Here, then, we must close the narrative of the rise and progress of Church music in England from Augustine's time to that of the thorough settlement of the Roman Church and its bishops in England.

Christianity revived by Augustine had, indeed, spread wondrously and gloriously. In this growth music had proved a great aid, since, of the many churches throughout England, there was not one, probably, at this time, whose clergy and congregation alike were not bound together by the musical sympathies engendered by the Gregorian chant.

Truly this gift of Gregory's to the Britons was priceless, especially if we consider what sacred musical art might have remained without it. Nor was Church music to be hastily taken from the charge of the clergy and monks who had nurtured it to its healthy existence. For several centuries—until the advent of the first of the glorious roll of English Church composers—sacred music, *i.e.*, music of the choir and chancel, remained in the hands of the clergy.

No specific sign of progress marks this long period, and no single name stands out among the generations of priest-musicians, monks and singers who daily chanted the services through all these years. Indeed, apart from the ecclesiastical chant, the clergy would seem to have left the art to the outside world, for the genesis of harmony appears to have sprung from the northern parts of Europe, and it was not until several centuries after it had been freely adopted for secular purposes that it was admitted into the service of the Church. Year after year the vaulted roofs of the churches rang with the old-accustomed strains from the deep-toned throats of the monks—and many of them possessed wondrous voices indeed.

The apparent standstill is easily accounted for. The Church had her settled services, with the approved musical ritual direct from Rome. Obedient to authority, the clergy were content with this, their duty being to preserve, and not to alter, either tone or inflection. It would have been little short of a rebellious act, or even heresy, to tamper with the service music, and the labours of the monks would be directed largely to copying and duplicating the service books, rather than to the inventing of new melodies and cadences—no light task if we remember that writing was the accomplishment of the few, and that the needs for choir books in both old and new churches were great. Of all this early monastic industry scarcely a remnant remains, though, happily, its influence has been lasting, and is yet traditional in many a church library throughout the land.

Not only did missal, gradual, psalter, and antiphonaria need to be copied and disseminated this while. The art of musical notation, which had

Invention of Notation. hitherto been in a crude state, was commanding the attention of musical minds, and was soon to be shaped for all time by the splendid discoveries of Guido d'Arezzo (*circa* 950-1025 A.D.) and Franco of Cologne (*circa* 1000-

$$\sim \smallsmile\!\!\! \int \big) \int \big\backslash \big\backslash \sim \cdots + \tfrac{3}{3} \big\backslash \Gamma\!\Gamma \big\}\big\}$$

Neume Characters, invented by St. Ephraim, a Monk of the Fourth Century, who originated the Neume System.

1075 A.D.). The primitive Neume* notation employed in writing the Gregorian chant was the system almost exclusively adopted by church choirs, monasteries, and academies formed for the dissemination of sacred song through the tenth, eleventh, twelfth, thirteenth and fourteenth centuries, for it was long before Guido's masterly and intelligible method of lines and spaces, or Franco's notes of various lengths,

* The word 'Neuma' is derived from the Greek πνεῦμα, meaning *breath*. The advantage of the Neume system over the alphabetical system of the Greeks and Romans consisted in its notifying more clearly to the priest where the inflexions and modulations were required in the chanting of the Gospel, Epistles, Psalms, etc.

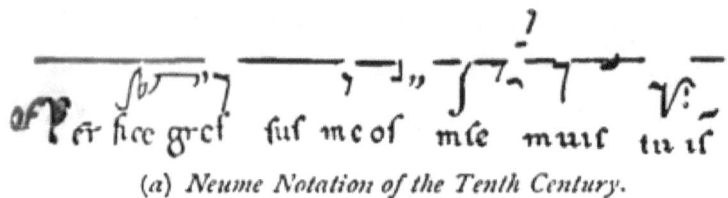

(a) *Neume Notation of the Tenth Century.*

Po · pu · le   me   ·   us   quid   fe · ci   aut

(b) *Neume Notation of the Eleventh Century, deciphered by Martini.*

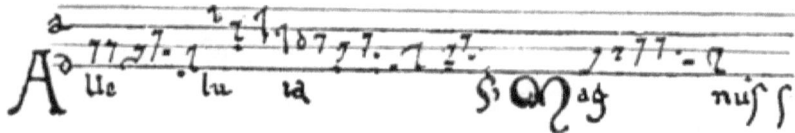

(c) *Neume Notation of Guido of Arezzo.*

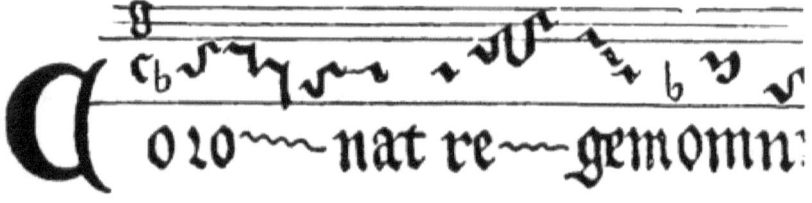

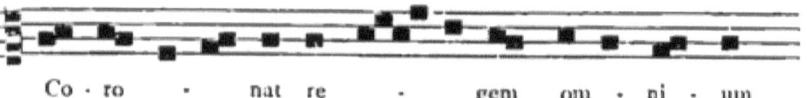

Co · ro   ·   nat   re   ·   gem   om · ni · um

(d) *Deciphered Neume Notation of the Latest Period.*

Neumata.

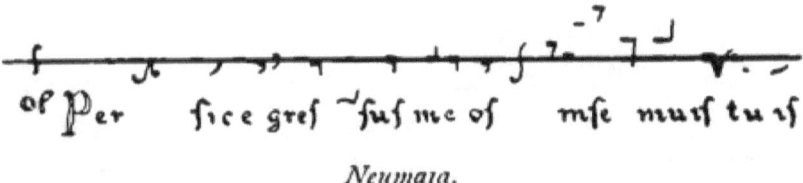

Ce · li Celorus   laudate   deum.

Translation.

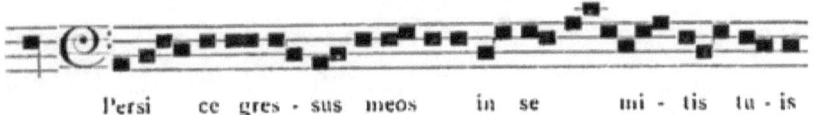

Neumata.

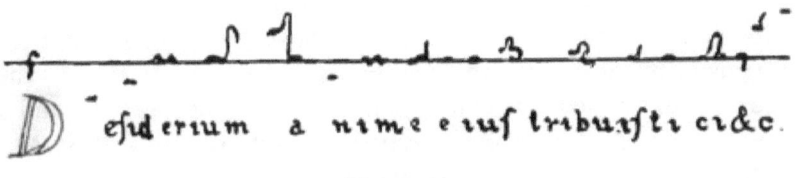

Persi   ce gres - sus meos   in se   mi - tis tu - is

Translation.

Neumata.

De-si-de · ri · um   a nime   e · ius tribuis ti e · i et

Translation.

became general.   Its characters suggested the value
and pitch of the tones, but coloured lines, as in the
examples *a, b, c, d,* had to be employed subsequently to
indicate the tonic or key-note.*   The clergy would be
the first to hear of such improvements in musical notation as Guido and Franco were giving to the world,
and slowly as the new fashion of writing music
would become known to the copyists in the monasteries, the manifest advantages of the stave and
measured notes would not be disregarded by the
heads of the abbeys and churches.

Guido d'Arezzo, *Inventus Musicæ,* as he was sur-
Guido   named, was probably the first to use the
of Arezzo. lines as well as the spaces of the stave,
and borrowing some syllables from a hymn to St.
John (written by Paul Diaconus), the patron saint
of singing in those days, he gave us the well-known
do re mi, etc., with which we ' sol-fa ' at the present

---

* The red line was introduced about the year 900.   All notes
written upon it were F's ; those above the line were higher ; those
below it being graver or lower.   There have been three accepted
systems of musical notation : (α) the Alphabetical letters ; (β) the
Neume ; and (γ) our present system of notes, lines, spaces, and a
stave.   Of these the Neume partially, and our present system
perfectly, illustrate the undulations of the melody.   The alphabet
method did not.   We owe our notes nomenclature, and the F, C,
and G clefs, however, to the primitive alphabet system.   An
ancient Office Book, used at Winchester Cathedral, is in the
Bodleian Library (775).   The MS. is attributed to the time of
King Ethelred II. (d. 1016), and has the plain chant notes written
upon lines and spaces of a stave with four lines.

time. The following shows the hymn as it was anciently sung, taken from a manuscript of Sens :

And which in modern notation would appear thus :

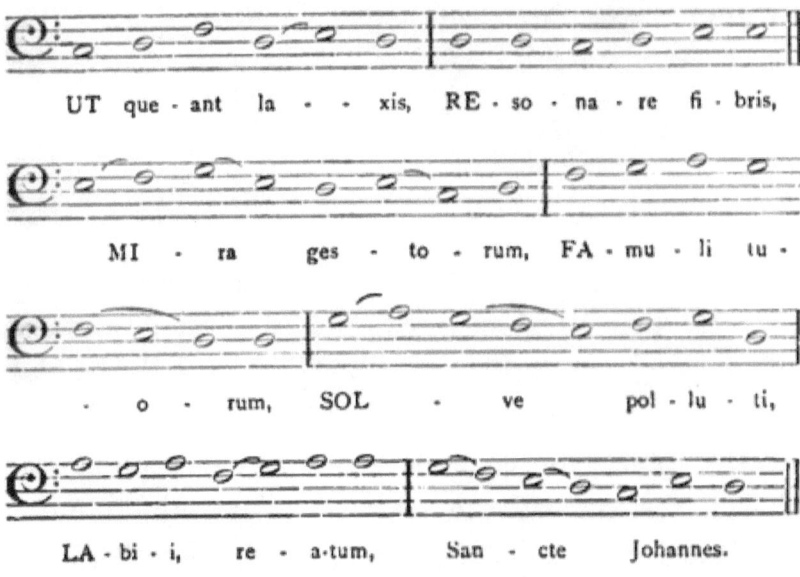

In the prologue to the Antiphonarium, Guido speaks of his invention as follows : 'By Divine assistance, I have pointed out such a method of notation that, by a little help from a master at first, an intelligent and studious person may easily acquire the rest by himself. And if anyone should suspect

GUIDO OF AREZZO.

my veracity in this assertion, let him come to our convent, let him make the experiment, let him examine the children under my care, and he will find that, though they are still severely punished for their ignorance of the psalms, and blunders in the reading, they can now sing correctly, without a master, the chants to those psalms of which they can scarcely pronounce the words.' He then explains the use of the lines and spaces, and tells us that 'all the notes which are placed on the same line, or in the same space, denote the same sound; and that the name of the sound is determined either by the colour of the line, or by a letter of the alphabet placed at the beginning of it: a rule of such consequence,' he adds, 'that if a melody be written without a letter (that is, a cliff, or coloured line), it will be like a well without a rope, in which,

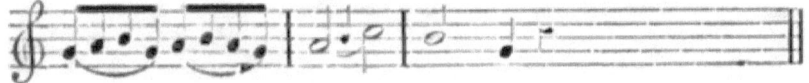

A so - lis or - tu us - que ad oc - ci - du - a Lit - to - ra ma - ris

planctus pulsat pec - to - ra; Ul - tra ma - ri - na ag - mi - na tris -

ti - ti - a Te - ti - git in - gens cum er - ro - re ni - mi - o.

Heu! me do - lens, plan - go!

NEUME NOTATION AND TRANSLATION.

Franci, Ro ma - ni at-que cuncti creduli, Luctu punguntur et magna mo-

les - ti - a, in-fan-tes, senes, glo-ri-o - si prin - ci-pes ; Nam clangit

or - bis detrimentum Ka - ro - li. Heu ! mi-hi mi-se-ro !

though there be plenty of water, it will be of no use.'

Franco of Cologne identified himself with the measuring of music, *i.e.*, the determining of the relative lengths of the notes. The hitherto unmeasured art, or *cantus planus*, he spaced out in the following powers, inventing the terms *maxima*, *longa*, *breve*, *semibreve*, and *minim*, to express the value of the notes:

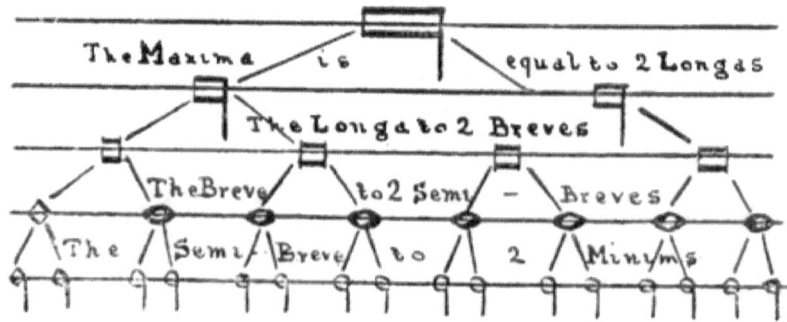

He also devised the following 'rests' or silences, giving each a relative value to its agreeing note.

It was not, however, until the fourteenth century that characters were used to express Time in music.

The Pause which fills 3 spaces is equal to a Maxima - - ·	
That which fills 2 spaces is equal to a Longa · · · ·	
That which fills 1 space is equal to a Breve · · · · -	
That which is placed above and fills half a space is equal to a Semi- breve	
That which is placed below and fills the half of a space is equal to a Minim	

A glance at the following illustration of the same period notation will show how nearly we then were to reaching our present characters or cyphers, which neither time nor invention seems able to improve.

Large.   Long.   Breve.   Semibreve.   Minim.   Semiminim.   Chroma.   Semichroma.

These notes proceeded in regular gradations, the large being equal to two longs, four breves, eight semibreves, etc. Any note written in red ink was diminished a fourth part; thus a red semibreve, instead of being equal to four semi-minims, was only equal to three. Thomas Walsingham, again referred to in Chapter VIII., mentions five characters as used in his day, viz., the *large*, the *long*, the *breve*,

the *semibreve*, and *minim*.   He adds : 'Of late a
new character has been introduced called a *crotchet*,
which would be of no use if musicians would only
remember that beyond the minim no subdivision
ought to be made,' to which criticism it only remains
to be asked : What would this ancient have said to
the quavers and demisemiquavers, together with the
whole range of musical fireworks of to-day ?

After the invention of the Time-table, music
became freed from its bondage.   We find that when
music meant merely the chanting a few sacred words,
such as a hymn, the natural measure of the words
supplied all the time that was necessary ; and long
and short notes, corresponding with this measure,
were sufficient for the purpose required.   But as the
art advanced, and more especially as florid counterpoint—or notes of various lengths sung by different
voices to the same syllable—became used, it was
necessary that characters should be invented to
express time in order to avoid confusion.

As against this doubtless well-deserved reputation
of Guido and Franco, some writers have urged that
hymn tunes exist of the period of Æthelred II.,
surnamed the Unready (978-1016 A.D.), with music
in staves of four lines and spaces, thus showing that
the English possessed, and used, lines and spaces
before the reputed invention of them by Guido.

A somewhat isolated name in English musical
history calls for notice here, since the bearer of it

proved a famous commentator of Guido. This is
John Cotton, supposed to be an Englishman, and
whom Gebertus conjectures to be the same as
John   Johannes Scholasticus, a monk of Treves,
Cotton. who lived about 1050. He was the author
of a tract entitled 'De Arte Musica,' which he dedicated to Fulgentius Episc. Anglorum—an English
Bishop whose name it is otherwise difficult to trace.
Whether Cotton lived as early, and was of English
nationality, has been doubted; but there is much in
favour of such a belief. There is a good English
ring, for instance, about the name of 'John Cotton,'
and he would easily acquire the classical appellation
'Johannes Scholasticus' from the fashion of re-
naming learned men upon their entering foreign
monasteries. Again, he must have lived soon after
Guido, since Cotton acts as his commentator, and
recommends the Harmonic Hand system, invented
by Guido, to those who wish to fasten the hexa-
chords upon their memories.

Burney states he saw in the Jesuits' College at
Antwerp* a Latin tract on music, of which Cotton
was the author. In the first chapter of this tract
Cotton   Cotton states that 'solmization by the six
MSS. syllables, *ut, re, mi, fa,* etc., was practised
by the English.' As it would have occupied some
little time to make this sol-fa method by Guido known,
it is probable that Cotton lived somewhat later than

---

* Burney, 'History of Music,' vol. ii., p. 96.

1050, which would agree with Burney's statement that the MS. tract was written in the twelfth century. The tract appears to have been duplicated, a second copy being in the Pauline Library at Leipzig, and a third in the Vatican.

Burney declares the work to be the most ample and complete treatise, as well as one of the most ancient on the subject of music, that has been preserved between the time of Guido and Franchinus (Gafurius) (1025-1521). The Padre Martini (1706-1734), who examined the subject very carefully, writes: 'After all possible diligence, and the most minute inquiry, I have not been able to discover any author who has given the intonations [of the Psalms] in notes anterior to John Cotton, who probably flourished in the twelfth century.' This same 'Father' Martini quotes a long passage from the eleventh chapter of the MS. tract to prove that the predominant and characteristic note of a chant used to be called the tenor, from *teneo*, I hold, or dwell upon. Hence the prominent position which the

ANGEL PERFORMING ON A STRINGED INSTRUMENT.

tenor clef or part has always taken in Church music. Ouseley, the latest authority of value, does not insist too strongly on the English nationality of this clever didactical writer; but, considering the prominence of Cotton's name in early musical history, we shall be quite justified in claiming the man and his work as an ornament of the First English School until some other country can prove that it has as strong a claim to Cotton as we have. This there will be great difficulty in doing.

An interesting anecdote is told of this John Cotton, who, resenting the inappropriate variations and ornaments in which it was the fashion with some of his contemporaries and others to indulge— probably these were the more musically educated monks who added their extempore harmonies to the *canto fermo*—likened them to revellers who, reaching home late at night, could not possibly tell next day by which way they came.

Here, then, we leave these early clerical musical workers battling with the mysteries of the new notation in which gradually the service-music was to be inscribed by those of the monks who best excelled in the art of writing and engrossing. We can imagine the anxious clergy carrying on the services, and sacred music continuing its secret influence for good during many troublous generations, when all other intellectual blessings were either withheld or banished from the reach of the people.

Whether it was that an improved order of Saxons

had been pouring into England when the country was fairly conquered, or whether the steady work of the clergy was beginning to tell in shaping the minds and dispositions of the people, not only in religious, but also in secular phases of life, it is certain that the Anglo-Saxon as settled and reared in England was a different being from the conquering Teuton of three and four centuries before. He altered wondrously into the counterpart of the

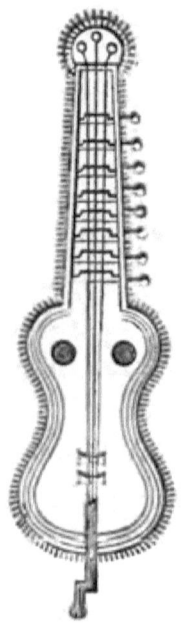

Englishman of to-day. Of course the Church was responsible for most of this changed, happy condition of things ; but not a little was brought about by the later generations of Saxons who swarmed into England when once it was subjugated. All the germs of musical art, which the branches of the great Aryan race brought with them from the East, did not fall in Britain alone. The seed settled mainly on German soil, as genial for it in truth as British, and when music first gave signs of life in the Western world, the throbs were simultaneous in the districts touched by the march of the Orient emigrants. So that while music was prospering in Britain under the later Britons, there was growing up that same while in Germany an art which was destined to come into this country as an influencing factor in the national music.

ORGANISTRUM OF THE NINTH CENTURY.

If we remember, then, that while the original

Saxons were little better than savages, their later orders were comparatively civilized people, it is easy

Late Saxon Musical Influence. to understand the advent into England of many musical manners and customs which tended greatly to the advancement of musical method and practice throughout England—at this time much more peopled with Anglo-Saxons than with Britons. Among these habits were many resembling, and therefore easy of alliance with, those of the Britons. Settling among the conquered and almost exterminated people, they speedily affected the national musical character ; for the Teuton music was not without a style in strong contrast with Celtic music. It had a good-humoured heartiness, a manly simplicity and strength, together with an impress of sincerity, which rendered it a sure channel to the heart and emotions. The national airs of the Teuton races bear strong testimony to this view, as the following examples will show :

GERMAN PEASANT SONG.

RUSSIAN SOLDIER'S MELODY.

Then there was another and a more affecting element coming into the island which was certain to impress the national musical character. This not outwardly, but in a closer and less seen way. Defiant and detestable as the muse of the original Saxon buccaneers for the most part was, it improved appreciably as each generation came and went. Much was forgotten, too, by the side of the softer sentiment pervading the musical strains to which the Teuton mother, sister and daughter gave expression. This domestic music exists in every tribe and every people. The cradle - song, lulling

GUIDONIAN OR HARMONIC HAND.

the infant to sleep ; the plaint of the maiden, dreaming of her far-off lover at the wars ; the child's tuneful measure at her every step—this natural music, which knows no particular age, nor people, came with the sterner Saxon muse. Whenever met, it is like the air we breathe—is as varied as the wants and aspirations which fill every mind ; and it was this softer feature in Saxon music that drifted into England to help to mould the present English musical character. We can only surmise as to its nature, since no domestic music of such early times has come down to us. We shall not be far wrong in concluding, however, that it was music of that homely kind and inborn origin which is to be heard in the nursery and at the spinning-wheel to-day, music which comes and goes we know not how or whither ; music, albeit, which makes a silent and imperceptible, yet lasting, impression upon all who hear it.

Principal Authorities.

'Early English Church History'	Bright.
'*Historia Ecclesiastica*'	Bede.
'History of England'	Lingard.
'Music and the Anglo-Saxons'	Wackerbarth.
'Dictionary of Music and Musicians'	Grove.
'Essays on English Church Music'	Mason.
'The Organ : its History and Construction'	Hopkins-Rimbault.
'History of Music'	Burney.
'History of Music'	Hawkins.
'*L'Art Harmonique aux XIIe et XIIIe Siècles*'	Coussemaker.
'History of Music'	Kiesewetter.

CHAPTER VI.

LATE SAXON AND EARLY NORMAN MUSIC.

Alfred, King and Musician — Spying the Danish Camp —
Baldulph and Athelstan feigning Music—Alfred founds
Oxford University—John, the First Music ' Professor '—The
Coming of the Danes—Christian Shrines and Sanctuaries—
Canute's Taste for Music—The Monks of Ely—Gunhilda's
Wedding-music—Ælfric—Aaron—Church Music under the
Danes—Church Music still influencing the People—Popular
Street Songs — Westminster and Waltham Abbeys—The
Coming of the ' Conqueror ' — Norman Ecclesiastics —
William's Visits to the Churches—A Singing Squabble at
Glastonbury—Music among the Normans—Native Music
under Norman Rule—Crellan, Soldier-musician—Music under
William II.—Chanting at Shrewsbury School—Winchester
Cathedral—Henry I. punishing a Minstrel—Rahere, Musician
to Henry I.—John of Salisbury—Church Music in Stephen's
Reign—Town Amusements in Henry II.'s Reign.

No name in British musical story possesses greater
charm than does that of Alfred, surnamed the
Great (849-901 A.D.), King of the Saxons, since it

Alfred— King and Minstrel. is with him that we are introduced to
one of the most interesting stories in
earliest English musical life. Alfred was
not only a warrior, but the legislator of his people ;

he was also a patron of music and the arts, a natural taste for which we find being stimulated early in life by his fond mother Osburga. She, anxious that her children should learn to read, once showed them a Saxon poem elegantly written and beautifully illuminated, which she promised to the one who should first learn to read it. This proved to be Alfred.

He stands the first among those enlightened English monarchs whose prescient rule has seen the true advancement of their subjects only in their social and moral greatness; a spirit well reflected—need it be mentioned?—in the person of our present gracious Sovereign.

ALFRED THE GREAT.

Flourishing towards the end of the ninth century, Alfred, among other parts which well fitted him to rule, was an excellent musician. Contemporary writers, like his tutor and biographer, Asser, Bishop of Sherborne (died 910 A.D.), Friar John, and Grimbald the monk—Mass Priests—all speak in glowing terms of Alfred's musical ability, and of his encouragement of the art among his people. At the death of Ethelred he was called to the throne by the unanimous voice of the West Saxons, and from that day to the time of his death he was occupied mainly in combating the successive incursions of the Danes.

Victory did not always favour him, and it was consequent upon a crushing defeat that we get the story of how he, cautious and solicitous for the **Alfred and the Danish Camp.** welfare of his kingdom, determined to first learn the strength of the enemy ere risking another overpowering by numbers. Pondering, probably during his secure winter retreat among the marshes of Somerset, he conceived the idea of spying out the Danish camp, and it was in connection with the carrying out of this resolve that Alfred comes before us in the double capacity of a fearless, cautious strategist as well as a talented musical Monarch, full of concern for his people. Disguising himself as a minstrel, for he had a master hand for the harp, he, unbeknown to any of his soldiers, made his way towards the Danish encampment, and, little by little, so ingratiated himself with the sentinels by his singing and harp-playing that one night (878 A.D.) he found himself a welcome guest in the very heart of the camp of the Danes. He does not appear to have excited suspicion among his foes; on the contrary, the Danish chief, and those who sat at his table, were charmed by his singing to the harp accompaniments. This is scarcely to be wondered at, inasmuch as before he was twelve years old, Alfred could sing a variety of Saxon songs, which he had learned from hearing them sung by others. He was provided with a good store, therefore, to entertain Guthrun, the Danish leader, and his soldiers.

Bale (1495-1563) asserts that King Alfred excelled in music, and his information was derived probably from ancient MSS. which, though existing in his time, are now lost. Sir John Spelman (died 1643), who wrote the ' Life of Alfred the Great,' confirms Bale, adding : ' King Alfred provided himself of musitians, not common or such as knew but the praticle part, but men skilful in the art itself, whose skill and services he yet further improved with his own instructions.'

Some writers question the truth of this story of Alfred and the Danish camp, attributing to it a legendary nature ; but apart from the evidence of contemporary historians, it is quite consistent with the spirit and musical custom of the age. To explore the Danish camp in the disguise of a harper would be no impossible proceeding in the case of a race as well disposed towards harmony as were the Danes. Moreover, there appears to have existed a sort of freemasonry among musicians in those days ; the man who could harp and sing could gain admittance to company wherever he went, whatever his nationality. One nation received the musician of another with every welcome, provided he was sufficiently talented to please by song or tune. It had long been customary for the Saxons to show favour

11

to the Danish scalds, and it was with no difficulty that the Danes extended a similar friendship to a wandering minstrel of talent, even if a Saxon, wherever he was met. No doubt the plan of subjecting the security of a camp to such a risk was extremely bad generalship, but less ingenious military devices have been resorted to successfully to the same end since those times. On many grounds, therefore, credence should be given to the story. Ingulph, contemporary with the Conqueror, Henry of Huntingdon, Speed, William of Malmesbury, as also the best modern historians, relate the story and accept it as trustworthy—this especially as it is now known that the incident was not without a precedent.

Even as early as the first invasion of Britain by the Saxons a similar occurrence is recorded by a native historian who wrote later. Colgrin, son of that Ella who was elected King or leader of the Saxons in the room of Hengist, was shut up in York, and closely besieged by Arthur and his Britons. Baldulph, brother of Colgrin, wanted to gain access to him, and to apprise him of a reinforcement which was coming from Germany. He had no other way to accomplish his design but by assuming the character of a minstrel. He therefore shaved his head and beard, and, dressing himself in the habit of that profession, took his harp in his hand. In this disguise he walked up and down the trenches without suspicion, playing all the while upon his instrument as a harper. By little and little he advanced near to the walls of the city, and, making himself known to the sentinels, was in the night drawn up by a rope.* The date of this incident is reputed to be the year 495 A.D.

If further proof were needed of the power of music as a passport in the times which we are considering —times when the enmities of nations could be forgotten, or the vigilance of war eluded, by the spell even of a stranger's song —it is furnished in an instance parallel with that recounted of King Alfred. About sixty years after Alfred's adventure a Danish king made use of the same disguise to explore the camp of our King Athelstan. With his harp in his hand, and dressed like a minstrel, Aulaff, or Olave, King of the Danes, went among the Saxon tents, and, taking his stand by the King's pavilion, began to play, and was eventually admitted. There he entertained Athelstan and his lords with his singing and his music, and was at length dismissed with an honourable reward, though his songs might have disclosed the fact that he was a Dane. Athelstan was saved from the consequences of this stratagem by a soldier who had observed Aulaff bury the money which had been given him, either from some scruple of honour or superstitious feeling.

Aulaff in King Athelstan's Camp.

* Geoffrey of Monmouth.

As soon as Aulaff was out of danger, the soldier recounted the circumstances to Athelstan, and to the charge of perfidy indignantly replied : 'No! I have shown that my honour is above temptation ; and remember that if I had been perfidious to him I might also have proved perfidious to you.' The King accepted the apology and shifted his camp. Werstan, Bishop of Sherborne, with his troops, arrived shortly afterwards, and pitched upon the identical spot, with the result that they were attacked in the night and killed to a man.

But Alfred's musical example and worth is not to be remembered merely on the strength of a pleasant story. In his zeal for the advancement of **Alfred and Oxford University.** learning and culture, he is credited with the founding of Oxford University. Here he inaugurated the first school in England for the purpose of teaching and diffusing a knowledge of the art of music. Theoretical as well as practical music was taught therein, for it is on record that in the year 886 A.D. the King bestowed on the afore-mentioned Friar John, one of the teachers of theory, the title of Prælector-Professor of Music, which is probably the first instance of the use of that term. It would have been quite in keeping for Alfred to have so done. He was sufficiently learned in musical theory to instruct his own 'musitians' in study and performance, and apart from the custom of the times, whereby every gentle-

man learnt music, there is no doubt whatever that
Alfred practised, and was a proficient performer on
some instrument, probably the harp.   In the King's
own words, ' Instrument-playing was common among
the Anglo-Saxons, and it was shameful to be ignorant
of it.'

Asser mentions Alfred's fondness for the oral
Anglo-Saxon poems and songs, which he learnt by
rote, and then sang to an instrumental accompaniment.   On the whole, therefore, this English King's
musical reputation will bear scrutiny.

It is recorded among the annals of the Church at
Winchester that Alfred founded a musical professor-
ship at Oxford.   This small beginning has developed
into that great music school of the University which
has wrought such good for the art in England, and
from which so many famous British composers have
taken their musical degrees.   King Alfred, with his
Chair   harmonious tendencies and culture, greatly
of Music. aided Church music, and no doubt it was
as much in the cause of sacred as of secular art that
he founded the Chair of Music at Oxford which
Joannes Monachus—Friar John of St. David's—
was the first to fill.*

* Some writers dispute Alfred's connection with the University
foundation, and state that it is supported only by documents
known to be forged, just as the stories attributing the foundation
of Cambridge to Cantaber, a mythical Spanish prince, or to
Sigebert, King of the East Angles in the seventh century, are by
some held to be the stupidest of historical fabrications.   Much

We have seen that, according to Bale, Alfred's knowledge of the art was by no means a superficial one, and this can be well imagined when we are told that that royal personage was able to improve critically upon no less an authority than Bede. The matter was Bede's description of the sacred poet Cædmon's embarrassment when the harp was presented to him in turn, that he might sing to it—'he hearpan singan.' Bede writes: 'Surgebat a media cœnâ, et egressus, ad suum domum repedabat.'

Alfred, literary critic that he was, espied the point, however, and adds that Cædmon not only arose, but arose *for shame*—'aras he for sceome '—thus conveying the fact that it was a disgrace, as then it really was, and should be now, to be ignorant of the musical art. Musicians may ever be proud of this diligent, heroic King, who thought it nought but a privileged duty to read the Psalms to the people in church in the absence of ecclesiastics and nobles who, amid the severity of the times, had fled either to France or to the shelter of Rome. As might have been expected of such a Prince, his Court, like those of other high personages of the time, afforded

---

the same kind of argument could be advanced, however, in respect to some of the most important truths, and if letter and seal had to be produced for everything which we are asked to believe, we should soon be robbed of many of our most cherished possessions. It seems to us more than probable that Alfred really was identified with an educational movement, including music, at Oxford, which has since grown into that great seat of modern learning.

shelter and succour for the minstrel. The name of one of these has come to us, Geraint, blue-robed bard of the chair and harper to King Alfred, A.D. 880, and is noteworthy inasmuch as he is reputed to have been the author of a grammar. Unquestionably the name of Alfred, good as he was great, is a worthy one in English musical history.

The Danes made their first descent upon England in 787 A.D. They were sea-kings and freebooters, fierce heathen from Denmark and the Scandinavian **Coming of the Danes.** lands, who from the eighth century to the eleventh poured into England, seeking, like the English themselves three centuries earlier, a definite settlement. They landed first in Northumberland, where they sacked churches, slew priests and wrecked the mother church at Lindisfarne. Especially did they wreak their fury upon Christian shrines and sanctuaries, spreading universal misery and want wherever they went. Year after year these Danes flocked here, until at the close of the ninth century half England was Danish.

A little later they had secured the throne, and Canute the Great was King (1017-1036 A.D.). Canute—or, as his name is sometimes spelt, Cnut **Canute.** —was a terrible destroyer. He repented, however ; and when he afterwards became a Christian, he ordered churches and monasteries to be built of stone and mortar in all places where himself or his fathers had burned the churches or minsters during their wars with the Anglo-Saxons.

Canute had a soul and ear for music, as an interesting story which has descended to us tends to prove. One day, attended by the Queen and his Court, he was journeying by water toward Ely, where he was to attend the Feast of the Purification of the Virgin. Passing by the abbey church, he heard the monks chanting their 'hours,' and as the sound of the music grew closer it so charmed the King that he commanded those who were rowing the royal barge to stay their oars, in order that attention might be directed to the singing. Some writers say that the King was so enraptured that he then and there broke into song, and sang the following extempore lines. This seems unlikely, however, as the fragmentary stanza preserved to us points to another author :

> Meuie runᴣen ᷐e Munecheſ binnen Ely.
> ᷐a Cnuꞇ chinᴣ ꝑeu ᷐eꝑ by.
> ꝑope᷒ eniꞇeſ noeꝑ ꞇhe lanꞇ.
> an᷒ heꝑe ꝑe Þeſ Munecheſ ſænᴣ.

Which translated runs :

> 'The monks of Ely sweetly sung,
> Whilst Cnut the King there row'd along ;
> Row near the land, knights (quoth the King),
> And let us hear the song they sing.'

Another version is :

> 'Sweetly sang the monks of Ely,
> While Cnut the King was passing by ;
> Row to the shore, knights, said the King,
> And let us hear these churchmen sing.'

The question of the influence of the Danes upon the English musical art and mind is one easy of disposal. If any effect resulted, it was for the worse rather than for the better, for their plundering meant a retrogression towards barbarism, and a decline in learning and culture. All that was beautiful they destroyed, so that that conspicuously religious Prince, King Alfred, has left it on record that 'before the ravages of the Danes he had seen the churches of England full of ornaments and books, nearly all of which they destroyed.' How much of musical worth and merit disappeared through these severities it is impossible to estimate. Such a wholesale destruction, not less than that later ruthless havoc wrought by Cromwell, would have been sufficient, however, to have effected the most complete effacement of all musical identity.

Very scanty, if, indeed, any, are the references to music at this time. the English being well occupied, as can be imagined, in keeping the Danes as

Music under the Danes.

much as possible at bay. Here and there a name especially identified with music has penetrated the gloom of the Danish devastation. The name of Gunhilda, the daughter of Hardicanute, has come down from this period. She was the fairest woman of her time, and when given in marriage to the Emperor Henry III., all the thanes—both English and Danish—accompanied them to the seashore. The songs which were composed for the occasion continued to be sung by the people at their convivial meetings, and preserved the memory of Gunhilda through many succeeding generations.

Another noteworthy personage was Turketal (952 A.D.) a royal clergyman and chancellor, who, choosing to become a singing monk, distributed all his wealth, and made a public profession of religion under the roof of Croyland Monastery, where he received the investiture from Edred the King, together with a blessing pronounced by the Bishop of Dorchester.

About this time flourished Ælfric (*circa* 955-1006 A.D.) the writer, the last great name connected with our literature before the Conquest. One of the

Ælfric. first pupils in the monastic school of Ethelwold at Abingdon, he became an instructive, trustworthy author. His works, which include 'Homilies on the Saints and Fathers of the Anglo-Saxon Church,' and his 'Constitutions of the Monks of Eynsham'—where was an abbey, founded by Ethelmer, of which Ælfric was Abbot — are especially of interest to those concerned with musical lore and learning. In his day the delivery of works written for the oral instruction of the people was in a sort of recitative—half sung, half spoken. Thus Ælfric's writings are characterized by an alliteration and rhythm somewhat allied to the rhythm of first English verse.

But one other name remains to be mentioned. This is that of Aaron, or Aron (born *circa* 1000, died 1052 A.D.). He was a Scottish musical writer who was Abbot of St. Martin's, at Cologne, in the year 1042 A.D. Little more is known of him, yet his memory may well be preserved as the first of that long list of men who have found a pleasurable occupation in writing upon the art of music.

We have but scant information respecting the fate of Church music under the Danes. The Gregorian chant had obtained too firm a hold, however, **Sacred Music under the Danes.** in the churches of the country to be permanently dislodged by civil matters like war and strife. It might be stifled by the disturbed times, but it could never be wholly eradicated, and, as we know, it has not been. There is every reason to believe that this Roman Church music, with any remnants of that music used in the old British churches, was the sole ecclesiastical art during Danish times here. The Psalms of David could certainly be heard to the impressive tones and endings for ever to be associated with the name of St. Gregory. The National Library of Paris contains an Anglo-Saxon paraphrase of the Book of Psalms, a part of which, from Psalm li. to cl., is attributed to Aldhelm in the eighth century. There are other Anglo-Saxon MS. psalters in the Cotton Collection of musical manuscripts. These, the famous ' Kentish ' psalters, the collection of Latin hymns of the Anglo-Saxon Church, preserved in a manuscript in the library of the Dean and Chapter of Durham, clearly show that psalms and hymns were sung in the Anglo-Saxon Church. How far they were understood would be a difficult matter to enter upon.

Many and varied were the ways in which the Church, and therefore her services and music, continued to influence the social manners and customs

Music Superstitions.
of the people. The farmer, for instance, took his religion with him into the field. As a charm against bad times, he obtained and sprinkled holy water upon the soil, and murmured a Paternoster; while not infrequently he took pieces of sod to church to have four Masses, perhaps in reference to the four Evangelists, chanted over them. Then he replaced the earth in the ground, amid the chanting of the hymns and the *Magnificat*, in the hope that the morsels blessed might leaven the whole extent of his acreage towards a bounteous harvest. Music and medicine joined even in a cure for demoniacs. A collection of herbs, made into a liquor, had seven Masses chanted over it, and was then pronounced equal to its work. One—-the final —direction only was enjoined : it was imperative that it should be drunk out of a church bell !

As with the Saxons, so with the Danes. The Northmen—Danes and Scandinavians—could not permanently resist the Church. It was the great

civilizing agent, and, with its cosmopolitan influences,
was a great power in the land. Sacred music
especially proved once more a most potent agent
for good in the imperative work which the clergy
had before them. When Guthrun signed the famous
Treaty at Wedmore and was baptized, with Alfred
as his godfather, hundreds of Danes followed the
example of their chief. Northumbria, Mercia, and
East Anglia were allotted them by the ' Peace '
Treaty, and in these provinces they were gradually
transformed from roving pirates into agricultural
settlers. To their credit be it said, they commenced
rebuilding the churches wherein sacred music was
wholly kept alive, for the outside world people were
mostly given to the singing of common, secular
songs.

One that used to be sung about the streets of
London in William of Malmesbury's day (*circa*
1095-1143 A.D.) had for its subject the marriage of
Gunhilda, the daughter of Hardicanute, already
referred to. Other Saxon rhymes or songs popular
among the common orders are mentioned by Robert
of Brunne. One concerned Gryme the fisher, the
founder of Grimsby ; another referred to Hanelock
the Dane, and his wife, Goldeburgh, daughter to
King Æthelwold—all, unhappily, irretrievably lost.
Would that some of these songs of the people had
had the good fortune to descend to us !

Little more remains to be written of this period of

English musical growth.   Before passing to the
consideration of music under the Normans, however,
two names call for record.   The one is that of the
pious King, Edward the Confessor (succeeded 1042,

**Edward
the Con-
fessor.**

died 1066 A.D.), more fitted for a Norman
cloister than the English throne, who introduced Norman architecture into England,
and built the choir and transepts of Westminster
Abbey, which was consecrated a few days before his
death.   The other name belongs to Harold (succeeded
and died 1066 A.D.).   He, anxious to advance the cause
of the secular clergy in opposition to King Edward's
care for the regular clergy, built Waltham Abbey as
a collegiate foundation in 1062, and provided for the
maintenance of a dean and twelve canons therein.
The former of these buildings has been closely identified with English ecclesiastical music, especially in
in regal and great civil solemnities ever since.

When, on Christmas Day, 1066, William the
Norman was crowned King at Westminster Abbey,
a great social victory was gained in England.   One

**William
the Con-
queror.**

of the first institutions to be affected by
the change was the Church, to which we
stand so much indebted for much of the
vitality which music possessed during the earlier
stages of its history in this country.   All the
bishoprics, abbacies, and livings were filled with
Norman ecclesiastics, prominent among whom were
Bishop Odo, Remi (Bishop of Lincoln), and the

Abbot Nicholas. These clerical introductions meant a great revival of the observances of religion, and therefore of sacred music. To use the words of William of Malmesbury, 'You might see churches rise in every village, and monasteries in the towns and cities built after a style unknown before.' The monkish chronicler says that 'William built and endowed churches in abundance. Scarcely did his own munificence or that of his nobility leave any monastery unnoticed. . . . The monastic flock increased, and monasteries arose on every side.'

William himself set a good example. He bore his King's helmet thrice every year into the church. At Easter it was at Winchester; at Pentecost, Westminster Abbey; and in midwinter at Gloucester. Then there

WILLIAM I.

accompanied him all the rich men over all England Archbishops and Bishops, Abbots and Earls, Thanes, and others. Mass was chanted and hymns sung to overpowering outbursts of Gregorian tone and inflexion.

Among the changes inevitable with newcomers of any age was one which, judging by its reception, appears to have struck terror into the hearts of those

immediately affected by it.   This change was none
other than an alteration in the style of singing.   It
is curious how in those early times the question of a
musical innovation met with much the same fate as

Squabble at Glastonbury. such things often do nowadays.   The
instance of a free fight in the choir-stalls
will rarely find its parallel in modern
times, however.   Holinshed, writing of Church
matters in William's reign, mentions a strife which
existed between Thurstan, Abbot of Glastonbury, a
Norman, and his monks : 'One cause thereof was,
for that the Abbot would have compelled them to
have left the plaine song or note, for the service
which Pope Gregorie had set foarth, and to have
used another kind of tune devised by one William
of Fescampe.'   Words came to blows, and at one of
the services 'the Abbot got armed men about him,
and falling upon the monkes, slew three of them at
the high altar, and wounded XVIIJ.   Howbeit the
monkes for their part plaied the pretie men, with
formes and candlesticks, defending themselves as
well as they might ; so that they hurt divers of the
Abbot's adherents and drove them out of the quier.'
Quite a pretty little musical squabble !

Of the social life and manners of the first Normans
in England we have but scant information, and the
period is particularly barren in musical data and
material ; but a gentleman was expected to be able
to perform upon some instrument of music.   The

Bayeux tapestry furnishes a representation of the proceedings at funerals. The corpse of King Edward is there shown being carried on an open bier on the shoulders of eight men, whilst on either side is an acolyte ringing two bells. Then the corpse was watched by priests, who sang from the *Officium Defunctorum* the Antiphon, 'Placebo Domino in regione vivorum.'

Scarcely a single musical name has descended to us belonging to this period, when graver matters probably occupied men's minds. It is easy to

English Music under the Normans. imagine, too, that the Englishman was reserved, if not positively silenced, musically, especially remembering the far-reaching grasp and rapacity of the Norman. In remote districts, and in places where the nature of the country provided a safe spot, however, the national art would be kept alive; but the old inhabitants, whether descendants of Britons or Saxons, would retreat as far as possible from the reach of the Norman influence or interference. By this means not a little of the old musical spirit and practice would be preserved.

Crellan was one of the old bards of the country who flourished about this time (1086 A.D.), and is heard of only in his death-scene as the harper of Prince Gryffydd ab Cynan. He was killed—soldier-musician that he was—while fighting in the cause of his Prince, who in peace times had fostered and provided for him.* This is the Gryffydd ab Cynan to whom Dr. Burney refers in his 'History of

---

* About the year 1042, this Prince issued rules and regulations respecting the bards and minstrels, among which were the following: That no one person was to exercise two callings, as poetry and playing on the harp or crwth. That no bard or minstrel was to possess more than the value of *ten shillings*, either in horses or cattle, or expensive apparel, under penalty of forfeiting it to the King—for *rich* men seldom devote themselves to study! An itinerent minstrel was not to go to the house of a gentleman, nor a chief minstrel to the house of a plebeian. It was the office of the itinerant minstrel to rebuke, to mock, to deride, and to entreat, by means of reproach, and all that under the pretence of singing; for which he was to receive a penny, on his acknowledging himself to belong as a mere weed to the bards; and a gibe from the company was to be given to him, that he might make light of the devil, who enticed him to idleness, riotous living, and sloth! The chief minstrel of the country was to have the marriage fines of the daughters of minstrels; he also was to have the presents of young women, when they married; that was four-and-twenty pence.

When the King was desirous to hear a song, the chief minstrel was to sing two songs, the first in the hall, addressed to God, and the other respecting the King.

When the Queen wished to hear a song in her apartment, the domestic bard was to sing three songs to her, *with a moderate voice*, not to occasion any disturbance in the hall. The chief minstrel must be acquainted with all the laws both of poetry and music, and be able to sing both in *harmony* and *concord*, also in cross consonancy (*query* counterpoint) and alliterations; be fond of entertaining subjects, and fertile in wit; also to be able to retain long in his memory the praise of the nobles. The graduated probationary pupil must know *ten concords, one fundamental, five concords of accompaniment, and eight tunes*. The disciplined pupil must know double the above. The master pupil must know three times as many, and be able to explain them. The chief

Music.'* Dr. Burney examined an old manuscript transcribed in the time of Charles I., which was

minstrel must know four times as many, and be acquainted with all the canons and their rules ; also the *system of canons as it is set forth in the book of science.* He must be able to compose a piece for himself, and be able to give an explanation of every part of it : such as every division and subdivision ; every quantity and rest, and every change of the drawings, and key-notes, *hidden and apparent;* and to show them forth warranted from his own performance, musically and masterly, so that the doctors and chief minstrels may conscientiously adjudge and elect him to be an author and master in science.

The tunes which are named on the mixed or minor key are thirty-one in number ; those on the *sharp* key, A, twenty-seven ; those on the *flat* key, F, ten. The contending concords, named on the mixed key, B, are eleven ; the concords in the flat key, F, seven, and those on the sharp key, A, eighteen.

That no pupil compose a song without showing it to his master, to know from his judgment that it be correct, before it be sung aloud to anyone, that it may not bring shame either on the master or the pupil.

Bards and minstrels are to be of a friendly conversation, peaceable, obliging, humble, and fond of doing good offices ; and all who are true subjects of the King and his magistrates should countenance and patronize the bards and minstrels.

The pupils to inquire of their masters, a month before each festival, where they are to go, lest too many go to the same place ; and that but one go to a person whose income does not exceed *ten pounds* (!), and two to him who has *twenty pounds !*

Order of Bards and Minstrels.—There are eight kinds of bards and minstrels : four graduated, and four frivolous.

The first four are—1. Bards who wear the band of their order ; 2. Harpers ; 3. Performers on the crwth ; 4. Vocalists. The four kinds of frivolous ones are—1. The piper ; 2. The juggler ;

---

* Vol. ii., p. 110.

reputed to be a transcript of 'the music of the Britons, as settled by a Congress, or meeting of masters of music, by order of Gryffydd ab Cynan, Prince of Wales, about the year 1100, with some of the most ancient of the Britons, supposed to have been handed down to us from the British bards.' The document is in letters with a line between the treble and bass. It contains pieces for the harp in full counterpoint. The music is written in a notation by letters of the alphabet, and is so curious that an

3. The drummer; 4. The fiddler, or player on the crwth with three strings. The gratuity of each of these is one penny, and they are to perform standing. The singer ought to know how to tune a harp, or crwth, and accurately sing several musical lessons through their regular parts. He should also be acquainted with the four-and-twenty metres of poetry, and be able to correct any old piece of poetry which he may receive incorrect from another. He should likewise know how to serve from the kitchen to the table of a person of dignity and power, and to carve every fowl that comes before him. And his office at a royal wedding is to serve at the table of the bride; a white covering is to be about the harp or crwth which he brings with him.

The Club-head Vocalist is one who sings without being able to play on an instrument. He is to stand in the middle of the hall, and beat time with his club, and sing a poem or ode with the beats.

Royal Weddings.—A notice of a year and a day is given to the bards to prepare themselves to attend royal weddings; and the chief minstrel is appointed the *butt* of the rest, and he gives them an entertaining subject to exercise their poetical talents upon. After dinner the chief minstrel sits in a chair, and those who put questions to him stand. They are permitted to say against him, in poetry, anything they choose, and on the morrow he answers them on the subject for the amusement of the company.

example may well be reproduced, together with the learned historian's reproductions in modern notation.

MOST ANCIENT SPECIMENS OF WELSH MUSICAL NOTATION EXTANT.

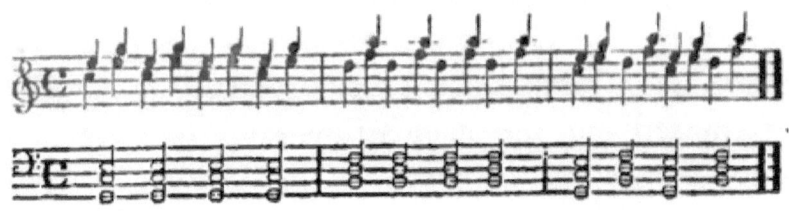

Translation in Modern Notation.

Translation in Modern Notation.

*Translation in Modern Notation.**

Dr. Burney considers that the harmonies were added by the transcriber,† but such a supposition seems improbable, since it would defeat the purpose of transcribing the manuscript—viz., to show the state of music at the time of the conference. Had the transcriber modernized the music, he would in all probability have modernized the notation. The honesty of the transcriber is not doubted, so that the music of this MS. may be safely regarded as the

* The patriotic Owen Jones Myvyr first published these specimens in the 'Archæology of Wales,' a valuable work in three volumes, printed at an expense of £2,000.

† Robert ap Haw of Bodwigen, in the Isle of Anglesea, from William Penllyn's book. William Penllyn was among the successful candidates on the harp at the Eisteddfod, or session of the bards and minstrels appointed in the ninth year of Queen Elizabeth's reign at Caerwys, in North Wales, where he was elected one of the chief bards or teachers of instrumental music

genuine Welsh music which the existing bards had in the tenth century, counterpoint and all.*

Unhappily, William of Malmesbury, when he comes to the reign of William Rufus (1087-1100), chronicles a different story to that of William the Conqueror's care for the churches. According to the chronicler, the rites and honours of the Church were brought to a low ebb, too humiliating and disgraceful to contemplate, and though several important churches were built or restored in this reign, such was owing more to the piety and liberality of their wealthy founders than to any encouragement accorded by the King. Most of these benefactors were powerful Norman Churchmen who followed upon the Conquest, imbued with a deep love for church-building, and bent upon making the Church a power not less formidable than the State. Several of the names identified with these reconstructions show how the Norman ecclesiastics were gradually strengthening their position.

Church Musical Influence.

* It is to be regretted that any doubts have grown around this Welsh MS., which, when Dr. Burney wrote, was in the possession of Richard Morris, Esq., of the Tower. Early musical MSS. are all too scanty, and have suffered deplorably in this country. Of course they were particularly liable to destruction, because, as notation improved, the older MSS. would become illegible, and therefore useless to the generality of musicians. The blind zeal of conquerors and bodies like the Puritans led to the destruction of any parchment or paper partaking of a musical character.

About this time lived Henry of Huntingdon (*circa* 1083-1155), to whose industry we are indebted for much relating to social life, and especially to music in England. He was Archdeacon of Huntingdon, and his chief work, the 'Historia Anglorum,' which extends to the reign of King Stephen, is especially valuable, inasmuch as it incorporates the narratives of popular songs and stories the originals of which have been lost. He is not always an exact chronicler, but as he went to the old songs of the people for many of his facts, he will always be entitled to respect on that account.

Contemporary with this chronicler was Ordericus Vitalis, born in 1075 A.D., who is associated with musical doings at this time. He was sent to a **Ordericus** school at Shrewsbury, and, among other **Vitalis.** matters, was taught chanting under a priest of royal blood, named Siward. Later on he went to St. Evroult, an abbey buried in the forests of Normandy, from which religious house he, forty years afterwards, wrote: 'I have cheerfully borne the light yoke of the Lord for forty-two years, and walking in the ways of God with my fellow monks . . . have endeavoured to perfect myself in the devices of the Church and ecclesiastical duties.'

Winchester Cathedral, which has always been associated with the social life of this country, and therefore with its religious and musical growth, was the point for which the Conqueror's youngest son,

Henry I. (1100-1135 A.D.), made when he left his brother William's dead body where it fell through Tyrrel's shaft in the New Forest. He seized the

Henry I. ecclesiastical treasure wherewith to ease the way to a speedy coronation in London, where, by gifts and bribes, he was crowned King, while Robert was away in the Holy Land with Peter the Hermit's Crusade. The coronation

took place at Westminster Abbey to the chanting of the Gregorian Mass and Canticle music by the Norman monks and singing-men. The exiled Anselm, Archbishop of Canterbury, whom King Rufus had banished, was recalled; and that same energy for church-building

HENRY I.

which had distinguished his father and brother marked also the character and reign of Henry, who no doubt saw, as they had done, the wisdom of strengthening the Norman ecclesiastical reach and influence.

We hear little relating to music in general in this reign; but one incident that stands recorded redounds but little to the credit or magnanimity of the Monarch. A luckless Norman minstrel, Luke de

Barre by name, fell into his power, and Henry determined to make him suffer. 'He has never done me homage,' said the King, 'but he has fought against me, and has besides composed facetious and indecent songs upon me, and sung them publicly, thus often raising the loud laughs of my worst enemies.' So saying, the King ordered the minstrel's eyes to be pulled out; but the terrified musician escaped from his tormentors, and, rushing thereto, dashed his brains out against the wall.

Matilda, Queen of Henry I., was, according to William of Malmesbury, so fond of music that she expended all her revenues upon it, and oppressed her tenants to pay her minstrels.

The name of one important musician that reaches us is that of Rahere. He was the King's *jongleur*, and founded the priory of St. Bartholomew, Smith-

Rahere, Jongleur to Henry I. field, which church, as recently restored, shows something of its original beauty. From this foundation it is clear that a royal jester, minstrel, or *jongleur*—whatever we may term him—was no mean or ill-paid personage in Henry I.'s day, for there are probably few among favoured musicians of to-day whose earnings would enable them to build and endow such a foundation as is the St. Bartholomew's charity.* As Henry I.

* In the history of Thomas of Reading, Rahere is said to have retained 'a company of minstrels, *i.e.*, fiddlers, who played with silver horns.' These would also be the King's servants, under the

had Rahere attached as *jongleur* to his Court, we may assume that musicians filled similar positions in the households of all great personages of the time, so that social music was by no means discountenanced this while by the nobility in England. We may be sure, too, that the old love for domestic music remained as strong as ever among the lower orders, and that around the hearths of many a remote Saxon and British homestead—far removed from the new fashions of the Normans—the family circle consoled itself with the musical delights, vocal and instrumental, which its members had intuitively acquired, and which their forefathers had practised long before them.

John, surnamed 'of Salisbury,' to distinguish him from other Johns, belongs to this reign. The name is so closely identified with early English music that **John of** it deserves notice. Born about the year **Salisbury.** 1110, John went as a youth to Paris. He attended Abelard's lectures at the Mont St. Geneviève, and became a scholar in the Montier la Celle Abbey, in the diocese of Troyes.

As secretary of Theobald, Archbishop of Canterbury, he came to know Becket, the Chancellor of England, of whose will he was an executor. In 1176 he was Bishop of Chartres, a high post for

direction of Rahere, and constituting a band of musicians who would be required chiefly on the great occasions, and other than those when Rahere performed privately for the King's amusement.

one to have risen to who, in Henry I.'s time, was, as an old chronicle puts it, 'being handed over to a clergyman's charge to learn his Psalms.'

From John of Salisbury we learn that the great ones of his time imitated Nero in his extravagance towards musicians. He avers that they 'prostituted their favour by bestowing it on minstrels and buffoons.' John died October 25, 1180.

The following passage which the same John penned about the year 1170 affords some idea of the pleasure the people of the time took in part-singing :

'The rites of religion are now profaned by music; and it seems as if no other use were made of it than to corrupt the mind by wanton modulations, effeminate inflexions, and frittered notes and periods, even in the *Penetralia*, or sanctuary, itself. The senseless crowd, delighted with all these vagaries, imagine they hear a concert of Sirens, in which the performers strive to imitate the notes of nightingales and parrots, not those of men; sometimes descending to the bottom of the scale, sometimes mounting to the summit; now softening, and now enforcing the tones, repeating passages, mixing in such a manner the grave sounds with the more grave, and the acute with the most acute, that the astonished and bewildered ear is unable to distinguish one voice from another.'

John was clearly one of the old conservative

school in music—apt to grow excited and to speak vehemently respecting the new-fangled musical notions which he saw, slowly but surely, creeping in.

During the terrible civil wars between the kind, engaging, but ambitious Stephen (1135-1154 A.D.) and Henry's daughter, the Empress Maude, the country was little disposed for practising music. The hauberk or coat of mail, lance, with sling and bow, claimed more attention than the harp and viol, which were placed aside awhile, when, according to an old record, 'all England wore a face of desolation and misery.

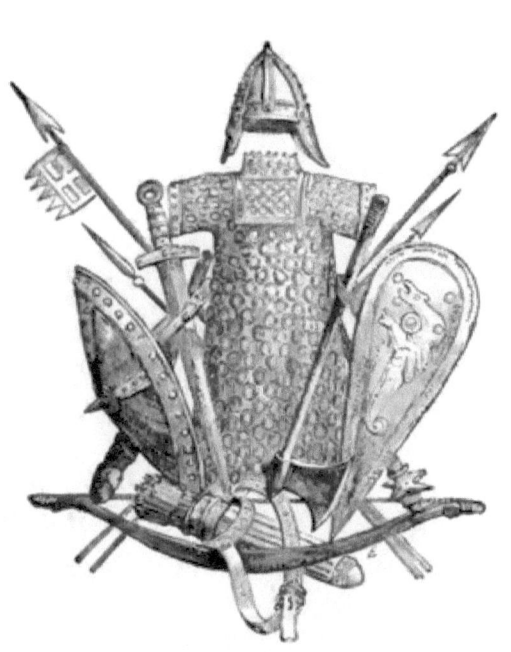

NORMAN ARMOUR.

Multitudes abandoned their beloved country, and went into voluntary exile; others, forsaking their own houses, built wretched huts in churchyards, hoping for protection from the sacredness of the place. Whole families, after sustaining life as long as they could by eating herbs, roots, and the flesh of dogs and horses, at last died of hunger; and you might see many pleasant villages without a single inhabitant.'*

The reign of Stephen witnessed an extraordinary extension of the monastic system, which meant a corresponding growth of ecclesiastical music, and possibly of domestic music, if the monks elected to enjoy its

STEPHEN.

practice. The exercise of the art, whether in its sacred or secular form, afforded little ground of offence to noble or serf, and it is extremely improbable that the art fell away even during a period when anarchy reigned unbridled in Britain. Certainly Church music did not decline. Happily the clergy and churchmen were diligent. With sword in hand they laid the stone and guided the trowel, so that even amid the deplorable struggles which marked Stephen's reign, when the work of devastation must have extended to, and effaced the beauty of, many a church, new ones sprang up with all that frequency and extent of beautiful architectural dimension and detail which has made this period a glorious one in the history of constructive building art and ornament.

* ' Gesta Regni Stephani.'

The stern and stirring Norman period is not without interest and value as a phase in our national musical history. It is true that it has furnished us **Norman Music Material.** with little actual musical material in the shape of manuscripts of either sacred or secular art. As far as regards sacred music this can be explained : this, unlike secular music, was liberally transcribed and duplicated, but it is only the fewest who, in the matter of books, think of any age other than that in which they live. If book and manuscript serve the purpose of their own generation, the majority of mankind are content not to trouble about the wants of another. Further, one has only to have some acquaintance with the wear and tear, avoidable and unavoidable, to which choir-books in daily use are subjected by choristers, to understand the discrepancy that would follow between the wearing-out and the duplicating processes, especially at a period when copying had to be done by the slow art of penmanship.

Still, this Norman epoch has given us the minstrel element—of which more anon—which, although it existed in England long before, and long after, the Norman Conquest, is particularly identified with this time, when a great stimulus was given to secular music, and especially to that form of it known as the art of the *improvisatore*, a spontaneous music and song which the genius and grace of the

minstrel could call up as if by magic, just as occasion
required.

Then we must not forget such unmistakable and
material help to the cause of music as was supplied
in the prolific erection of churches wherever the
quick eye of the Norman churchman discovered
a choice site ; the situations of many of our oldest
churches well attest the shrewd judgment and discretion which these ecclesiastics displayed in this
matter.   The more churches there were the more
sacred music there was bound to be.   In Fitz-
Stephen's contemporary description, written a few
years later (about 1174 A.D.), there were as many as
one hundred and thirty-nine churches in London.
Throughout the country they were relatively
numerous, so that here alone would be a great
outlet for musical exercise, since King and Queen,
chivalrous noble and pious lady, Bishop, Abbot,
priest, and commoner—all flocked to the church for
Matins, Mass, and Evensong.

Perhaps there was little else than the Gregorian
music to the Mass, and the chants to the Canticles,
Litanies, and Misereres, to be heard, but the music
and the services would be on a scale corresponding
with the extent of the abbeys and churches, and as
many of these were of great splendour we may conclude that the heritage—as regards its spirit if not its
letter—which the Roman Church bequeathed at a
later period to the Protestant Church was one that

was truly worthy of the high purpose which it fulfilled as an accompaniment and adornment to the office of Divine service.

This Church music undoubtedly existed, and was used and practised daily in the principal towns and centres ; while secular art was kept alive by the minstrel or bard, who, either comfortably housed in his patron's hall or castle, or moving from place to place in the country, was as jealous of his art as were the ecclesiastics of theirs.

This same Fitz-Stephen, in his graphic account of London during the reign of Henry II., describes the town amusements at the several seasons of the year. He particularly mentions the water and riverside revels at Easter, where 'the maidens as soon as the moon rises dance to the guitar and with their nimble movements shake the ground.'

Nor was this all. What of the people's music and all that uncontrolled harmony and melody which was as prevalent among the various classes then as it is now? We are wont to keep little reckoning of all this natural music which comes and goes in the case of each one of us with a lifetime. But it exists around us, though all unnoticed and neglected by the historian. In these early Norman times men and women, maidens and youths, possessed their wide and varying sentiments just as they do now. Of course they broke into song. The lover with his plaint, the nursery lullaby, the maid at her wheel, the peasant's drone as he tilled the soil, the milkmaid's song—all these were then as now.   And was every knight and lady dumb?   Did the guard as he strode the lonely battlement never hum a tune to lighten the weight of his coat of mail or hauberk ; or when these were removed for a season, would he not have broken out into some song — rude or polished—that had grown up with him from his childhood?   Surely there was all this untutored art in its many thousand shades of emotion and expression.   There was the same human heart then as now, and that fount of all that is joyous and all that is sad will, in every season, overflow and pour forth its message in many a strange mood and key through that chaste and adequate medium which music alone supplies.

PRINCIPAL AUTHORITIES.

'Life of Alfred the Great'	Spelman.
'Chronicles'	Ingulph.
'History of Ely'	Bentham.
'English Songs'	Warton.
'Popular Music of the Olden Time'	Chappell.
Anglo-Saxon Chronicle.	
'History of Music'	Burney.
'Norman Conquest'	Freeman.
'Dissertation on Romance and Minstrelsy'	Ritson.
'Short History of the English People'	Green.
'*Roman de Rou*'	Wace.
'Specimens of Various Styles of Music'	Crotch.
'Chronicle'	Holinshed.
'*Historia Anglorum*'	Henry of Huntingdon.
'*Gesta Regni Stephani.*'	
'Social England'	Cassell.
'Dictionary of Music and Musicians'	Grove.

CHAPTER VII.

MINSTRELSY FROM NORMAN TO LANCASTRIAN TIMES.

MINSTREL! The word is fuller with music than many a more pronounced term in modern tone art

phraseology. Its mere mention thrills the imaginative mind into a realm of fancy concerning a singularly
beautiful and romantic phase of early English musical

Min-   life. How the school-boy and girl loves
strelsy. to linger over the brief references to
the minstrel and his art in the primer or history-
book! How, as we grow older, the minstrel has
still a charm for us; and whenever the word 'minstrelsy' meets our eyes, all our musical nerves and
instincts seem to vibrate within us! The music of
the 'waits,' rough and coarse as it too often is—a
musical feature which still clings to the Yule season
—never fails to arrest the attention of old and young
as a remnant, it is thought, of ancient English music
and custom. Unfortunately the terms 'minstrel'
and 'minstrelsy' have been indiscriminately used
for every sort of musician and performance, of whatever age. We have to consider the minstrels here
as a great body of itinerant performers who flourished
between the Conquest and three centuries later.

Popularly the 'waits' of to-day are regarded as
minstrels of the kind which obtained long before
music became that great art which early musicians
like the Elizabethan composers made it; and many
people there are who see more music in the snatches
of tune which startle the crisp night air, beneath our
window-casements, at Christmas time, than they
perceive in the performance of a modern symphony.
We need not disagree. It would be harsh to dispel

an illusion which springs out of the fulness of a good heart—as all hearts are at the Christmas season. It is the odour of the old minstrelsy which flavours the modern imitation, and for that reason we are content to overlook not a little that is musically bad in these midnight musicians. The modern 'waits' and carol-singers are a survival—slight, perhaps—of old time methods which no one wishes to see die out, although it is to be regretted that the 'artists' at these nocturnal musical performances do not treat us to something of a higher order than is their wont. The extravagant raspings of flute and viol, and crude vocal harmony — generally extemporizations — are only to be regarded charitably, and no one, we hope, would seriously think or judge of musical England by such searchings and gropings.

The minstrel—a name we do not get until after the coming of the Normans, though in person he was here with the Saxons—was distinguished for his skill in instrumental music only, and it was left to him to borrow his story from any source—provided it pleased his patrons. Many of these English musicians could and did compose songs themselves, but as in the lapse of years the art declined, the later singers fell back upon the compositions of others. It was ever rare, however, to find a minstrel who could not invent a few stanzas as occasion and opportunity required. We must not hurriedly pass them by, for they were a great feature

in early English social life. To them, too, we owe
most of the old heroic ballads which we cherish.
'The minstrels,' says Percy, 'were the successors of
the ancient bards who under different names were
admired and revered from the earliest ages, among
the people of Gaul, Britain, Ireland, and the North,
and, indeed, by almost all the first inhabitants of
Europe, whether of Celtic or Gothic race ; but by
none more than by our own Teutonic ancestors,
particularly by all the Danish tribes.'*

The term 'minstrel,' from the Norman French
ministraulx, came into use in England with the
Conquest with that great influx of the minstrel

Norman   element that followed in the van of the
Minstrelsy. army which William, Duke of Normandy, brought with him (1066 A.D.). It is from the
Norman settlement that the history of the minstrel,
who, as we shall see, long survived in this country,
conveniently dates. No doubt the Briton and the
Saxon possessed a musician who, under another
name, performed precisely similar offices for the
State and the people as did the Norman minstrel ;
both countries' musicians were equally fortunate,
too, in the favour and esteem in which they were
regarded by the people at large, and the patron-
nobles in particular.

There was little, if any, artistic superiority in one
over the other ; and, save in the matter of the

* 'Reliques of Ancient English Poetry' (Percy).

tongue they spoke, one national musician was very like another. Throughout North-West Europe there was, and had long been, this musical necessity—a performer who, whether under the name of bard, scóp, scald, or minstrel, played much the same *rôle*, and was similarly regarded in whichever country he trod and travelled. Thus he was a 'minstrel' wherever he lived, and wherever he went, and writers have not troubled to make any more careful distinction when referring to either the British bard and harper, or to the later harper-scald of the Saxon.

The Normans did not introduce poetry and song into England, as is generally supposed, but the visitors from Northern France gave a great impetus to impromptu music here. The art was already in a sturdy state when the descendant of Rollo the Ranger stepped on English soil to win immortal fame as the 'Conqueror.' That independent style of melody which we have seen was inherent in and peculiar to the ancient Britons still lived, as do traces of it even to this day. Nor was Anglo-Saxon music withering. All England was still alive with the doings of King Alfred, who had explored the Danish camp. The old Saxon gleemen plied their trade for centuries after the Conquest, for the Norman music for many years affected not so much the lower orders—who could not understand it—as the nobility. Thus it was for awhile an art for the knight and patrician— not for the plebeian— so that the common music at the rural entertainments, fairs, and such like, long remained English and not Norman. The 'fun of the fair,' with the jigs and the dance tunes, were English features for many centuries after the arrival of the Conqueror. When we meet with the Normans, however, we not only become possessed of the name 'minstrel,' that has been inaptly applied to the travelling musician of a much earlier period, but we are introduced to much of the habit and custom of the minstrel as he existed in a flourishing land just outside our own.

With this fresh performer a new and different character of music was introduced into England, which mixed well with the native and Saxon art. Like many other of the Norman influences this new musical element was destined to have a considerable and permanent effect upon English musical art. One result of it was the increased favour accorded to secular music and the minstrel's art in particular. So much was this the case that minstrels became a distinct order of men for many years after the Norman Conquest, men who gained their livelihood principally by singing verses to the harp at the houses of the great. Further, the Norman minstrel brought the romantic spirit largely into play, and weaved it inextricably into our national lyrical art. This was a great gain.

'The *menestrier*, *menestrel*, or minstrel,' says Ritson in his 'Dissertation on Romance and Minstrelsy,' was 'he who accompanied his song by a musical instrument, both the words and the melody being occasionally furnished by himself, and occasionally by others.' The same author is of opinion that there were different orders of minstrels. He writes : ' That the different professors of minstrelsy were, in ancient times, distinguished by names appropriated to their respective pursuits, cannot reasonably be disputed, though it may be difficult to prove. The *trouveur, trouverre*, or *rymour*, was he who composed *romans, contes, fabliaux, chansons* and *lais ;* and those who confined themselves to the composition of *contes* and *fabliaux*, obtained the appellation of *contours, conteours*, or *fabliers.*'

The minstrels, firmly established in England by the Norman Conquest, flourished as long after as the sixteenth century. They became a real factor in the national musical character, and it will be evident that no such body of men could exercise their profession in the palace of the king, the hall of the noble, and in the outdoor world, without deeply impressing all who heard the song and music. What was sung and played would cling with remarkable tenacity to and operate upon the minds and actions of all who heard it. At the outset we ought to possess an adequate idea of the minstrel and the many-sided nature of his calling. This has been well set out by Le Grand. ' This profession,' he says, ' required a multiplicity of attainments, and of talents, which one would at this day have some difficulty to find re-united, and we have more reason to be astonished at them in these days of ignorance : for besides all the songs old and new, besides the current anecdotes, the tales and fabliaux, which they piqued themselves on knowing, besides the romances of the time which it behoved them to know and to possess in part, they could declaim, sing, compose music, play on several instruments, and accompany them. Frequently even were they authors, and made themselves the pieces they uttered.'

He sang the lighter and shorter chansons, and that he was a skilled musician is clear from the following extract from an Anglo-French poem :

'Ge sai juglere de vielé*
Si sai de muset† et de frestele‡
Et de la harpe et de chifonie§
De la gigue‖ de larmonie¶
Et el saltiere** et en la rote.'††

The minstrel was with the English and Normans the successor of a previous musician. William's ancestor Rollo hailed from Norway and Denmark, where Norwegians held the scalds in high esteem. Many of these went into the Norman duchy to become Normans, and to change their musical title to that of *minstrel*—the name which they brought to England, and which has ever since remained here.

* Viol.	† Bagpipes.	‡ Flageolet, or Flute.
§ Hurdy-gurdy.	‖ Fiddle.	¶ Tambourine.
** Dulcimer played with the fingers.		†† Zither.

From the Domesday Book we learn of the bounty of William I. towards his private joculator or bard in Gloucestershire—' Bardic Joculator Regis ' ; while a still more famous minstrel's fame and reputation have made him quite a national figure.

The name of one warrior-musician more eminent, more daring than the rest that followed William has come down through history. This was the herald-minstrel Taillefer. His intrepidity and

Taillefer. courage as a soldier matched his skill in music, and beseeching his ducal patron to be allowed to do so, he led the onslaught on King Harold and the English upon that memorable day when the sun went down at Senlac, and the dead bodies of the Saxon King and his hus-carls were mantled by the night. The preliminary to the onset was brilliant and characteristic. The fearless, careless minstrel rode before the Norman foot-soldiers playing with his spear, casting it, indeed, in jaunty fashion into the air and catching it again by its iron head, the while he chanted songs in praise of Roland by Charlemagne and other heroes of France. Roland's feats and achievements in wars with the Saracens well qualified him to frame a stirring battle-song, the grandeur and stimulating nature of which it is said aided the Conqueror greatly on this memorable field-day. Three times the hero-minstrel did thus ; then, poising the mighty weapon, he hurled it with such great force that it fell into the midst of his enemies, and, fixing one Saxon, brought him to the dust. Then came the awful rush—Taillefer, the first to strike a blow, was the first on William's side to fall on English soil.

The 'Song of Roland' ('Chanson de Roland'), though often referred to in musical and general literature, may well receive some notice here. It was originally composed if not by, at least

The Song of Roland.

in honour of, Roland, Count of Mans and Knight of Blairs—eight feet in stature —who was slain in the Valley of Roncesvalles as he was leading his uncle Charlemagne's army from Spain to France (A.D. 778). A version of the story was made in a poem in the Anglo-Norman tongue of Turold, an English minstrel, *circa* 1140 A.D. As in most of the early romances, the largest portion of this poem consists of battle scenes, which are told with somewhat of Homeric vigour. It was obviously an earlier version, however, that Taillefer chanted. Unfortunately not a little uncertainty and misrepresentation have gathered round this famous item of history, both as regards its words and tune or notation. The celebrated composition, or one bearing the title, whatever or whosesoever it was, was preserved as late as the fourteenth century, when it was sung at the Battle of Poictiers (1356 A.D.). There the French soldiers sang it within hearing of their King, John, and upon his reproaching one of them with singing it at a time when there were no

Rolands left, the murmur went round that Rolands would still be found if they had a Charlemagne at their head.

There are several metrical romances on the subject of Charlemagne of considerable antiquity still extant, and one of these may, possibly, be the 'Song of Roland.' It is at least curious that while this particular composition should have escaped the vigilance of historians, another song, a 'Lament,' also inspired by the famous Charlemagne (742-814 A.D.), and written in memory of his death, is still in existence.

The story of Taillefer is not mentioned by any contemporary historian, and whether Turpin, Archbishop of Rheims (died 800 A.D.), who appears to have been first responsible for the narrative of Roland, was himself relating the prowess of Roland in his own words, or repeating those which had emanated from Charlemagne's nephew himself, is a point which will probably never be cleared up. In the fifteenth century there was a song entitled '*L'Homme Armé*' which was popular, and Dr. Burney (1726-1814), our famous, but not always accurate musical historian, who wrote long afterwards, conjectured that it was the '*Chanson de Roland.*' M. Bottée de Toulmon proved it to be only a love-song, however, composed by Tinctor, the Belgian composer (1434-1520). The same authority considers the so-called 'Song of Roland' to have been a 'Chanson de Geste,' a metrical historical romance. This is not unlikely. Great men who were scholars, from Charlemagne downwards, were wont to collect and learn by heart all that tended to perpetuate the memory of the wars and acts of the Kings who had preceded them. Such fragments soon grew bulky, and led to such compositions as another reputed 'Chanson de Roland,' a copy of which is in the Bodleian Library, containing something like four thousand verses. It is needless to remark that Taillefer would scarcely have been burdened with such a weight of learning when he played that famous *rôle* which cost him his life before the Saxon battle-axe. What he sang, with his loud voice, probably were such parts of songs of the period in praise of Charlemagne, Roland, and other heroes as he had learned, selections which would be calculated to stir the fire of the Norman soldiers, and animate them for the terrible fray immediately before them. They were pitched in French rhyme, something akin to the following, which Wace, the Jersey man, and typical representative of the Norman-French poets in England, sang :

> 'Taillifer, qui mult bien chantout
> Sor on cheval qui tost alout,
> Devant le Duc alout chantant
> De Karlemaiqne e de Rollant,
> E d'Oliver e des vassals
> Qui morurent en Rencevals.'*

---

* ' *Roman de Rou.*'

Which, translated, runs as follows :

> ' Telfair, who well could sing a strain
> Upon a horse that went amain,
> Before the Duke rode singing loud
> Of Charlemagne and Rouland good,
> Of Oliver and those vassals
> Who lost their life at Roncevals.'

Dr. Burney felt constrained to print some sort of version of a Roland song in his bulky ' History of Music,' and based one on some fragments for which he was indebted to the Marquis de Paulmy, but neither the words nor the tune make any claim to, or indeed possess, the merest flavour of antiquity. This strain is amusing, and on that account, and as furnishing a specimen of Dr. Burney's powers as a happy translator, are worth reproducing *in extenso :*

MILITARY SONG ON THE FRENCH CHAMPION, ROLAND.

I.

> ' Let every valiant son of Gaul
>   Sing Roland's deeds, her greatest glory,
> Whose name will stoutest foes appal,
>   And feats inspire for future story.
> Roland in childhood had no fears,
>   Was full of tricks, nor knew a letter :
> Which, though it cost his mother tears,
>   His father cried, "So much the better !
> We'll have him for a soldier bred,
>   His strength and courage let us nourish ;
> If bold the heart, though wild the head,
>   In war he'll but the better flourish."
>   Let every, etc.

2.

'Roland, arriv'd at man's estate,
    Prov'd that his father well admonish'd :
For then his prowess was so great
    That all the world became astonish'd.
Battalions, squadrons he could break,
    And singly give them such a beating,
That seeing him whole armies quake,
    And nothing think, but of retreating.
                    Let every, etc.

3.

'In single combat 'twas the same :
    To him all foes were on a level :
For ev'ryone he overcame,
    If giant, sorcerer, monster, devil.
His arm no danger e'er could stay,
    . Nor was the goddess Fortune fickle,
For if his foe he did not slay,
    He left him in a rueful pickle.
                    Let every, etc.

4.

'In scaling walls with highest glee,
    He first the ladder fixt, then mounted :
Let him, my boys, our model be,
    Who men or perils never counted.
At night with scouts he watch would keep,
    With heart more gay than one in million,
Or else on knapsack sounder sleep
    Than gen'ral in his proud pavilion.
                    Let every, etc.

5.

'On stubborn foes he vengeance wreak'd,
    And laid about him like a Tartar ;
But if for mercy once they squeak'd,
    He was the first to grant them quarter.

The battle won, of Roland's soul
 Each milder virtue took possession ;
To vanquish'd foes he o'er a bowl
 His heart surrender'd at discretion.
     Let every, etc.

6.

'When ask'd why Frenchmen wield the brand,
 And dangers ev'ry day solicit,
He said, 'Tis Charlemagne's command,
 To whom our duty is implicit ;
His ministers and chosen few
 No doubt have weigh'd these things in private,
Let us his enemies subdue,
 'Tis all that soldiers e'er should drive at.
     Let every, etc.

7.

'Roland like Christian true would live,
 Was seen at Mass, and in procession ;
And freely to the poor would give,
 Nor did he always shun confession.
But Bishop Turpin had decreed
 (His council in each weighty matter)
That 'twas a good and pious deed
 His country's foes to drub and scatter.
     Let every, etc.

8.

'At table, Roland, ever gay,
 Would eat and drink, and laugh and rattle ;
But all was in a prudent way,
 On days of guard, or eve of battle.
For still to king and country true,
 He held himself their constant debtor,
And only drank in season due
 When to transact he'd nothing better.
     Let every, etc.

14

9.

'To captious blades he ne'er would bend,
    Who quarrels sought on slight pretences :
Though he, to social joys a friend,
    Was slow to give or take offences.
None e'er had cause his arm to dread,
    But those who wrong'd his prince or nation,
On whom whene'er to combat led
    He dealt out death and devastation.

      Let every, etc.

10.

'Roland too much ador'd the fair,
    From whom e'en heroes are defenceless,
And by a queen of beauty rare
    He all at once was render'd senseless.
One hapless morn she left the knight,
    Who, when he miss'd her, grew quite frantic ;
Our pattern let him be in fight,
    His love was somewhat too romantic.

      Let every, etc.

11.

'His mighty uncle, Charles the Great,
    Who Rome's imperial sceptre wielded,
Both early dignity and state,
    With high command, to Roland yielded.
Yet though a gen'ral, count, and peer,
    Roland's kind heart all pride could smother ;
For each brave man, from van to rear,
    He treated like a friend and brother.

      Let every,' etc.

To these words he assigned the following tune,
which is singularly deficient in those stirring properties which Taillefer's song must have possessed
to have affected the soldiers, or to have won the

commendation that tradition has assigned to it. It contains, too, some horrible consecutive octaves.

CHANSON DE ROLAND.

Sol-dats François chantons Roland, de son Pa - is il fut la Gloi-

re; Le nom d'un Guerrier si vail - lant est le sig - nal de la victoi-

re. Ro-land e - tant pe-tit Gar-çon fai-soit sou-vent pleur-er sa

Mere, Il é-toit vif et polis-son tant mieux, disoit Monsieur son Pè-

re; À la force il joint la va-leur, nous en fer-ons un mi-li - tai -

re.   Mau - vaise tête a - vec bon cœur   c'est pour re-us-

sir à la   guer - re.

Of much truer ring is the following harmonized melody, which unquestionably possesses an old-time character, and is sufficiently inspiriting to have stirred less impressionable beings than the picked soldiers that flocked under William's banner, a holy banner that had received the blessing of the Pope himself, and beneath which the Norman priests attached to the army, and the soldiers, sang psalms and chanted litanies and misereres the whole long night preceding Senlac:

CHANSON ROLAND.

Dr. Crotch has printed the above tune in the third edition of his 'Specimens of Various Styles of Music,' but he does not trace its source, and is unable to vouch for its authenticity.

As the Norman settlement proceeded, the music of Norman France became more and more distributed among the English. It leavened the

musical inclinations of the inhabitants, but it can
never be urged that it displaced the old art of the
country. This remained as permanent as ever
Influence within the breast of Briton and Saxon.
of the The Norman influence lent some polish
Norman
Music. to the Brito-Saxon art, undoubtedly, but
it did not dispel the old musical spirit of the natives,
or mar the enthusiasm with which they were wont
to recount in song the glorious achievements and
records of past ages. Great dwellings existed which,
if not entitled to rank as baronial hall and castle, yet
were scarcely ever without their pedestal galleries
for the minstrels, from which at feasts, and upon
auspicious occasions, singers and instrumentalists
delighted the assembled guests :

> ' Illumining the vaulted roof
> A thousand torches flam'd aloof ;
> From many a cup, with golden gleam,
> Sparkled the red metheglin's stream ;
> To grace the gorgeous festival,
> Along the lofty window'd hall,
> The storied tapestry was hung.
> With minstrelsy the rafters rung,
> Of harps that from reflected light
> From the proud gallery glitter'd bright.
> To crown the banquet's solemn close,
> Themes of British glory rose ;
> And to the strings of various chimes
> Attemper'd the heroic rhymes.'

The minstrel's was, indeed, a privileged calling,
and all the recognition accorded to it—and this was

no small measure—grew out of the natural love for
music in the hearts of the people. No matter the
country, no matter the people, everyone then, as
now, loved music *per se*, and whatever was the form
in which it was presented, it was welcomed with such
heartiness and such unmistakable signs of pleasure
that no one was in doubt.

This is easy to imagine. The Western world was
emerging from a state of night into day. The
change was gradual, but it was real, and the tendency
of it all was towards a 'sweetness and light' yet
imperfect even in our day. Music was a great factor,
and it appealed to the heart of noble and serf alike.
Wherever the minstrels took music, there it soon
was in the ascendant. Especially was this the case
in England. For many years, indeed, is the history
of our country associated with the minstrel in person
and practice, and this happy state covered the reigns
of many of the English kings. It is a pity that they
ever declined. They did so, however, and this
mainly from causes which originated from among
themselves. They resorted to everything and anything to amuse their patrons, stopping at nothing
that would gratify their purses and appetites.

A curious anecdote shows at once the readiness and
resource of the minstrel, and the kind of patron with
whom he had betimes to deal. Before the minstrel
was the jongleur, and the difference is expressed in
the following story : A minstrel once appeared at a

castle gate and asked permission to enter and eat. The porter asked him what he was. He replied, 'God's servant.' On this being told to the lord of the castle, he said if that was the case he should not be admitted. When the minstrel heard this, he took the *rôle* of the jongleur and said he was Satan's servant, on which he was told he might enter, 'because he was a good fellow.'

The last state of the jongleur was a sad one indeed. He became a stroller and vagabond, and having to face all sorts of auditors, he often supplemented his musical powers with tricks, sleight of hand, and buffoonery. In a MS. in the British Museum (Add. ii. 694) two jongleurs are represented as dancing in very curious clogs. One plays the viol while the other is performing tricks with a peacock and brandishing a knife. As early as the time of Henry III. (1216-1272), the jongleurs, who sang the songs composed by the trouvères, or troubadours, were falling into disrepute, the genteeler and more talented minstrels being more in accord with the greater civilization of the times.

It is easy to realize that the great wave of romantic musical art which came over with William I. did not **Effect of** disappear with the Norman rule. On the **Min-** contrary, it became a striking feature in **strelsy.** after English social life. Scene after scene is presented wherein the minstrel stands out so prominently as to appear rather strange to us with our present notions. We can hardly fully realize the close relationship that then existed between patron and minstrel, or the sympathy that one had with the other. Minstrelsy was long a power in the land, and the doings of the minstrel and the attention bestowed upon him become items of interest throughout the reigns of several sovereigns. A few instances are worthy of note.

As early as the reign of Henry II. (1154-1189 A.D.) the record has been traced of one Jeffrey, also called Galfridus Citharædus, who received a corrody or annuity from the Benedictine abbey of Hide, near Winchester, as a reward, no doubt, for the exercise of his musical talents on important occasions. Another name of musical note of this time (1180) which has been preserved, is that of Einion, the priest, who wrote *Dwned*, or Book of Minstrelsy.

The name of the gallant and chivalrous monarch, Richard I., is indelibly associated with minstrelsy in England. A liberal patron of poets and minstrels, he loved sweet music, and could himself **Richard I. and Blondel.** exert the tuneful lyre with cunning skill. Like the Monarchs of his day, he owned his court of minstrels, where his musical tastes were mainly gratified by a favourite minstrel, whose name was Blondel de Nesle.

This King of many parts ascended the throne in the year 1189. Shortly before, the generous Sultan Saladin had been victorious in the battle of Tiberias, and had reconquered Jerusalem and the Holy Sepulchre. The European Christians felt it to be their duty to avenge this defeat, and deemed it indispensable to declare war again with Saladin. Richard Cœur de Lion, the most valiant and chivalrous prince of the time, was particularly anxious to show his bravery and his sincere devotion to the holy cause. To be enabled to procure the necessary means, he

RICHARD I.

not only sold his own jewels and treasures, but disposed of the domains and jewels of the Crown. 'I would even sell London,' he said, 'could I but find a buyer for it.'

Owing to his intrepidity, which had in it a touch of the romantic, and to his innate desire for adventures, he was called 'Cœur de Lion' (Lion-heart), and became one of the most famous and admired heroes of that chivalrous time. His very name was dreaded and feared by the Saracens and the Turks, so that mothers threatened their crying children with it in order to quiet them. When the horses of the Arabs shied or became restive, the riders, in giving them the spur, exclaimed, 'Dost thou fancy thou canst see King Richard?' It is scarcely possible to give a more decided proof of Richard's influence, and the great power his name exercised upon his enemies. The romanticists of the period found something so admirable in the deeds of the chivalrous King that they could not help fancying that Richard was in the actual possession of Kalibur or Escalibor, the magic sword of the great warrior King Arthur; although it is related in other books that, according to the wish of Arthur, his shield-bearers threw his famous sword, after his death, into the sea.

It is the story of the imprisonment of the 'Lion-hearted' upon his return from the Crusades, and his subsequent discovery by Blondel, which forms a narrative so attractive to young minds and old in the life of this fearless English King.

During the siege of Ascalon, Richard had offended the Duke Leopold of Austria so greatly that the latter (although not sufficiently brave to demand satisfaction with the sword from such a valorous antagonist as the Lion-hearted Richard) went home, determined to take revenge, without placing himself in any immediate personal danger. He had not long to wait. Leopold had nursed in his breast the remembrance of his quarrel with King Richard whilst in Palestine, and suddenly he got his enemy within his reach. Escaping the Paynim foe, the Red Cross hero was wrecked in the ship which brought him to European shores, near Aquileia. This mishap necessitated his passing through the

Duke's dominions in order to reach England, to accomplish which he took the precaution to disguise himself as a pilgrim. Notwithstanding his forethought, he was discovered, and forthwith confined in prison.   The place of immurement was the fortress of Dürnstein, surrounded by the Emmersdorf country.   Poised on the crest of a well-nigh perpendicular rock, it stood one of the most formidable among the castles of the age. The Danube swept by, and lashed the base of the gigantic fabric. There was a tower which still remains—a monument of the skill and daring of mediæval builders—wherein the English King was imprisoned.

Blondel, following his master from Palestine, had lost sight of him in the wreck, being himself driven into the lagunes of Venice ; but, faithful singer, he no sooner reached *terra firma* than his thoughts turned to the whereabouts of his royal patron.   Not finding any clue, he determined that he would travel the whole of Europe to find his beloved master, and it was in carrying out his resolve that Blondel heard, quite by accident, the rumour that his King was imprisoned.   Suddenly he remembered the circumstance of his master's old disagreement with Duke Leopold, and starting off for Austria, after many searchings and more misgivings, he learnt of a most notable prisoner suffering confinement in the stern castle of Dürnstein.

Now did Blondel's heart beat for joy.   He felt

sure he had all but found his royal patron. How
could he reach him ? Bribes or fair-dealing would
only frustrate the end he had in view. At last he
bethought him to approach a window in the tower,
from which he hoped and suspected the imprisoned
one might catch his voice. This was so. In the
stillness of the night he preluded on his instrument,
and began to sing a romanza composed by Richard
himself in Palestine at a time when ardent love for
the beautiful Marguerite, Countess of Hennegau,
filled his whole heart. Blondel began :

> ' Fierce in me the fever burning,
> Strength and confidence unmanned,
> Eyes, though dark their sight is turning,
> Yet discerning
> Through the gloom Death's pallid hand
> Grimly stretched across from out the spectral land ;
> Then came my Love so bright and true,
> And Death and fever quickly withdrew.'

Here the minstrel stopped ; as each verse of the
song had a refrain, he was sure that, if the captive
was really Richard, he would now betray himself
in singing the refrain.

Blondel's supposition proved correct. A voice,
hollow, yet well practised in the art of singing,
answered from the prison :

> ' I know with full assurance
> That Woman's gentle care
> Brings comfort, hope, endurance,
> In time of deep despair.'

'When to arms the trumpet sounded,
Swift I rushed amid the fray,
Where the heaviest blows abounded,
Till surrounded
By the foe, I stood at bay;
Powerless sank my arm, black night obscured my day;
On Love I called, nor called in vain,
And victor rested on the plain.'

The same voice replied:

'I know with full assurance
That Woman's gentle care
Brings comfort, hope, endurance,
In time of deep despair.'

Blondel finished with the last verse of the song:

'When the air is rent asunder
By the furious battle-cry,
When the lightning and the thunder
Raise our wonder
And alarm, resigned am I;
Never from my heart shall trust and courage fly;
Though danger still my steps pursue,
Love always bears me safely through.'

The voice again answered:

'I know with full assurance
That Woman's gentle care
Brings comfort, hope, endurance,
In time of deep despair.'

Great was Blondel's joy, as now there was scarcely
a doubt that it was his beloved Royal master who
had answered him; but to make quite sure, he
improvised a fourth verse to the same melody:

> ' Foul revenge and envy waken
> 'Gainst the Lion coward spite ;
> Trapped, he is to prison taken,
> All forsaken ;
> Faith guides Blondel's search aright ;
> Lionheart ! soon shines before thee,
>   Freedom's light !'

And at once the voice of the unseen captive replied likewise in improvisation :

> ' Were lovely Margot now with me,
> This dungeon would a heaven be !
> For—I know with full assurance
>   That Woman's gentle care
> Brings comfort, hope, endurance,
>   In time of deep despair.'

Then did Blondel feel certain that he had found his patron and King. He sped to England, and told his story to the barons and nobles. Without loss of time a treaty was entered into for Richard's ransom, and though the enormous sum of £300,000 was demanded, it was collected and cheerfully paid in order that England might once more become possessed of her lawful valorous sovereign.

A lay, or song of complaint, is attributed to Richard I. during his imprisonment in the Tour Tenebreuse, or Black Tower. The following stanza shows its style and drift :

> ' No wretched captive of his prison speaks,
>   Unless with pain and bitterness of soul ;
> Yet consolation from the Muse he seeks,
>   Whose voice alone misfortune can control.

Where now is each ally, each baron, friend,
  Whose face I ne'er beheld without a smile ?
Will none, his Sov'reign to redeem, expend
  The smallest portion of his treasures vile ?'

As we all know, the King was set free, and came
again to England. When he died, a troubadour,
named alike Gaucelm and Anselm Faidit, who had
followed in his train to Palestine, wrote a poem on
the death of his benefactor. Here are the grateful
bard's words and music :

plore. The valiant Richard, England's mighty king, The fire and chief of all that's good and brave, Of tyrant Death has felt the fa - tal sting: A thousand years his equal may not bring, The world from meanness and con - tempt to save, The world from mean - ness and con-tempt to save.

This song breathes the spirit of affection and loyalty that existed between minstrel and patron, even when as distantly distinguished as were this King and subject, in those palmy days ere minstrelsy gave way before the methods and principles of a theoretical and scientific art.

Another musical event in Richard I.'s reign was the discovery and release of the captured heiress of D'Evreaux, Earl of Salisbury, from her relations in Normandy, by a knight disguised as a harper, who carried her off in triumph, and presented her to the King. He gave her in marriage to his natural brother, William Longespée, who thus became Earl of Salisbury in his wife's right.

The story of King Richard and Blondel will prepare the reader for the many privileges extended to minstrels ; nor will he be surprised to find that eventually these favours became so numerous, far-reaching, and so abused, that legislative control had to be exercised over them.

One singular privilege concerned with minstrels and minstrelsy dates as far back as the reign of King John (1199-1216 A.D.), and was confirmed in **Privileges of the Minstrels.** modern times as recently as the seventeenth year of George II.'s reign. It arose out of the Midsummer Fair at Chester, the institution of which is traced to the time of Edward the Confessor, when Leofric, Earl of Chester, among other grants in favour of the

Abbey of St. Werburg in that city, established a
fair on the festival of the saint to whom it was
dedicated, and ordained that the persons of vagabonds of every description, and even culprits, who
should assemble there during that solemnity, should
be safe, provided they were not guilty of any new
offence.

This privilege happened to prove of singular
advantage to Earl Randal, who in 1212 A.D.,
during the reign of King John,
was unexpectedly besieged by
the Welsh in Rhuddllan Castle, in
Flintshire. The loose people at
the fair were summoned together,
through the aid of Robert de
Lacy, Constable of Chester, who,
with pipers and other minstrels,
led them into the castle, and by
their number and appearance,
rather than by their prowess, so

FIFTEEN-STRINGED HARP
OF THE TWELFTH CEN-
TURY.

terrified the Welsh that they fled instantly.   ' In
memory of which notable exploit,' we are told, ' that
famous meeting of such minstrels hath been duly
continued to every midsummer fair ; at which time
the heir of Hugh de Dutton, accompanied with
divers gentlemen, having a penon of his arms borne
before him by one of the principal minstrels, who
also weareth his surtout, first rideth up to the east
gate of the city, and there causeth proclamation to

be made that all the musicians and minstrels within
the County Palatine of Chester do approach and play
before him.   Presently, so attended, he rideth to
St. John's Church, and having heard solemn service,
proceedeth to the place for keeping of his court,
where the steward, having called every minstrel,
impanelleth a jury, and giveth his charge ; first to
inquire of any treason against the King, or Prince
(as Earl of Chester) ; secondly, whether any man
of that profession hath exercised his instrument
without licence from the lord of that court, or
what misdemeanour he is guilty of ; and, thirdly,
whether they have heard any language amongst
their fellows, tending to the dishonour of their lord
and patron, the heir of Dutton.   Which privilege
was anciently so granted by John de Lacy, Constable of Chester, son and heir to the above
specified Roger, unto John de Dutton and his heirs,
by a special charter, in these words, "*Magisterium
omnium liccatorum et meretricum totius Cestreshire,*"
and hath been thus exercised time out of mind.'

Among the many occupations of minstrels was
an attendance at important marriages.   In the year

**Employ-
ments
for
Minstrels.** 1290 A.D. Eleanor, Queen of Henry II.,
witnessed such felicitous events as the
marriage of her two daughters, Joan and
Margaret.   Both ceremonies were conducted with
much splendour, and minstrels from all parts flocked
to Westminster.   It is improbable that they took

any active musical part in the religious service, since
the choral establishment
of the Abbey would have
been adequate for the
occasion ; and it is more
likely that the minstrels'
services were required for
the rejoicings and festivities that followed the ceremony.

HENRY II.

From the records of
these auspicious occa-
sions, we read that several
'kings of the minstrels' were present. These were

PERFORMER ON A CIRCULAR
PSALTERY OF THE TWELFTH
CENTURY.

Grey of England, Caupenny
from Scotland, and Poveret,
the minstrel of the Mareschal
of Champagne, who, when not
occupied on account of their
superior merit in solo performances, planned and conducted
the minstrelsy in chorus, and
were responsible for the conduct of the music and the be-
haviour of those who per-
formed it. That some such
arrangement was necessary
becomes evident when we remember the large
numbers in which the minstrels gathered together

upon special occasions.   Thus, at the nuptials of
Henry II.'s daughter Margaret there were over four
hundred minstrels, English and others, engaged.*

The policy, with its consequences, of the lofty,
intrepid, and inflexible prelate—Thomas à Becket—
in this reign have cast some little light upon the
musical features of the time.   Thus, when in 1159

Noble.   Churchman.   Yeoman.   Peasants.   Soldiers.

ENGLISH COSTUMES, TIME OF HENRY II.

the future 'Archbishop and priest of God' went to
Paris to negotiate the marriage between the eldest
son of Henry II. and the daughter of Louis VII.,

* And such numbers might easily have been increased in the
manner suggested by Du Cange.   'In the Middle Ages,' he writes,
'these men swarmed so about the houses and courts of the great,
and princes spent such large sums on them, as completely to
their coffers.'

he entered the French towns 'preceded by two
hundred and fifty boys on foot, in groups of six, ten
or more together, singing English songs, according
to the custom of their country.'

The foul murder episode takes us into the old
Cathedral. It was dim twilight—the hour of vespers,
which, indeed, had already commenced. At the
sound of the psalmody of the choir, a voice exclaimed : 'To the church—it will afford protection.'
The alarmed monks forced the Archbishop with pious
violence through the cloisters into the church, where
they, trembling with fear, concealed themselves
under the altars and behind the pillars of the church.
Becket met his murderers as he descended from the
chapel of St. Benedict into the transepts. He passed
them, and took up his station against a column between the altars of St. Mary and St. Bennett, where
in a few moments he was cruelly butchered.

We learn, from an old record, that Henry III.
(1216-1272 A.D.), in the thirty-sixth year of his reign,
gave forty shillings and a pipe of wine to Richard,
his harper, and also another pipe of wine to Beatrice,
the harper's wife—'et in uno dolio empto et dato
Beatrice uxori ejusdem Ricardi.'

Given not a little to the fine arts, Henry,
though stupid and weak as a sovereign, and quite
unequal to the troublous spirit of the times, yet
favoured music, painting, and architecture. Some
of our best Cathedral architecture dates from his

reign ;* illuminated Prayer-Books, missals, and the like, afforded engrossing labour for the cultured minds of his period. We find one Henry d'Avranches, probably a Norman Frenchman, dignified with the title of Master Henry the Versifier, an appellation which has been held to imply a character somewhat different from the Royal minstrel or joculator. In the years 1249 and 1251 A.D. are to be found orders on the Treasurer of the Royal Household to pay this 'Master Henry' one thousand shillings, probably a year's stipend. Thus music was befriended by this King.

The next Sovereign, Edward I., 'Longshanks' (1272-1307 A.D.), was more addicted to tiltings and tournaments than to the pleasure and profit which music afforded. He appears to have retained some patronage of the art, for we hear of his minstrel not following his avocation merely, but actually guarding.

---

* Among the principal churches in the Early English style of architecture built in this reign are : Wells Cathedral, built by Bishop Joceline, 1225-1229 A.D. ; Lucock Abbey, Wilts, built by Ela Longespée, Countess of Salisbury, and afterwards Abbess, 1232-1238 A.D. ; Southwell Minster choir, built by Archbishop Grey, 1232 A.D. ; Ely Cathedral Presbytery, built by Bishop Northwold, 1235-1252 A.D. ; Ashbourne Church, Derbyshire, 1235-1241 A.D. ; Netley Abbey, built by Bishop Peter de Roche, A.D. 1239 ; Nine Altars Chapel, Durham Cathedral, built by Bishop Poore, 1242-1290 A.D. ; Glasgow Cathedral choir, built by Bishop Burdington, 1242-1248 A.D. ; Chetwode Church, Bucks, an Austin priory, 1244 A.D. ; choir and transepts, Westminster Abbey, rebuilt by Henry III. at his own expense ; Crowland Abbey, built by Abbot Ralph de Marche, 1255-1281 A.D., and several others.

and avenging an injury to, the person of his master. A short time before Edward I. ascended the throne

Edward I. saved by a Minstrel. he was accompanied by his harper to the Holy Land. Upon an occasion at Ptolemais, Edward had the misfortune to be wounded with a poisoned knife, whereupon his harper, 'Citharædus suus,' who must have been in close attendance upon his Royal master, and is worthy of praise for his alertness, hearing the struggle, rushed into the Royal apartments, and,

striking the would-be as-sassin on the head with a tripod or trestle, beat out his brains, thus ade-quately requiting the insult to the King.

It would be thought that such a signal service would not be forgotten by the Sovereign, and would have inclined him favourably towards musi-

EDWARD I.

cians generally. This does not appear,

Massacre of Welsh Bards. according to some writers, to have been the case. The bards had not lost their primitive influence over the people in the time of Edward I., who, it is said, became so irritated at the continual insurrections and disturbances fomented by their songs, that he caused many of them to be hanged. This reputed massacre of Welsh bards, it

must be stated, is not generally believed. To Sharon
Turner, who studied Anglo-Saxon history minutely,
it 'seems rather a vindictive tradition of an irritated
nation, than a historical fact. The destruction of
the independent sovereignties of Wales abolished
the patronage of the bards, and in the cessation of
internal warfare and of external ravages they lost
their favourite subjects and most familiar imagery.
They declined because they were no longer encouraged.' This so-called massacre,, then, may be
taken as a fable, the best authority for which will
hardly bear scrutiny.

The reader will be struck with such an array of
minstrels as the 426 who gathered together when
Edward I. created some young knights ; and it can
easily be imagined that their musical performances
would be of an extremely effective and beautiful kind,
inasmuch as they were probably all picked harpers
and songmen reputed for their skill in music. There
is an interesting record relating to their accommoda-
tion and that of the guests on this occasion, to the
effect that 'the Royal palace, although large, was
nevertheless small for the crowd of comers,' where-
fore the 'full Court' was held by King Edward
simultaneously at Westminster and the New Temple.
The topography of the time no doubt admitted of
the whole stretch of land, from Westminster to the
City, forming a part of the Royal demesne—inter-
sected by another palace at the Savoy—the line of
approach being the pleasant waterway of the Thames.

As to the music, the very nature of the minstrel's art would be almost a guarantee of success. There were no harsh instruments employed; drums, cornets, and tubas, if known, were eschewed for an accompaniment of a much more graceful and charming kind. The instrument *par excellence* was the human voice in solo and chorus. It had an accompaniment and support in the harp, singly or in bands, with strings plucked in wondrous fashion— the whole framing into a harmonious combination of the most ravishing music, which heightened itself at moments until the very bounds of ecstasy were reached. *Similia similibus curantur.* Then would the harpers change their key, and with one grand sweep of cunning string whirl back the heart and brain to soberer mood—fit prelude, as they well knew, to an impassioned outburst of chorus harp-music, wild in its flights, surpassing in its transporting delights, and so thrilling that King, Baron, and noble rose to their feet, fired with the enthusiasm that had grown within them. Such spontaneous outbursts of natural, unrestrained musical passions were not infrequent among the harpers when banded together, who seemed moved by a common sympathy to float their vast harmony upon the wind's wings, and preferably in the full chorus form described.

As if by right, and fully deserving enduring fame, the names of not a few of these harper-singers— musical minds who constituted so picturesque a feature in a particularly stern period in our country's

history—have come down to us.   There were North-
folke and Carleton, Lambyn Clay, Fairfax—a name
that appears again among fifteenth-century musicians
—Merlin and Richard Wheatacre ; then we meet
with Richard de Haleford, Adam de Werintone,
Adam de Grimmeshawe, Hanecocke de Blithe—
musical celebrities with surnames weaved, after
Norman fashion, from the localities in which they
resided.   Sometimes only the Christian name of the
harpers is given in these old records, thus : Lawrence,
Matthew, Richard, John and Geoffrey ; while other
peculiarities of their enumeration are such suffixes
as Guillaume ' sans manière,' Reginald ' le menteur,'
or ' Perle in the Eghe,' ' Makejoy,' etc.   Occasionally an unmistakable distinction of locality is
recorded—like John ' de Salopia,' Robert ' de Scarde-
burghe,' and Robert ' de Colecestria,' and sometimes
the minstrel is identified by reference to his patron,
as ' harper of the Bishop of Durham,' ' Abbot of
Abyngdon,' ' Earl of Warrene,' etc.

Wages in those days constituted a not less important matter probably than they do now. Certainly
the entries of disbursements and receipts tend to
Minstrels' prove this.   Original records, such as the
Payments. Wardrobe Books, showing the Royal
Household expenses, preserved in the custody of
the Queen's Remembrancer, furnish, happily,
abundant information on this point.   When, for
instance, King Edward I. held his *cour plenière* at
the Feast of Whitsuntide, 1306 A.D., to confer the

honour of knighthood upon his son, Prince Edward, and several young nobles, there were present six kings of the minstrels, viz., Le Roy de Champaigne, Le Roy Caupenny, Le Roy Boisescue, Le Roy Marchis, Le Roy Robert, and Le Roy Druet. The first five received each a sum equivalent in present-day money to £50, while Le Roy Druet was paid £30. The list of money states that five marks, or £3 6s. 8d. (the mark being 13s. 4d.), was the sum paid to each chief minstrel.

On the occasion of the marriage of Queen Eleanor's daughter Margaret, the bridegroom gave, very generously, the sum of £100 to be distributed amongst the 426 minstrels present. This pleasant task was willingly undertaken by Walter de Storton, and each musician received the substantial sum of £3 10s. 4d. for his services at the wedding festivities. Altogether some £200, or £3,000 of our money, was expended upon the music at this brilliant social function. One shilling in those days is computed to have been worth fifteen shillings at the present time. A simple calculation will show, therefore, that a liberal estimate was then put upon the musician and his art that would do infinite credit to many who find themselves in quest of 'a little music' nowadays, especially to that class of really well-to-do people who, wittingly or unwittingly, act towards the musician as if his only care was to air himself and his art, untroubled and unconcerned with such mundane matters as flour and firewood.

Another excellent method that appears to have obtained with patron and minstrel was one which, probably, set that fashion which is not altogether effaced yet awhile.   Not content with paying the minstrel-labourer the worth of his hire, the appreciative patron went to the expense of obtaining some enduring token which he could bestow upon a favourite performer.   We learn this from an entry that occurs in the accounts of the executors of Queen Eleanor (1291 A.D.).   It is a record of a disburse-

EDWARD II.

ment of thirty-nine shillings for a cup, purchased for presentation to a distinguished performer among the King's minstrels.

Passing from Edward's reign to that of his son, Edward II. (1307-1327 A.D.), we find unusual attention and consideration being bestowed upon the minstrel and his art.   In the year 1309 A.D., at the feast of the installation of Ralph, Abbot of St. Augustine's, Canterbury, seventy shillings (or £52 10s.) was expended on the minstrels who accompanied their songs with the harp.   That excellent method, indicated by the word 'grant,' or gift—the absence of which on a national scale has so impeded the legitimate advancement of modern

musical England—comes conspicuously before us.
These grants occasionally took the sensible shape of
real estate, and not improperly and without doubt
not undeservedly, the native musician was often
singled out for this favour. Thus, Le Roy Robert,
who was the English King of the Minstrels, figures
as the recipient of many money grants, while to
' Roy de North,' the King's minstrel, whose real
name appears to have been William de Morlee—
Morley is a name that afterwards becomes famous
amongst Elizabethan composers — are conveyed
several houses that once had belonged to John le
Boteler, surnamed Roy Brunhaud.

Nor were those who had the welfare of the
minstrels at heart unmindful of their exterior.   These
providers of music for indoors and outdoors were

The Minstrels' Dress. clothed as well as fed—wearing, indeed,
a special and costly attire of velvet, satin,
silk, and furs of ermine. Besides the
large sums of money which were paid them by the
nobles, the minstrels received gratuitously these
expensive habiliments. Froissart (1337-1410), speaking in his ' Chronicles ' of the condition and magnificence of the Count de Foix, states that on one
Christmas Day at his Court there were seated at
the table four Bishops, Viscounts, knights, and his
own kinsmen. In the hall were many minstrels,
'as well those belonging to the Count as to the
strangers who were present. This day the Count

MINSTRELS' PILLAR, ST. MARY'S CHURCH, BEVERLEY.*
(*Photograph by Messrs. F. Frith and Co., Reigate.*)

gave to the minstrels and heralds 500 francs among them ; he also clothed the minstrels of the Duke of Torraine with cloth of gold trimmed with ermine ; the dresses were valued at 200 francs.'

The Earl of Lancaster in Edward II.'s time used to expend much money on the liveries of his minstrels. The representations on a column and arcade in Beverley Minster indicate the style of the minstrels' dress. When walking or travelling in the open air they slung their instruments—which were light—over their shoulders, suspended by a silken tape or cord, and so protected the harp and crwth from unfavourable weather or undue gaze under the customary loose outer cloak or surtout. They had piked boots or shoes, which, on special occasions, were tied to the knees with chains of silver. That it was a characteristic costume consistent with the grace and beauty of the art of which they were the exponents is probable, while it is certain that, after the fashion of the costumes of the period, it was as picturesque as it was conspicuous.

Trokelowe,* the chronicler, gives us a curious passage relating to minstrels, which shows that women even were not denied the order :

'When Edward II. this year (1306) solemnized the Feast of Pentecost, and sat at table in the

---

* Trokelowe (John of) was a monk of Tynemouth, who died about 1343. He continued the *Chronicle of Rishanger.* His *Annals* extend from 1307 to 1323.

great Hall of Westminster, attended by the peers
of the realm, a certain woman, dressed in the
habit of a minstrel, riding on a great horse, trapped
in the minstrel fashion, entered the hall, and going
round the several tables, acting the part of a
minstrel, at length mounted the steps to the Royal
table, on which she deposited a letter. Having
done this, she turned her horse, and, saluting all the
company, she departed. When the letter was read,
it was found to contain certain animadversions on
the King's conduct, at which he was greatly
offended. The door-keepers being called and
threatened for admitting such a woman, readily
replied that it never was the custom of the King's
palace to deny admission to minstrels, especially
on such high solemnities and feast days.'

That the dress of the minstrels was of a superior
class is all but established by a reference to the
subject in a poem treating of the period of
Edward II., and cited by Stowe (1523-1603).
Therein knights of the day are warned to adhere
to their proper costume, lest they be mistaken for
minstrels. If the clothes worn by each order of
society would tend to such a misapprehension, they
must have been similar in cut and texture, unless,
indeed, the nobles, emulating the minstrels, discarded
their own apparel, and adopted that in the style of
the musicians.

Here is the allusion :

> ' Knytes schuld weare clothes
> I-schape in dewe manere,
> As his order wold aske,
> As well as schuld a frere*
> Now thei beth disgysed,
> So diverselych i-digt,†
> That no man may knowe
> A minstrel from a knygt
> > Well ny
> So is mekenes falt adown
> And pryde aryse an hye.'

The minstrels were not music-makers only. They appear to have been artists to their finger-tips, and their language seemingly found vent and expression not in string and tone only, but even in stone. If minstrels were not the actual craftsmen, and only the donors, then there must have been the soul of music, and great veneration for the art in the hearts of our nameless and forgotten countrymen who sculptured such wondrous and almost incomparable work as the west front of Wells Cathedral (1230-1235 A.D.), wherein the workers introduced, in almost speaking stone, the angels chanting the *Gloria in Excelsis.*

In thirty-two quatrefoils are angels in descent, variously disposed, chanting *Gloria in Excelsis.* They hold in their hands mitres, crowns, and scrolls —emblems of temporal and eternal rewards to those who listen faithfully to their message of salvation.‡

---

* Friar.   † Bedight.
‡ Bishop Ralph de Salopia founded the College of Vicars Choral, or Singing Men, in the year 1329, and endowed the

Time has effaced the workmanship, but enough remains to speak the soul of the workers. Cromwell's forces greatly damaged the carvings.

Again, if an actual example of masonic musical work is demanded, that exquisite example in Beverley Minster already referred to well attests it.

Chappell, in his remarks on English minstrelsy, thus describes the Beverley Minster pillar : 'Five men are thereon represented, four in short coats, reaching to the knee, and one with an overcoat, all having chains round their necks and tolerably large purses. The building is assigned to the reign of Henry VI., when minstrelsy had greatly declined, and it cannot therefore be considered as representing minstrels in the height of their prosperity.

They are probably only instrumental performers (with the exception, perhaps, of the luteplayer) ; but as one holds a pipe and a tabor, used only for rustic dances, another a crowd or treble viol,

---

singers with the manor of Welleslegh and other estates. By his will he gave them 20 quarters of wheat, 20 quarters of barley, 20 quarters of oats, 10 oxen, 10 cows, and 100 sheep. He also gave the choristers (boys) 10 quarters of wheat, 2 oxen, 2 cows, and 20 sheep, besides which he built a house for the residence of themselves and their master on the west side of the cloisters. Founder's Day is still kept up. On November 8 every year, the priest-vicars, vicars-choral, and choristers repair to the vicar's chapel, and there hold a service in commemoration of Bishop Ralph de Salopia.

a third what appears to be a bass flute, and a
fourth either a treble flute, or perhaps that kind of
hautboy called a wayght, or wait, and there is no
harper among them, I do not suppose any to have
been of that class called minstrels of honour, who
rode on horseback, with their servants to attend
them, and who could enter freely into a king's palace.
Such distinctions among minstrels are frequently
drawn in the old romances. For instance, in the
romance of Launfel we are told, " They had men-
stralles of moche honours," and also that they had
" Fydelers, sytolyrs (citolers), and trompoteres." It
is not, however, surprising that they should be rich
enough to build a column of a minster, considering
the excessive devotion to, and encouragement of,
music which characterized the English in that and
the two following centuries.'

But a still more important example of stone
carving bearing upon native music is to be seen in
St. Mary's Church, Beverley. This is where the
best minstrels' pillar stands, though all authorities
that have come under my notice have either noticed
only the Beverley Minster pillar, or mixed up the
two.

The pillar in St. Mary's Church is the eastern-
most pillar of the nave on the north side. Its history
is somewhat as follows :

' In 1520 the central towers of the church fell, and
destroyed a great part of the nave, especially the

north aisle. The restoration of this was effected by various voluntary offerings. All the corbels of the pillars which now support the nave bear inscriptions recording the names of those who gave to the re-building. Thus on the two westernmost pillars we read, "Klay and his wife made these two pillars and a half." On the fourth and fifth pillars, "These two pillars made good wives." On the sixth—"the minstrels' pillar"—"This pillar made the minstrels." Just below the capital, on a series of small brackets on the shaft of the pillar, are sculptured and still dimly-coloured figures of five minstrels. And it is supposed that they represent members of a certain guild or fraternity of minstrels or gleemen which flourished in Beverley.'

The inscription, in the writing of the period, seems to signify that the column was made by the minstrels, just as a poesy more distinctly expressed on a modern bell might run, ' Taylor of Lough-borough made me.'

Another ancient and curious, though barbarous privilege in favour of English minstrels, which should be mentioned, was granted by John of Gaunt, Duke of Lancaster, from his Castle of Tutbury in the year 1381 A.D. The occasion was the inauguration of the first English King of the Minstrels. ' During the time of which ancient Earls and Dukes of Lancaster, who were ever of the blood Royal, great men in their time, and had their

A Tutbury Custom.

abode, and kept a liberal hospitality here at their house of Tutbury, there could not but be a great concourse of people from all parts hither ; for whose diversion all sorts of musicians were permitted likewise to come to pay their services ; amongst whom, being numerous, some quarrels and disorders now and then arising, it was found necessary, after a while, they should be brought under rules, divers laws being made for the better regulating of them, and a governor appointed them by the name of a *King*, who had several officers under him, to see the execution of those laws, full power being granted them to apprehend and correct any such minstrels appertaining to the said Honour, as should refuse to do their services in due manner, and to constrain them to do them ; as appears by the charter granted to the said King of the Minstrels by John of Gaunt, King of Castile and Leon, and Duke of Lancaster, bearing date the 22nd of August in the fourth year of the reign of King Richard the Second, entitled the "*Carta le Roy de Minstrala*"; which being written in old French I have translated, and annexed it to this discourse, for the more universal notoriety of the thing, and

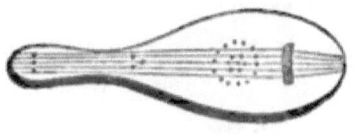

THIRTEENTH-CENTURY LUTE.

for satisfaction how the power of the King of the Minstrels and his officers is founded, which take as follows :

'"John, by the Grace of God, King of Castile and Leon, Duke of Lancaster, to all them who shall see, or hear these our letters, greeting—Know ye, we **John of** have ordained, constituted, and assigned **Gaunt's** to our well-beloved the King of the Min- **Charter.** strels, in our Honour of Tutbury, who is, or for the time shall be, to apprehend and correct all the minstrels in our said honour and franchise, that refuse to do the services and minstrelsy, as appertain to them to do from ancient times, at Tutbury aforesaid, yearly. on the days of the Assumption of our Lady, giving and granting to the said King of the Minstrels for the time being full power and commandment to make them reason- ably to justify and to restrain them to do their ser- vices and minstrelsies in manner as belongeth to them, and as it hath been there, and of ancient times accustomed. In witness of which thing we have caused these our letters to be made patent. Given under our privy seal, at our Castle of Tutbury, the 22nd day of August, in the fourth year of the reign of the most sweet King Richard the Second."

'Upon this, in process of time, the defaulters being many, and the amercements by the officers perhaps not sometimes over-reasonable, concerning which and other matters controversies frequently arising, it was at last found necessary that a Court should be erected to hear plaints, and determine controversies between party and party, before the steward of the

Honour, which is held there to this day, on the
morrow after the Assumption, being the 16th day of
August; on which day, they now also do all the
services mentioned in the above said grant, and
have the bull, due to them anciently from the Prior
of Tutbury, now from the Earl of Devon ; whereas
they had it formerly in the Assumption of our Lady,
as appears by an " Inspeximus " of King Henry the
Sixth, relating to the customs of Tutbury : where
amongst others, this of the bull is mentioned in these
words : " That there is a certain custom belonging
to the Honour of Tutbury that the minstrels, who
come to Matins there on the Feast of the Assumption of the Blessed Virgin, shall have a bull given
them by the Prior of Tutbury, if they can take him
on this side of the river Dove, which is next Tutbury ; or else the Prior shall give them 40d., for the
enjoyment of which custom they shall give to the
lord, at the said feast, 20d."

'Thus, I say, the services of the minstrels were
performed, and privileges of the bull enjoyed anciently on the Feast of the Assumption : but now
they are done and had in the manner following :
On the Court day, or morrow of the Assumption,
being the 16th of August, what time all the minstrels
within the Honour come first to the bailiff's house of
the Manor of Tutbury (who is now the Earl of
Devonshire), where the steward for the Court to be
holden for the King, as Duke of Lancaster (who is

now the Duke of Ormond), or his deputy, meeting
them, they all go from thence to the parish church
of Tutbury, two and two together, music playing
before them, the King of the Minstrels for the year
past walking between the steward and the bailiff,
or their deputies, the four stewards, or under
officers of the said King of the Minstrels, each with
a white wand in their hands, immediately following
them, and then the rest of the company in order.
Being come to the church, the Vicar reads them
divine service, choosing Psalms and Lessons suitable
to the occasion. The Psalms when I was there,
(1680) being the 98th, 149th and 150th; the first
lesson Chronicles ii. 5, and the second, the fifth
chapter of the Epistle to the Ephesians to the 22nd
verse. For which services, every minstrel offered
one penny, as a due always paid to the Vicar of the
Church of Tutbury upon this solemnity.

Service being ended, they proceed in like manner
from the Church to the Castle-hall or Court, where
the steward, or his deputy, taketh his place, assisted
by the bailiff, or his deputy, the King of the Minstrels sitting between them; who is to oversee that
every minstrel, dwelling within the Honour and
making default, shall be presented and amerced;
which that he may the better do, an *O! Yes!* is
then made by one of the officers, being a minstrel,
three times, giving notice by direction from the
steward to all manner of minstrels, dwelling within

the Honour of Tutbury, viz., within the counties
of Stafford, Derby, Nottingham, Leicester and
Warwick, owing suit and service to his Majesty's
Court of Music here holden as
this day, that every man draw
near and give his attendance, upon
pain and peril that may otherwise
ensue ; and that if any man shall
be essoigned of suit, or plea, he
or they should come in, and they
should be heard. Then all the
musicians, being called over by a
court-roll, two juries are impan-
elled, out of twenty-four of the
sufficientest of them, twelve for
Staffordshire, and twelve for the
other counties ; whose names
being delivered in Court to the

A MINSTREL.
(*From the Arundel MSS.*)

steward, and called over, and appearing to be full
juries, the foreman of each is sworn, and then the
residue, as is usual in other courts, upon the Holy
Evangelists.

'Then to move them the better to mind their
duties to the King, and their own good, the steward
proceeds to give them their charge ; first commend-
ing to their consideration the original of all music,
both wind and string music, the antiquity and excellence of both, setting forth the force of it upon
the affections by divers examples. How the use of

it has always been allowed (as is plain from Holy
Writ) in praising and glorifying God ; and the skill
in it always esteemed so considerable, that it is still
accounted in the schools one of the liberal arts, and
allowed in all Godly Christian Commonwealths ;
where, by the way, he commonly takes notice of the
statute, which reckons some musicians among rogues
and vagabonds, giving them to understand that
such societies as theirs, thus legally founded and
governed by laws, are by no means intended by that
statute ; for which reason, the minstrels belonging
to the Manor of Dutton, in the County Palatine of
Cheshire, are expressly excepted in that Act. Ex-
horting them upon this account to preserve their
reputation, to be very careful to make choice of such
men to be officers amongst them as fear God, are
of good life and conversation, and have knowledge
and skill in the practice of their art. Which charge
being ended, the jurors proceed to the election of
the said officers, the King having to be chosen out
of the four stewards of the preceding year, and one
year out of Staffordshire, and two out of Derbyshire ; three being chosen by the jurors, and the
fourth by him that keeps the Court, and the deputy
steward, or clerk.

' The jurors departing the Court for this purpose,
leave the stewards with their associates still in their
places, who in the meantime make themselves merry
with a banquet, and a noise of musicians playing to

them, the old King still sitting between the steward
and the bailiff as before ; but returning again, after
a competent time, they present first their chiefest
officer by the name of their King ; then the old King,
arising from his place, delivereth him a little white
wand in token of his sovereignty, and then, taking
a cup filled with wine, drinketh to him, wishing him
all joy and prosperity in his office. In the like
manner do the old stewards to the new ; and then
the old King riseth, and the new taketh his place ;
and so do the new stewards of the old, who have
full power and authority, by virtue of the King's
steward's warrant, directed from the said Court, to
levy and distrain in any city, town corporate, or in
any place within the King's dominions, all such fines
and amercements as are inflicted by the said juries
that day upon any minstrel, for his or their offences
committed in the breach of any of their ancient
orders, made for the good rule and government of
the said society. For which said fines and amercements so distrained, or otherwise peaceably collected,
the said stewards are accountable at every audit ;
one moiety of them going to the King's Majesty, and
the other the said stewards have for their own use.

 ' The election, etc., being thus concluded, the
Court riseth, and all persons then repair to another
fair room within the castle, where a plentiful dinner
is provided for them ; which being ended, the
minstrels went anciently to the Abbey-gate, now to

a little barn by the town-side, in acceptance of the bull to be turned forth to them, which was formerly done (according to the custom above mentioned) by the Prior of Tutbury, now by the Earl of Devonshire ; which bull, as soon as his horns are cut off, his ears cropt, his tail cut by the stumple, all his body smeared over with soap, and his nose blown full of beaten pepper ; in short, being made as mad as it is possible for him to be, is let loose. After solemn proclamation made by the steward, that all manner of persons give way to the bull, none being to come near him by forty feet, any way to hinder the minstrels, but to attend his or their own safeties, every one at his own peril. He is then forthwith turned out to them, anciently by the Prior, now by the Lord Devonshire, or his deputy, to be taken by them and none others, within the County of Stafford, between the time of his being turned out to them, and the setting of the sun the same day ; which if they cannot do, but the bull escapes from them untaken, and gets over the river into Derbyshire, he remains still my Lord Devonshire's bull ; but if the said minstrels can take him, and hold him so long as to cut off but some small matter of his hair, and bring the same to the Mercat Cross, in token they have taken him, the said bull is then brought to the bailiff's house in Tutbury, and there collared and roped, and so brought to the bull-ring in the High Street, and there baited with dogs. The first course being allotted for the King, the second for the honour of the town, and the third for the King of the Minstrels; which, after it is done, the said minstrels are to have him for their own, and may sell, or kill, and divide him amongst them, according as they shall think good.

'And thus this rustic sport, which they call the bull-running, should be annually performed by the minstrels only; but, now-a-days, they are assisted by the promiscuous multitude, that flock hither in great numbers, and are much pleased with it, though sometimes, through the emulation in point of manhood that has been long cherished between the Staffordshire and Derbyshire men, perhaps as much mischief may have been done in the trial between them as in the Jeu de Taureau, or Bull-fighting, practised at Valentia, Madrid, and other places in Spain; whence, perhaps, this custom of bull-running might be derived, and set up here by John of Gaunt, who was King of Castile and Leon, and Lord of the Honour of Tutbury.'*

But minstrelsy in England, like most other things, had its fluctuating periods. For long it was held in the highest possible esteem, and was, indeed, favoured by high and low alike. At one time there seemed to be no prospect of its ever waning. It was at once the schoolmaster and newspaper of the people, for most of the learn-

Decline of Minstrelsy.

---

* Plott, 'History of Staffordshire,' cap. x., sect. 69.

ing that was acquired outside the Church came from the minstrel narrator, while he was also the mouth-piece of all matters and occurrences in the outside world. Then he carried messages from land to land, from master to mistress, from swain to lover—messages not concealed and circumscribed by the remorseless machinery of a Government Post-Office, but intelligence conveyed by word of mouth, and often in instrumentally-accompanied song ; messages varied, embellished, and expanded according to the issue and sympathies which they were intended to prompt. Thus was the minstrel a responsible public servant, with the affairs of the King and the peasant in his hands, and able, if so minded, by a word or inflexion to defeat or to gain any end desired.

Little wonder that he was feasted and fed, and escorted to a high place at the banquet ; and none less surprising is it that his trained eyes, to the discomfort of some far-off lover, caught betimes the nervous maiden's with mutual consent long ere the rightful lover's tale had passed the messenger's fervid lips.

Music from remote antiquity has proved a sure aid in capturing many hearts, and to sing or to harp has ever been a necessary requisite in the character of a perfect prince or a complete hero. During the early periods of music in every country, the wonder and affections of the people have been gained by surprise at its charms. It was so in England with the minstrels; but as in the course of generations these became numerous, and the art and accomplishment less surprising, they began to be lightly regarded and appreciated, and to lose favour. From this and other causes, the minstrel slowly declined in public and private estimation, and from being seated at the tables of kings, and helped to the first 'cut,' they were eventually reduced to the most abject state, and ranked among rogues and vagabonds. Quite an analogy with the ancient Greeks. Their first musicians, it will be remembered, were gods; the second, heroes; the third, bards; the fourth, beggars!

Perhaps the chief contributory cause of the fall and ultimate banishment of the minstrel orders socially and morally arose from among themselves more than from elsewhere, or from any such cause as a new education, or an outburst of controlled musical method and fashion. The downfall might have been delayed for many years save for the **Causes of** pernicious element that gathered round **Decline.** minstrels and minstrelsy by reason of their very attractiveness. 'Familiarity breeds contempt,' and the success attending the profession of the minstrels, and the adulation and favours showered upon them by men and women alike in every rank of society, overcame the minstrels. They were killed with kindness, choked with praise. They

17

became pampered and spoiled children of luxury, who, little by little, took liberties with, and stole upon the kindness and indulgence of their patrons and patronesses until, gradually losing all sense of chivalry, refinement, and delicacy of sentiment they eventually passed into a condition characterized by licentious irregularity and vices of the worst kind.

What had occurred in the kingdom of Charlemagne happened in England. There the *trouvères* had passed from love-ditties to songs of a licentious, satirical and libellous character, which came to be so gross that proclamations were issued forbidding them to be sung, especially within the precincts of the churches. In great disgrace the English minstrels were deservedly allowed to remain. Hence the obloquy which for so many years afterwards attended the following of music as a profession in this country, and which reputation only the persistent example of musicians of the latter half of the nineteenth century has permanently removed.

The first serious check which the minstrel orders received was in the reign of Edward II. In the year 1315 A.D. it was deemed necessary to issue a

Legislative Minstrel Control. royal warrant for the better regulation of minstrels. Their numbers had increased so greatly, and their demands had become so alarming, added to which dissolute and dangerous people had assumed the minstrel character, that the following order was promulgated:

' Edward by the grace of God etc. to sheriffes etc., greeting. Forasmuch as many idle persons, under colour of minstrelsy, and going in messages and other faigned business, have been and yet be received in other men's houses to meate and drynke, and be not therewith contented yf they be not largely consydered wyth gyftes of the lordes of the houses etc. We wylling to restrayne suche outrageous enterprises and idlenes &c. have ordeyned that to the houses of prelates, earles, and barons none resort to meate and drynke, unlesse he be a Mynstrel, and of these mynstrels that there be none except it be three or four Mynstrels of Honour at the most in one day, unlesse he be desired of the lorde of the house. And to the houses of meaner men that none come unlesse he be desired ; and that such as shall come so, holde themselves contented with meate and drynke, and with such curtesie as the maister of the house wyl shewe unto them of his owne good wyl, without their askyng of any thyng. And yf any one do against this ordinance, at the firste tyme he to lose his Minstrelsie, and at the seconde tyme to forsweare his craft, and never to be receaved for a Minstrel in any house. Geven at Langley the 6th day of August in the 9th year of our raigne.'* A very salutary order indeed !

When we come to the reign of Queen Elizabeth (1558-1603 A.D.), we shall find that among the other

* Leland Coll. (Hearne).

wise acts of this Queen one was intended to purge
the minstrel order of some of the opprobrium which
it had no doubt deservedly gained. This was the
ordering of a commission, consisting of certain knights
and esquires of the Principality, authorizing them, by
open proclamation, to summon all persons intending
to live 'by name or colour of minstrels, rhythmers or
bards.' There was also a provision whereby such
as should be found worthy to exercise the profession
of music could be licensed. Such a step must have
proved very beneficial, as it would have had the
effect of ridding the ranks of incompetent performers
and mere mountebanks.

Needless to say, however, that a class which had
grown into public favour, and had won the hearts of
the people so much as had the minstrels, would not
be easily controlled ; also, whether they were good
or bad, musically and morally, they were almost
the sole amusers and entertainers of the people.
Naturally they would die hard, whatever restrictions
governed them, and this really proved to be the
case.

The new rules and regulations for minstrels had
for awhile the desired effect, so much so that the
musicians and their art rose again in the estimation
of the wealthy. We find them taking once more an
active part in public and private social functions.
Thus, on the Sunday before Candlemas, 1377 A.D.,
the friends of the young Prince Richard, son of the

Black Prince, arranged a mummery exhibition for his entertainment. A large gathering of minstrels was requisitioned. 'In the night,' relates the scribe, 'one hundred and thirty citizens, disguised and well horsed, in a mummery, with sound of trumpets, sackbuts, cornets, shalms, and other minstrels, and innumerable torchlights of waxe, rode from Newgate through Cheape, over the Bridge through South- wark, and so to Kennington besides Lambeth, where the young Prince remained with his mother, and the Duke of Lancaster, his uncle, the Earles of Cambridge, Hertford, Warwicke, and Suffolke, with divers other lords.'*

Thus did the minstrels pursue their craft for several further generations. They were, indeed, on the decline, but they disappeared very gradually, and even at our own day they can hardly be said to have quite died out. In remote country places remnants of their orders survive in the person of the itinerant musician who travels from village to village, entertaining the villagers with instrument and song, fiddling for the dance in the manor barn at weddings and such-like festivities, and providing generally the only music the inhabitants either hear, or hire, from the outside world. What really wrought the greatest change in the minstrel and his art, however, was the advent of scientific music, *i.e.*, a systematized art. From the time that this set in, and the fourteenth

* Stowe, 'Survey of London.'

century composers and theorists began their work,
minstrelsy was doomed, linger as it might and did.

That they died hard can easily be imagined.
There was much about the minstrel and his art
that won noble and lowly born alike; and with all
their faults and failings the minstrels had long
rendered services not easily to be forgotten. Otherwise, how could they have reached that pinnacle of
estimation in which they were so long regarded?

We read in the household book of the Earls of
Northumberland of the regulations for the minstrels;
and Bishop Percy, one of that family, in his 'Hermit
of Warkworth,' says:

> 'The minstrels of thy noble house,
>   All clad in robes of blue,
> With silver crescents on their arms,
>   Attend in order due.'

Beyond a few further references in the course
of our story, we must here bid adieu to the minstrel
and his wondrous and captivating art, not for-
getting how great a blank such narratory musical
material filled for many years when the people had
little else than their rustic music, with the Mass and
Service tones chanted by the priests and monks.
We must not look unkindly upon either minstrels or
their art, but for which many a cherished story might
have perished untold, and not a few of the threads
of early English history would have proved seriously
wanting. They kept the national chronology in

stormy times, when written records were few and far between. The deeds of soldier, bard, and sea-warrior were preserved in what such singers sang. These minstrels moulded the stories of the epochs —narratives of terrible onslaughts and victorious repulses—into acquisitive verse, and blended with it characteristic music such as gave life and colour to all that they told. Needless to say that such accompaniments breathed the true national spirit! The English people were made, and their music untainted, so that the soul-stirring melodies which helped the stories' current, the harmony that was swept by many a soft wind, was the true English music—notable for its freshness and vigour, and that peculiar ring of distinctiveness which can still be traced, and which indisputably gives its home and origin to no other country but Old England.

PRINCIPAL AUTHORITIES.

' Anecdotes of Music '	Burgh.
' Antiquities of Chester '	Leycester.
' Baronage '	Dugdale.
' History of Staffordshire '	Plott.
' Relicks of the Welsh Bards '	Jones.
' Essay on National Song '	Ritson.
' Order of the Garter '	Anstis.
' Popular Music of the Olden Time '	Chappell.
'Chronicles of England, France, and Spain'	Froissart.
' Survey of London '	Stowe.
' History of Music '	Burney.

The Monthly Musical Record.

' *Recueil de l'Origine de la Langue et Poésie Française* '

CHAPTER VIII.

FIRST POLYPHONY, OR PART-WRITING: MUSICAL GRAMMAR AND AUTHORSHIP.

WITH the coming of the Plantagenets we approach a period in the national musical life which provides evidence that when Music, 'heavenly maid, was young,' England played the chief part towards making it what it now is, the greatest, if youngest,

of the arts.   Men large in mind, and with trained
reasoning powers, rose up to grapple with perhaps

**Polyphony,
or Part-
writing.**

the most difficult of the many aspects
of music.   They were not only performers, vocal or instrumental, of merit
or otherwise, nor did they elect to fulfil merely the
useful function of becoming historians of the art and
its workers : they did immeasurably more.   They
devoted their talents and learning to fathoming the
real nature of music, tracing its mathematical bases
and scientific conditions, until in time a perfectly
reasonable art was built up for all nations and all
ages.   Such a profound study, with the unravelling
of the many abstruse points which it involved, could
alone suffice to make Music a universal language
—a medium not less powerful or effective, and
eminently more beautiful than even Literature itself
—for expressing every shade of emotion which the
human mind realizes or can appreciate.   Obviously
it was a great work, and as a result of much patience,
perseverance, and genius, music was lifted out of
obscurity into the clear light of reason and order.
From the art of the improvisatores it became the
study of scientists and calculating theorists.   Englishmen had all to do with this mighty evolution, and
many are the writers, and numerous the MSS., which
can be arrayed before the student to prove that, in
furthering the earliest stages of music, our country
took such a share as to justify its claim to a supre-

macy over all other countries as far back in the history of the art as the twelfth century.

This application of theory and method to music made but slow progress, especially in its early stages, when it stood a strange and new thing, by the side of the improvised art of the minstrels, which, with all its grace and fervour, had held for generations past a strong hold on the ears and hearts of the people.   We have seen something of the rise, progress, and decline of minstrelsy ; and fortunate indeed was it that while the minstrels' art was spreading and influencing the national taste a new form of regulated and comprehendable musical art, to supplant it, should be gradually emerging from the hearts and minds of men who were to prove themselves the first of England's disputative musicians and theorists.

The new style of regulated music grew for a long time side by side with minstrelsy, and when at length it entered men's minds that the study of music, as a science, afforded a profitable and engaging pursuit for even the most learned, there proved no lack of gifted and diligent inquirers into sound values and mathematical ratios, such as the science of music involves.   Now began to grow in earnest that great art-phase of our social national life, covered by the comprehensive term—Musical England.

At last, therefore, we are on solid ground.   There exists no more need for doubt or speculation about our subject, since the *terra firma* of English musical history is reached. The nature of this footing, and the date at which it was attained, place England indisputably two hundred years in advance of any musical nation existing at the time.* This enviable position cannot be reviewed save with feelings of the greatest pride and satisfaction, especially since by an unhappy sequence of fashionable taste and craze, or, if not that, of sheer neglect and contemptuous indifference on the part of those from whom better things might have been expected, the voice of musical Britain has been allowed, until the present Queen's reign, to drop out entirely from the musical councils of Europe. Happily, the country is now fast regaining its rightful place in this respect. When we consider the low estimate in which England, as a musical nation, has been popularly regarded on the Continent, it must afford every patriot mind the liveliest satisfaction to be able to point the scornful to a period when this country, as incontrovertible evidence proves, was leading the way in musical learning. Two or three precious pieces of testimony have survived to show that England played the major part in making the art of music that vast medium of thought and expression which it now is. One item of proof—'Sumer is icumen in'—gives England, as we have said,

* If we accept the Cornish hymn to St. Augustine with its music, we are three hundred and fifty years ahead.

a precedence of something like two centuries in the creative department of music. This is no trifling possession !

The aim and end of all music is the expression and inciting of feeling, passion, emotion—whatever it may be called ; and although melody is eminently adapted to the utterance of sentiment and feeling, its great power as a medium is enhanced beyond measure immediately it is associated with the sister element — harmony. With melody and harmony combined—and especially according to prescribed rule and method—an illimitable sphere of musical possibility opened out. The natural outpourings in which the minstrels and others before them indulged, afforded the liveliest pleasure to all who heard them, because such improvisations were the outpourings of really gifted artist-minds ; that they partook of many desirable musical properties is also certain enough ; but, after all, the reach of such art was prescribed, and it perforce passed away with those who practised it. The remembrance of it alone remained. Directly music became a written art that could be expressed in understandable characters, then its position was wholly altered. With a melody legible and on a writing substance, another melody and another could be built upon it at the will and temperament of the composer, and thus penned, all would become permanent art-work. Such was exactly what took place in musical England after the best period of the minstrels. Harmony discovered and reduced to a scientific study—peculiarly suited as it was and is to many voices—a scope was immediately afforded to musical expression such as the fondest dreams of the improvisatores and minstrels could hardly have realized.

To go to the actual source, harmony seems to have arisen in the first instance among the Northern tribes of Europe, and it was not for centuries after they had freely adopted it for secular **First Adoption of Harmony.** purposes that it was admitted into the music of the Church. Some writers endeavour to attribute the introduction of harmony into music to the influence of Christianity. So far as England is concerned, such a fixture would be wrong indeed, unless we elect to forego the musical reputation of the country prior to, say, Augustine's time. It is in the nature of things that wherever there is melody there harmony is close by, and it (though not perhaps a written art) must have been in practice here long before the news and influence of the great Passion-drama on Calvary could have spread to these shores. That Christianity greatly aided the development of harmony, however, is beyond question. Music is, of all the arts, the one most capable of reaching the emotions. It will rise up out of the deepest depths of the soul; it will sink into its most inward recesses. No wonder, therefore, that when the dark veil of Paganism lifted over Europe, and the glorious light of Christianity was discerned in the darkness, that the precious revelation began to be reflected in, and to find expression through music. Thus it was that harmony, *i.e.*, polyphonic or several-voiced music, adapted for young men and maidens, old men and children, set out on its grand march.

Before taking leave of the unwritten English musical art, it behoves us to consider an aspect of the national music which must have largely tinctured **Folk-** and flavoured the creations of England's **music.** first legitimate composers. Folk-music is a phase of every country's art which cannot but have permeated all early written music, just as the 'ding-dong' or turn of a successful song nowadays induces countless imitations. The unique position that folk-songs and traditional melodies occupied at a period when Western Europe was without music-science ; the great blank such must have filled before, and long after, the dawn of Christianity ; the element that folk music constituted in the foundation and development of the various European schools of music ; its value and aid as a faithful index of the minds, longings, and fancies of the people of the soil—all render it a valuable factor in the making-up of the national musical style and character. What colour and tinge this folk-music must have lent to the healthy minds of the first English expressionists ! Wherever the folk-song has lived and flourished

amid its pure air of nature, it has emanated from
the life of the people, and has grown out of the soil
that they trod. Hebrews, Greeks, and Romans, all
had these songs, and while the women lightened
their domestic pursuits with their country's melodies,
the men sung them as they tempered the war
weapon and ploughed the furrow.

With the migration of the German races, when
music as an art yet was not, the tedium of many a
monotony must have been dallied away to a soft
folk-theme, or an onslaught in battle intensified by
some grand, soul-stirring glee which the warrior
Teuton learned as he lived. His existence often was
under sparse roof save the broad canopy of heaven,
while his land-song glittered with rapine and
aggression. Rarely with him was it attuned in
peaceful vein, more often impelling its singers to
axe and oar with a dash which made Roman
enemies fear them as fierce and cunning foes, with
the sea for a war-school and the storm for a friend.

It is strains such as these, strains which have
sprung out of many of the worst feelings as well as
of the many varied and nobler moods of which human
nature is capable, that constitute Folk-music. Such
emanations sprang direct from the heart, and were
as psychologically true as music can be : the shep-
herd tending his flock, the soldier on the march, the
fisherman mending his nets, the sower casting seed,
the reaper joyous with his sickle—these chanted

and sang songs long before the age of scientific art, and all is reflected in a country's musical character.

The characteristic of the folk-song is the fidelity with which it reflects nature in its human and physical aspects. Unadorned by art, it speaks the

Nature of Folk-music.

simple minds of the people, and, as we muse over its tones, we not only picture the gaily-attired peasantry who sang it, but we seem to breathe the very air of the country to which it belongs. It tells of the existence and every-day life of workers, indoor and outdoor, whose character alone remains to us as we see it reflected in these faithful mirrors of times which every lover of his country cherishes.

British folk-music that has come down to us has all the mixture of influences which have been infused into us, and which have made us pre-eminent

British Folk-music.

as a people. The soft and fascinating nature of the strains of ancient British bards, as well as the good-humoured heartiness and manly strength and simplicity of the Saxon, can easily be traced throughout our national songs. Even more strongly marked in this folk-music is the Celtic character, with its impetuous, sensitive, and ardent swellings of wild melancholy and deep pathos, a feature which no conquest could stamp out nor even reach, hid away, as it perforce was, in the Welsh fastness and Highland stronghold.

As an art factor, the folk-song cannot be overrated. Breath of the sod, these natural outpourings, with their glow of truth and warmth, gave life to many kindred melodies for generation and generation. The early contrapuntists used the most popular folk-melodies as themes for their Masses and motets. That more of this British folk-music has not come down to us in notation is to be regretted. The possession of the roundelays, refrains, and dance tunes, many of which go back to the time of Henry VII., would throw a strong light on the habits and customs of our ancestors, and enable us to peep far back into the social life of 'Merrie' England.

BY CHANCE IT WAS.

16th Century.

By chance it was I met my love, It did me much sur-

prise, Down by a sha-dy myr-tle grove, Just as the sun did

rise; The birds they sang right gloriously, And pleasant was the

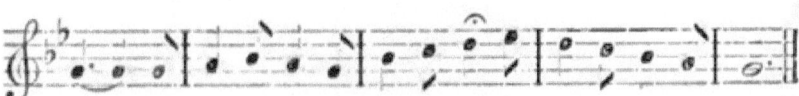

air, And there was none save she and I, A-mong the flowers fair.

18

FATHOM THE BOWL.

Ancient Welsh Harp Tune.

Come all you old minstrels wherever you be ! With comrades united in

sweet har-mo-ny, While the clear cry-stal fountain England shall roll, Give
through

me the punch ladle, I'll fathom the bowl ; Give me the punch ladle, I'll

fathom the bowl.

THE PAINFUL (FAITHFUL) PLOUGH.

Traditional.

Come all you jolly ploughmen, of courage stout and

bold, That labour all the winter in the stormy winds and cold : To

clothe your fields with plenty, your farm-yards to re-new, For to

crown them with con - tent - ment, behold the pain - ful plough.

These were the songs which found vent at the Whitsun-ales, May-games, Sheep-shearings, Harvest-homes, Christmas Feasts, Wakes and Weddings.

'This traditional music,' writes an authority upon West Country music, 'lies in superimposed beds. Among the yeoman and farmer class, a few, chiefly hunting songs, remain. . . . They know nothing of those in the social bed below, which is the most auriferous; and the old song-men who sing for their 'entertainment' in taverns do not know the songs sung at the firesides of the yeomen. . . . Our folk-music is a veritable morraine of rolled and ground fragments from musical strata far away. It contains melodies of all centuries down to the present, all thrown together into one confused heap.'*

The most remarkable example of early part music, if we except a hymn to St. Augustine, is the com-position known as 'Sumer is icumen in,' probably the greatest musical curiosity extant. It is the oldest piece of polyphonic and canonical composi-

* 'Songs and Ballads of the West' (Baring-Gould and Sheppard).

tion known to be in existence, and is reputed to be also the oldest song with musical notes attached

'Sumer is icumen in.'

to it. It is in the handwriting of the thirteenth century. The words form an old Northumbrian Round, and are in praise of the cuckoo, a favourite subject in every age, with both poets and musicians.

Wanley, an accomplished antiquary and musician, discovered the composition in 1709, and both Burney and Hawkins referred to and produced it in their musical histories, published later (1776). These writers attributed this musical curiosity to about the middle of the fifteenth century, but subsequent researches have proved that both Dr. Burney and Sir John Hawkins were in error, and that the MS. is beyond all doubt two hundred years older, *i e.*, of the latter part of the reign of Henry III. Sir Frederick Madden declared it to belong to the thirteenth century, and fixed its date *circa* 1250 A.D. The late Mr. William Chappell,* the accomplished antiquary and author of 'Popular Music of the Olden Time,' took a great interest in this remarkable composition, and now we know conclusively its real antiquity.

It was copied by a monk of Reading, named John Fornsete, a man of light and learning, whose name will ever adorn English musical annals. The latest date of his work is the year 1228, when the original

* Who reproduced the MS. with black stave-lines instead of red, as in the original.

could not have been very long composed. This
practically fixes the date of the copy. The author
of the music—and that talented countryman was
probably one of a small knot of gifted musical
workers who constituted the First English School—
gives the following curious directions for the performance of his piece, which he calls ' Rota': ' Hanc
rotam cantare possunt quatuor socii. Paucioribus
autem quam tribus aut saltem duobus non debet
dici ; præter eos qui dicunt pedem. Canitur autem
sic. Tacentibus ceteris, unus inchoat cum his qui
tenent pedem. Et cum venerit ad primam notam
post crucem inchoat alius ; et sic de ceteris. Singuli
vero et repausent ad pausaciones scriptas, et non alibi,
spatio unius longæ notæ.' It is, therefore, a six-
voiced canon, four in one, built upon two additional
parts, forming a ' Pes' or ground bass, the only
piece of music in six real parts known to exist before
the fifteenth century. The words of the song in
full are :

' Sumer is icumen in,
  Lhudé sing Cuccu.
Groweth sed, and bloweth
    med,
And springth the wde nu.
Sing Cuccu.
Awe bleteth after lomb,

Lhouth after calve cu ;
Bulluc sterteth,
Bucke verteth,
Murie sing Cuccu,
Cuccu, Cuccu.
Wel singes thu Cuccu ;
Ne swik thu nauer nu.'*

* Which means to say, Summer has come in, loud sings the
cuckoo. The seed grows, and the mead blows—*i.e.*, is in flower
—and the new wood springs. The ewe bleats after the lamb,

A transcription of this remarkable composition into the modern form of notation is given below, from which the reader will be able to judge of the sweet and pastoral nature of the music, and its adaptability to the words.

It will be observed that the composition is fairly free from errors of harmony, and that it is a strict

SUMER IS ICUMEN IN.

Su - mer is i - cu - men in, Lhu-de sing Cuc-cu.

Su - mer is i - cu - men

Sing Cuc - cu nu. Sing Cuc - cu.

Sing Cuc - cu. Sing Cuc - cu

the cow lows after the calf; the bullock starts, the buck verts—or leaves the wood for the grass—merrily sings the cuckoo. Well singest thou, cuckoo; may'st thou never cease.

SUMER IS ICUMEN IN (*continued*).

canon—in fact, it is, save the Augustine Hymn, the earliest example of canon known. It supplies also the earliest specimen of a ground bass, or 'Pes.' In every way it is a priceless documentary proof of English musical invention.* Bearing in mind its

* The original of this MS. is in the British Museum, Harleian Collection, No. 978, and in the same valuable codex will be found other documentary evidence of the existence of this genuine First English School.

SUMER IS ICUMEN IN (*continued*).

nu.   Sing   Cuc - cu.   Aw - e

blow-eth med, And springth the w - de nu.   Sing

- cu.   Grow - eth sed, and bloweth med, And springth the

- cumen in,   Lhu - de sing Cuc - cu.   Grow-eth

- cu.   Sing   Cuc - cu   nu.   Sing

- cu   nu.   Sing   Cuc - cu.   Sing

undoubted genuineness, it becomes a valuable piece of British musical evidence—quite enough to prove absolutely that, despite the persistent disregard of England as a musical nation by her Continental neighbours, this country can fearlessly lay claim to a precedence even in musical matters—to having, in fact, given the Western world its musical start in those far-off days when constructive music was in its first stages towards becoming the great art—the vast

SUMER IS ICUMEN IN (*continued*).

vehicle of refined, as well as unrefined expression which it now is.

One curious characteristic marks this composition. Though in praise of the cuckoo, no attempt is made to imitate that bird's call, one of the simplest of reproduction, since it is but a descending third interval. The temptation to introduce this into the music would certainly be more than many modern musicians would be able to withstand.

SUMER IS ICUMEN IN (*continued*).

Wel sing·es thu Cuc - cu ;   Ne swik thu na - ver nu.

Cuc - cu,   Cuc - cu. Wel sing - es thu   Cuc-cu.

Mu-rie sing Cuc-cu.   Cuc - - cu.

Bul-luc stert-eth, Buck-e vert-eth, Mu - rie sing Cuc-cu.

Sing Cuc - cu nu.   Sing   Cuc - cu.

Sing Cuc - cu.   Sing   Cuc - cu.

On the original are engrossed in red letters the
following instructions as to the singing of the 'Pes'
in two lower parts :

1. 'Hoc repetit unus quoties opus est, faciens pausacionem in fine.'
2. 'Hoc dicit alius pausans in medio et non in fine, sed immediate
   repetens principium.'

The Latin words which are written under the old
English ones suggest that the music was also used
for religious purposes. This was not, probably, the

original intention. It is more likely that the tune was seized upon, as often was the case with secular airs, for adaptation to words for sacred purposes. The added words are :

' Perspice christicola	Filio non parcens	À supplicio
Quæ dignatio	Exposuit mortis exitio	Vitæ donat
Cœlicus agricola	Qui captivos	Et secum coronat
Pro vitis vitio	Semivivos	In cœli solio.'

Possibly parchment may have been dear and scarce in those days, since a similar utilization of space occurs in the 'Angelus ad Virginem' MS. belonging to the same period.*

We have referred in a former chapter to Guido and Franco, and their wonderful inventions of solmization, notation, time characters, etc. With these

---

* In connection with the much and rightly lauded 'Sumer is icumen in,' mention should here be made of a composition of even earlier date, which the Rev. Dr. Mee brought under the notice of the Musical Association in a paper read by him in May, 1888. This MS. is a hymn to St. Augustine (No. 572, Bodleian MSS., Oxford), set for two voices, and believed by experts to have been written in Cornwall as early as the tenth century. This composition antedates 'Sumer is icumen in' by about one hundred and fifty years, than which it is certainly not less striking as an example of polyphonic composition. To quote a writer in the *Musical Times*,† 'it tells the same tale, *but in a far more striking way ;* for if both pieces are measured by the standards of their own time, it will be seen that the art shown in the eleventh century composition is far more extraordinary than that exhibited in the famous " Round."'

† August, 1895.

once provided, and such musical signs as the series
of black notes called a 'semibreve,' 'breve,' 'long'
and 'large,' the material of written music
was supplied.   One of the earliest,
probably the first writer upon the theory of music
after Guido and Franco, was an Englishman—
Walter Odington, or Odyngton, Monk of Evesham,
Worcestershire.   He was born, as we shall read
later on, at the close of the twelfth century, in the
reign of Henry III.—the date of one of his
theoretical writings being ascribed to the year
1240 A.D.

    Walter Odington.

An old authority, Dugdale, speaks of Odington
among learned Englishmen of the Order of St.
Benedict—*i.e.*, he was a Benedictine monk—'a man
of a facetious wit, who, applying himself to literature,
lest he should sink under the labour of the day, the
watching at night, and continual observance of religious discipline used, at spare hours, to divert himself with the decent and commendable diversion of
music, to render himself the more cheerful for other
duties.' This apology, however, for the time he
bestowed on music was quite unnecessary, since in
Odington's day, and long after, no monk or Romish
priest could hope to succeed in his profession if
ignorant of music, a rule which it is a pity has not
been enforced among Anglican clergy of later times.
Then it was, too, that in secular life a knowledge of
music was part of the compulsory education of a

gentleman, the art having second or third rank among the accomplishments.

The Odington MS. referred to is entitled '*De Speculatione Musicæ*,' and is preserved in the Library of Corpus Christi (which Burney calls St. Benet's) College, Cambridge. It forms part of the Parker collection of MSS., the gift of Archbishop Parker to the College. It is thus briefly described in Nasmyth's catalogue :

The 'De Specula- tione Musicæ' Tract.

CCCCX.

CODEX MEMBRANACEUS IN 4TO, SECULO XV. SCRIPTUS, IN QUO CONTINENTUR.

1. Summus fratris Walteri (Odingtoni) monachi Eveshamiæ musici de Speculatione Musicæ.
2. Imperfecta quædam de re musica Latine et Anglice.

Its first page only has been injured by time, and some vacuities have been left by the scribe, which seem intended to have been filled up with red ink. The work is divided into six parts or books, full particulars of which are given by Burney.* The first part, '*De Inequalitate Numerorum et eorum Habitudine*,' consists of ten chapters on the division of the scale and harmonical proportions ; the second part, with eighteen chapters, treats of ancient musical history, the Greek scales, harmonical proportions, etc. ; the third part is chiefly speculative, and touches such diverse matters as harmonics, proportions of

* 'History of Music,' vol. ii., p. 156 *et seq.*

organ-pipes, the casting of bells, and melody ; the fourth book concerns poetical feet and rhythms rather than music ; while the fifth part, of eighteen chapters, deals with the notes or characters used during his time, in chanting or plain song, as follows :

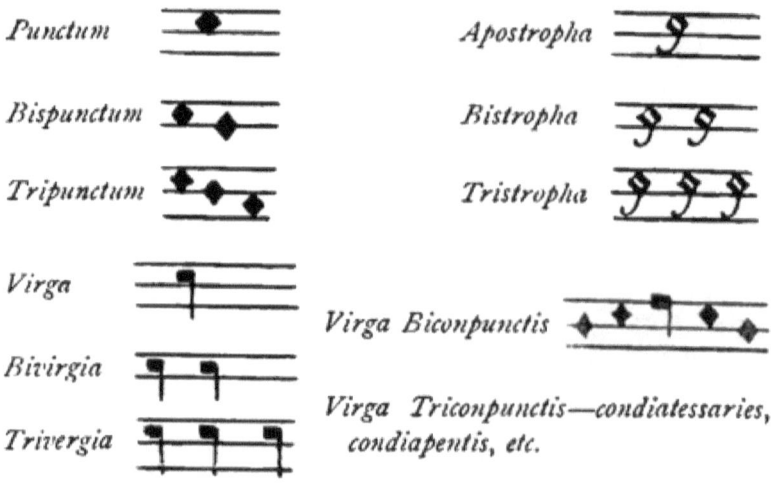

Punctum

Bispunctum

Tripunctum

Virga

Bivirgia

Trivergia

Apostropha

Bistropha

Tristropha

Virga Biconpunctis

Virga Triconpunctis—condiatessaries, condiapentis, etc.

which characters express almost every species of interval by a single character, and groups of notes by a single term of art, added to which is a description of different kinds of ecclesiastical chants, and the rules to be observed in their composition. Finally, in the sixth and last part Odington treats of organum, or the composition of additional parts to melodies, etc. There can be no doubt that this is a most remarkable work for its time, one which, in Burney's opinion, would prove to be 'the most ample, satisfactory, and valuable which the Middle Ages can boast.'

Thus did one of our own countrymen take up the
science and theory of music where it had been left
by Franco, thereby giving Britain the indisputable
England honour of supplying the next writer upon
and
Mensural mensural music following Franco of
Music. Cologne. Such an achievement must not
be lost sight of, especially in face of the contemptuous spirit in which it has been the fashion to
regard the part played by this country in the development of the art.

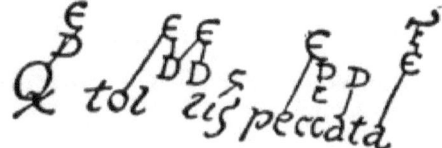

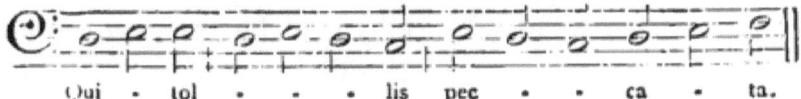

Qui · tol · · · lis pec · · ca · ta.

LETTER NOTATION OF GUIDO D'AREZZO, WITH DECIPHERING.

The reader will not be surprised to learn that
attempts have been made to depreciate, and even to
deny to England, the pre-eminent position to which
Odington's writings entitle her, some of the de-
tractors going to the extent of doubting the authenticity of both the man and the manuscript.

Let us take Forkel,* the musical historian, and
after him Kiesewetter, who roundly abuse Burney
for his defence of Odington. Forkel declares of

* Vol. ii., p. 415, *et seq.*

Odington that 'we know scarcely anything more of him than the name, and the existence of a treatise said to be his, but nowhere published;' while Kiesewetter is bolder still : 'I challenge all English critics to confess that they know nothing more of the monk of Evesham, if they know him only through their Burney. The praises which the Doctor [Burney] lavishes upon him are by no means conclusive. He is dazzled by patriotism, and his object can only be to flatter his countrymen when he says of the treatise in question, *that it would have made all works from the time of Boethius to Franco, even had they been collectively lost, unnecessary to the world.'*

This is strong, and a fair sample of the style of criticism that has been applied in the past regarding English musical work and influence.

A few fortunate features hinder such sweeping censure. The MS. itself can be handled and examined by trustworthy persons ; but perhaps the views of a later critic concerning the work and its author, an authority whose testimony is as valuable as that of any foreigner, will be the best answer to all objections whatever, and whenever raised. Sir Frederick A. Gore Ouseley, Mus. Doc., and late Professor of Music at Oxford University, in rightly making some interpolations to Naumann's ' History of Music,' wherein English musical history had, as

* ' History of Music,' p. 291.

usual, been neglected, says : 'Putting John Cotton on one side as doubtful, there still remain several well-known early theorists, concerning whose English nationality there can be no uncertainty at all. The earliest is Walter Odington, who was probably born somewhere between 1180 and 1190 A.D. He was a monk of Evesham, and was elected Archbishop of Canterbury in 1228 A.D., but the Pope disallowed the appointment. He is supposed to have lived till about the year 1250 A.D. In the library of Christ's College, Cambridge, there is the only known copy of his treatise, "*De Speculatione Musicæ*," the one work of his which has come down to us. This is a very valuable book, because it gives a very vivid and correct notion of the state of the art of music at the time it was written. It has been printed and edited by Coussemaker, the fertile French historian, in the first volume of his admirable "Collection of Ancient Musical Treatises," and is worth studying on account of the variety of topics it embraces. There can be no doubt that he was one of the most learned and versatile writers of his period.'[*]

That Burney should rejoice in such a work and be moved to praise its author is only natural and just, and every Briton with a spark of *amor patriæ* in his composition will rejoice in the book being a piece of native handicraft, if we may use the term. The MS., setting aside matters of comparison with Guido,

---

[*] Naumann's 'History of Music,' pp. 560, 561.

Franco, or any other, shows beyond all reasonable doubt that this country, at the time the work was written (about the year 1230 A.D.), was taking—we must repeat it—a far more active part, and greater share, in the development of the first stages of musical art than have ever been credited to us.

Happily, we can go much farther, however, in the making of our present story, as well as in establishing the claim that the English musical influence at this time was immensely greater than is commonly supposed. There need be no hesitation in thus making Britain's musical merits known, for it is only her just due. The old country has such an evident brilliant future before it that the recounting of its ancient musical achievements will show how strongly linked is the new with the old. Britain's place and influence in the past only needs to be adequately known and realized to fire her young harmonious life to splendid art-doings in time to come.

It must be allowed that hitherto this country has not followed Germany and Italy in their great creative art-reaches; but such regions might have remained undiscovered, unexplored, and unproductive, save for the great part played by England in the early stages of theoretical musical development. It was England that invented much, and kept much alive; it was this country that brought down the materials of modern music which the great tone poets of Germany have applied and handled with such glorious and immortal results. The whole musical world is under a great debt of gratitude to England for her pioneer musical work alone, and there is no other country that can claim so great a share in first musical development as can our own land.

Many excellent native scholars and musical disquisitionists, whose names and works deserved to be perpetuated, followed in the wake of Odington. Tunsted, John de Muris, and Torksey are notable among such tonal authorities.

Simon Tunsted (also spelt Tunstede) was an English Franciscan monk and Doctor of Divinity. He was born at Norwich about the year 1310, and **Tunsted.** died at Bruzard, in Suffolk, in 1369 A.D., so that he was probably alive in the reign of Edward I. He is one of the earliest native writers upon the theory of music, and there is every reason to be proud of him as a man of science and an able musician, inasmuch as no doubt whatever can be raised to cloud his personality as a leader of early English musical thought. Two works from his pen, '*De Musicâ Continuâ et Discreta cum Diagrammatibus*' and '*De Quatuor Principalibus in quibus totius Musicæ Radices Consistunt*,' are preserved in MS. in the Bodleian Library at Oxford. This latter treatise has been edited and produced by Coussemaker, the French historian. Burney states that Tunsted 'was in such favour for his learning and piety as to be unanimously chosen Provincial Master of all England.'*

John de Muris, or Murus, second in our list, flourished *circa* 1330 - 1400, and although some doubt has obtained respecting his nationality, a con-

John de Muris. census of opinion fixes it as English. While some writers have regarded him as a Norman and Italian, others have alluded to him as a highly-gifted French ecclesiastic. It is certain that he was a distinguished writer and musician who held the post of Chanter in the church of Notre Dame of Paris, becoming also a Doctor and Canon of the Sorbonne; and it is not unlikely that the holding of these appointments in France may account for his English origin being questioned.

He is known to have been the author of several valuable musical treatises, and some writers have sought to invest him with the honour of inventing

Muris and the Time-table. the musical Time-table; but Burney has disposed of that matter beyond reasonable doubt. In the first place, John de Muris, although a writer on Time characters in music, nowhere claims the honour of any inventions in the matter for himself. Among the MSS. which were bequeathed to the Vatican Library by one of the Queens of Sweden, there is, as Burney points out, a 'Compendium of Practical Music,' by Muris, in which the author treats of Time characters; but, instead of

* Burney, 'History of Music,' vol. ii., p. 395.

claiming honours for himself, the writer sets forth a chronological list of anterior musicians, who merited the title of inventors in musical notation. That Muris perpetuated and preserved much relating to notation that might otherwise have been lost is incontrovertible, and if it is for this labour only that he and other early English writers are celebrated, the honour paid them is well merited.

Undoubtedly the decision arrived at by Burney concerning these writings is just: 'Though he [Muris] has no title to the first invention of the time-table, he must certainly have been a great benefactor to practical music by his numerous writings on the subject, which doubtless threw new lights upon the art, as may be better imagined now from the gratitude of his successors, by whom he is so frequently quoted and commended.'*

We do not agree with the learned historian, however, when he depreciates Muris's writings merely because the lapse of years has rendered them 'totally useless and almost unintelligible' to a later generation.

The many musical works by Muris preserved in MS. include: '*Practica Cantus Mensurabilis,*' being **Muris'** a treatise on time or measured music; **Writings.** '*Ars Summaria Contrapuncti,*' or a compendium of counterpoint, in which the term 'counterpoint' is brought nearer to the time of Guido than

* Burney's 'History of Music,' vol. ii., p. 198.

is done by any other theoretical writer ; and a third
work, ' *Theoremata Musica Versibus Explicata*,' or
musical theorems explained in verse—all in the
Vatican Library.   His most valuable treatise is the
' *Tractatus de Musica*,' entitled likewise ' *Musica
Speculativa*.'   These manuscript writings by Muris
are to be found in the Bodleian, Corpus Christi
College, and British Museum collections, but in
some instances they appear to be duplicates, and
not all separate tracts.

Muris seems to have been a 'stickler' for accuracy
in matters musical, as an extract from the ' *Speculum
Musicæ*,' a folio work written on vellum, and containing six hundred pages, wherein, among other
matters, Muris dilates upon concords, well illustrates.
He censures the singers of his day who dare to
descant or compose—*i.e.*, make concords with their
voices by supplying another part to the tenor or
plain-song without any knowledge of scientific music.
In his eyes they murdered the pure, simple harmony
of his time, 'throwing sounds about at random, as
awkward people throw stones at a mark without
hitting it once in a hundred times.'   Here is the
good master Muris's Latin translated into sixteenth-
century English : ' Alas! in these our dayes, some
do stryve to glosse over theyr lacke of skyll with
silly sayenges.   This, cry they, is the *newe* method
of discantynge, these be the newe concordes.   Howbeit they grievously offend thereby both the hearing

and the understanding of suche as be skylled to judge of theyr defects ; for where we look for delight they do induce sadnesse. O incongruous sayenge ! O wretched glosse ! Irrational excuse ! O monstrous abuse ! O ! if the good old maysters of former tyme did hear suche descanters, what wolde they say or do? Out of doubte they wolde thus chyde them and say, "This discant, whereof ye now make use, ye do not take it from *me ;* ye do in no wyse frame your songe to be concordaunt with me ; wherefore do ye thrust yourselves in ? Ye do not agree with me ; ye are an adversary and a scandal unto me. O that ye wolde be dumb ! This is not *corcordynge* but most doatynge and delyrious discordynge." '

Such ruling is, of course, most excellent ; and as harmony at its best, at such an early stage, would sound rather incongruous to modern ears, an insistence upon an accurate rendering, free of any liberties with the original, may well be pardoned of the early authorities.

Another name that has escaped the general literary neglect of his period is that of John Torksey, or Torkesey, who rightly figures in the school of First **John** English musical authors. Burney refers **Torksey.** to a very scarce and curious volume of MS. tracts, neatly written on vellum, which, before the Reformation, belonged to the monastery of Waltham Holy Cross, in Essex, and containing a

series of nine treatises by several writers, all relating
to music.   These would appear to have been transcribed and collected by the Precentor of Waltham
Abbey (John Wylde), whose name appears on the
first leaf, and his initials, ' J. W.,' on the last.   This
MS. volume of tracts once belonged to Tallis, but
in Burney's day the valuable book was the property
of the Earl of Shelbourne, whose descendants may
possibly still hold it.*   One of these tracts, called
' *Musica Guidonis Monachi,*' is divided into two
books.   The first contains twenty-two chapters, in
which the author treats of the monochord, the scale,
the hand, ecclesiastical tones, solmization and clefs ;
and ends with a battle between B flat and B natural.
The prejudice and pedantry of the writer reach the
culminating point in the second book, where he
actually draws a parallel between the tone and semitone and Leah and Rachel, Jacob's wives.   In
another work entitled '*De Origine et Effectu Musicæ,*'
the author makes very great complaints against the
fashionable singers of the time, who, he says, ' corrupt and deform the diatonic genus, by making the
seventh of a key a semitone.'   It becomes a curious
study to see how the boldness of the musical inno-
vators here mentioned was kept in check by the
bigotry of those who founded their opinions solely
on tradition ; for, although many practical musicians
used the semitone, instead of the whole tone, before

* Burney's ' History of Music,' vol. ii., p. 413.

the key-note, in performance, none had the temerity to carry out the reform on paper. Perhaps the very fact of its being against the law gave an additional piquancy to the use of it; and thus we see that, whilst the ponderously learned were endeavouring to imprison the art within the narrow boundary of their own authority, it was, in fact, almost insensibly eluding their grasp, and moving onward into freedom and life beyond. Among the tracts, and numbered 'V.,' is one entitled '*Regulæ Magistri Johan Torksey*'; and another, 'VII.,' by Thomas Walsingham. Torksey's tract deals chiefly with the ancient time-table and notation of the period, concords, and discords. The author states that though there are only three specific square characters used in musical notation—the *large*, the *long*, and the *breve*—these are modified into six species of simple notes, thus :

to which are added the equivalent 'rests.'

By some means Torksey's name has become mixed with a John (or Thomas) of Tewkesbury, but there is little question of their being distinct personages. In the Bodleian Library is a MS. ascribed to Thomas (or John) of Tewkesbury, at the end of which it is stated that it was finished at the University of Oxford in 1351. A chapter occurs in it headed '*De Figuris inventis a Fran-*

cone,' setting out the labours of Franco in inventing
the time characters. Possibly the author of this
MS. was the same John of Tewkesbury, a musical
friar, who in the year 1388 presented the book
called the 'Four Principles of Music'* to the Minor
Friars of Oxford, by the authority and consent of
Master Thomas of Kingsbury; the latter doubtless
one who had a taste for collecting either original or
transcribed musical MSS. for the benefit of the
monks and abbey of Tewkesbury. On the whole,
there would seem to have been at least two musical
enthusiasts and *littérateurs* helping forward musical
matters at Tewkesbury at about this time: this
cultured friar and our original author, Torksey.

Robert Handlo must not be forgotten. He was
another of these native writers on music early in the
fourteenth century. Little is known concerning the
Robert life of this worthy beyond that he was the
Handlo. author of a musical treatise dated 1326
A.D., and entitled '*Regulæ cum Maximo Magistri
Franconis, cum additionibus aliorum musicorum,
compilatæ à Robert de Handlo*' — a commentary
upon Franco's tract—'*Ars Cantus Mensurabilis*,'
with additional discoveries of other musicians—
which latter the contents hardly justify. However,
it is a scarce tract, treating of musical time, notation,

* Tunsted, it will be remembered, was the author of this
work, '*Artis Musicæ Quatuor Principalia*,' which was much
duplicated, possibly, among others, by Torksey himself; hence its
authorship has been wrongly ascribed to him.

etc. Unfortunately, the original MS. was destroyed by fire when Ashburnham House, Westminster, perished. Happily, the treatise had been copied, however, by Dr. Pepusch—the industrious German musician working in England early in the eighteenth century — and his transcription is in the British Museum. Coussemaker has printed the tract in the first volume of his excellent collection, '*Scriptorum de Musicâ Medii Ævi.*'

Burney speaks depreciatingly of Handlo's work,[*] preferring the literal copying from Franco to the original annotations ; but, despite this, the book was evidently regarded as a standard text-book for several centuries—since Morley, the Elizabethan composer, recommends it, more than two hundred years after, in his 'Plain and Early Introduction to Practical Music.'

Another addition that must be made to the roll of distinguished English writers upon music is Thomas Walsingham. In what for distinction's sake we may term the Waltham Abbey volume of MS. tracts, there is one numbered '*VII. Regulæ Magistri Thomæ Walsingham.*' This treatise deals with the whole science of notation, time, etc., of music as it then existed. Burney speaks highly of the work : 'Walsingham has, indeed, taken great pains to remove this difficulty (the measuring of such ancient music

Thomas Walsing-ham.

---

[*] Burney, 'History of Music,' vol. ii., p. 195.

as was composed before the use of bars) by explana-
tions and numerous examples in notes ; and I do
not remember to have seen such light thrown on
the subject by any other author before Morley, when,
indeed, instruction, except for the perusal and performance of old Masters, was too late, as the time-
table had undergone many changes, and composers
had learned to express their thoughts in a new and
more intelligible manner.'* This was our Walsingham.

Another interesting work, numbered ' VIII.' in this
same volume of MSS., is ascribed to Lionel Power,
and is entitled 'Of the Cordis of Musike.' It
Lionel appears to have been written about the
Power. middle of the fourteenth century. Burney
speaks of it as 'a short treatise, written in English,
and with its Saxon letters bearing marks of considerable antiquity.' ' It seems to be the most
ancient musical tract that has been written,' records
the learned historian, ' or at least preserved, in our
vernacular tongue.'

Then he proceeds to give an extract from it :
' This Tretis is contynued upon the Gamme for hem
that will be syngers, or makers, or techers. For
the ferst thing of alle ye must kno how many cordis
of discant ther be. As olde men sayen, and as men
syng nowadayes, ther be nine ; but whoso will syng
mannerli and musikeli, he may not lepe to the

* Burney, 'History of Music,' vol. ii., p. 421.

fifteenth in no maner of discant ; for it longeth to no
manny's uoys, and so ther be but eyght accordis
after the discant now used. And whosoever will be
a maker, he may use no mo than eyght, and so ther
be but eyght fro unison unto the thyrteenth. But
for the quatribil syghte ther be nine accordis of
discant, the unison, thyrd, fyfth, syxth, eyghth,
tenth, twelfth, thyrteenth, and fyfteenth, of the
which nyne accordis fyve be perfyte, and fower be
imperfyte. The fyve perfyte be the unison, fyfth,
eyghth, twelfth, and fyfteenth : the fower imperfyte
be the thyrd, syxth, tenth and thyrteenth ; also these
maist ascende and decende wyth alle maner of
cordis excepte two accordis perfyte of one kynde as
two unisons, two fyfths, two eyghths, two twelfths,
two fyfteenths, wyth none of these thou maist
neyther ascende neyther descende ; but thou must
consette these accordis togedir and medele hem
wel, as I shall enform the. Ferst thou shall medele
wyth a thyrd a fyfth, wyth a syxth an eyghth, wyth
an eyghth a tenth, with a tenth a twelfth, wyth a
thyrteenth a fyfteenth ; under the which nyne
accordis three syghtis be conteyned, the mene syght,
the trebil syght, and the quadribil syght : and others
also of the nyne accordis how thou shalt hem
ymagyne betwene the playn song and the discant,
here folloeth the ensample—Ferst to enforme a
chylde in hys counterpoynt, he must ymagyne hys
unison the eyghth note fro the playn song, benethe

hys thyrd ; the syxth note benethe hys fyfth ; the
fowerth benethe hys syxth ; the thyrd note benethe
hys eyghth, even wyth the playne-song ; hys tenth
the thyrd note above, hys twelfth the fyfth note
above, hys thyrteenth the syxth above, hys fyfteenth
the eyghth note above the playn-song.'   All of which
is interesting, undoubtedly, to the student of theory,
and to all acquainted with the intricacies of primitive
harmony and counterpoint, but not over-entertaining
to the ordinary reader !

The sum and substance of this teaching as evolved
by Burney, out of the characters used by Master
Power, is the following, which, with its flavour of old
ecclesiastical music, is not unpleasing :

The treatise concludes with these words : ' Who
wil kenne hys Gamme wel, and the ymagynations
thereof, and of hys accordis, as I have rehersed in

this Treatise afore, he may not faile of hys Counterpoint in short tyme.'—LYONEL POWER.

The concluding tract, No. IX., in this remarkable volume of musical MSS. is by one Chilston. It is a 'Treatise of Musical Proportions : their Nature and Denominations,' 'ferst in English **Chilston.** and then in Latyne,' in which the author deals with the philosophy of music, and goes over much the same ground as the writers of the tracts already mentioned.

There was one more musical author of this First English School period—Ælred Theinred, or Thinred, by name, who wrote an interesting and fairly exhaustive dissertation on tones, keys, **Theinred.** and intervals. This musical treatise is entitled '*De Legitimis Ordinibus Pentachordorum et Tetrachordorum*,' and is preserved in the Bodleian Library. It bears date 1371 A.D. Of the life of Theinred little more is known than that he was a Benedictine monk, and Precentor of his monastery at Dover. His pen, however, has preserved his name, and provided one more feature of interest in the early annals of English music.

Here, then, is an array of pioneer authors, Englishmen beyond all reasonable doubt, who wrote upon native musical art, and helped to frame the grammar or science of written music at a period long before the time when other European countries took up the subject from Guido and Franco. The names of such men and their works deserve to be honoured and perpetuated, for they performed a great task at a critical stage of music's history—men and makers who it must be declared have been studiously avoided by foreign musical historians, and too easily forgotten by their own countrymen.

It will help the reader better to appreciate the musical situation that prevailed for a long time in England if this feature of 'Time' about which our **Musical** early authors thought and wrote so much **'Time.'** is explained. The first broad basis for time in music was the fixing of two kinds of measures only—one of three beats, called 'perfect measure,' the other of two beats, or 'imperfect measure.' In the mediæval age the word *Tempus*, or time, marked the relative durations of the breve and semibreve. *Modus* and *Prolatio*—two other laws in early time canon—affected the other known notes. This was an important step towards the perfection of time in music, and as such deserves attention under each head :

(*a*) Prolation was the system of determining the relationship of semibreves to the breve, or minims to the semibreve. The following examples will illustrate this, and afford the reader a sight of the circle clef, as well as the perfect and imperfect bars or measures.

The dot within the circle, or time signature, implied that the time was perfect. The absence of the dot showed it to be imperfect. A whole circle

meant major, a broken circle minor. (β) Modus
was applied to the system for dividing the *maxima*
note of mediæval music into *longs*, and *longs* into
breves. Like *Prolatio* and *Tempus*, three of a next
lesser quantity corresponded to one of the next
larger value, and constituted a trinary division, or perfect measure. When two
beats became the equiva-
lent, this was a binary
division, or imperfect measure. (γ) Tempus was the
dividing of breves into
semibreves.

Franco refers to notes
as 'perfect,' *i.e.*, of three
proportionate durations;
and 'imperfect,' or of two
equal durations, as above
stated. By this division
musicians were enabled to
compose either in duple
or triple measure. In
perfect time the breve was
of the value of three semibreves, while in imperfect
time the breve was equal to two semibreves. Perfect and imperfect time were by some writers also
denoted by a circle and semicircle respectively, without reference to dots.

Major Prolation (Perfect).

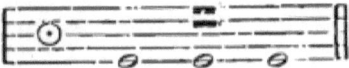

Minor Prolation (Perfect).

The same (Imperfect).

The same (Imperfect).

This circle ◯, one of the oldest time characters in

early modern music, was placed at the beginning of compositions, and indicated that the time of the work was triple, or perfect—and that each note corresponded to three of the next longest kind. Sometimes the ◯ had the figure 3 attached to it—◯₃.

A broken circle, C, indicated imperfect, or duple time—or a note equivalent to two of the next longest species. It was frequently figured C₂. From this broken circle came the C which marks all common time in modern music. The question of the major or minor key had to be gathered from the music itself. Besides this circle, mediæval musicians made use of the cypher $\frac{3}{1}$ to express the power of three semibreves for that of the breve : and of the cypher $\frac{3}{2}$ to express the power of three minims for the semibreve.

Thus, from these two broad divisions of time—the perfect and the imperfect—we derive the present two principal kinds of time : common time, with two or four equal parts in a bar, and triple time, with three equal parts in a bar—both of which can be subdivided into simple and compound.

Something should be said here relating to the musical instruments in vogue during the period **Grosse-** which we are considering. When in **teste.** the next chapter we turn to Chaucer, we shall find him throwing much light upon this interesting aspect of English musical practice, which, like other features of the art, had made great strides since the Norman ingress. The Normans brought several musical instruments, and while thoughtful minds like Odington, Torksey, and Walsingham were gathering the elements of music, and shaping them into intelligible grammatical form and principle for all ages, a growing love for musical colouring was deepening among the English people. They could not resist an intuitive passion for concords and sweet song, and as every new instrument came within their hearing, it was welcomed with delight, and soon found its especial friends. The harp was a particular favourite, and was regarded as an instrument of great virtue, as the following episode related of Grosseteste, the learned and pious Bishop of Lincoln, who died in 1253 A.D.,* indicates :

> ' I shall telle as I have herde
> Of the bysshope Seynt Roberde,
> Hys toname (surname) is Grosteste,
> Of Lynkolme, so seyth the geste.
> He lolde moche to hear the harpe,
> For mannes wytte it makyth sharpe.
> Next hys chambre, besyde hys study,
> Hys harper's chambre was fast thereby.
> Many times, by nightes and dayes,
> He had solace of notes and layes.

---

* A legend of bells heard in the sky by several people on the night of Grosseteste's death, in the autumn, testifies to the regard in which he was held by the people.

One askede hem the resun why
He hadde delyte in minstrelsy:
He answerede hem on thys manere
Why he helde the harpe so dere—
'"The vertu of the harpe, through skylle and ryght,
Wil destrye the fendy's* might:
And to the Cros by gode skeyl
Ye the harpe lykened weyl.
Therefore, gode men, ye shall lere
Whan ye any gleman here
To wurschep God at your powere,
As Davyd seyth in the Sautere,
In harpe and tabour and symphan gle.
Wurschep God, in trumps and sautre,
In cordes, in organes, and bells ringyng
In all these wurschepe the hevene-Kyng."'

We are indebted mostly to the art of illumination
for nearly all that we know respecting early English
musical instruments.   This art was largely followed

Early English Instruments. in England by the religious orders.   The
early poets and authors have left us many
references to the instruments in their
wondrous language, but it was the monks and patient
cultured souls in the convents and monasteries who
gave us the actual delineation of the instruments.
Through long hours of the day and night did the
monks in the scriptorium labour over the pages of
missals and religious books, which testify to the
loving zeal of those who painted their wondrous
colours and illuminations.   In this way have the
forms and details of instruments been recorded,

* Fiend's.

which might otherwise only have come down to us by name.

It is probable that the representations, where met with, in these old religious books are strictly accurate, so exact were the ungrudging workers who copied and engrossed them. These were almost invariably ecclesiastics, however, and this fact should be borne in mind in considering the development of early English musical instruments. The priests and monks were determinedly opposed to secular music, tending as it did to divert attention from sacred art, and for this reason would do nothing to perpetuate worldly instruments ; apart from which the fitness of things would permit them to introduce into the ecclesiastical books representations of such instruments only as were allowed in the Church service. Instrumental material was more extensive and varied, therefore, than the manuscripts and illuminations of the period would seem to show.

The organ was coming more into use in the churches, and favour was gradually extending to-

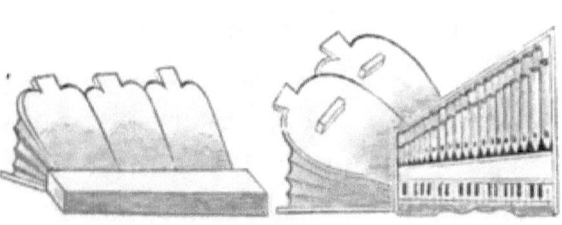

REGALS, OR SMALL PORTABLE ORGANS.

wards the regal, a small portable organ. Another name given to this instrument was 'portatives,' from the Latin verb *portare*, to carry. A reference to

it occurs in the poem of the *Hoblate*, written in
1450 A.D. :

> ' Clarions loud knellis,
> Portativis and bellis.'

This illuminating was performed in the scriptorium of the monastery. There, in charge of the
chartularius or superintendent, sat the artist-scribes,
who worked wondrous colourings
in the antiphonaries and missals.
The music was written with the
words in con-
nected   lines,
and over these
the neumes, or,
when invented,
the musical notes. The first letter
of every antiphon or psalm was
richly illuminated. Occasionally
one whole line, or even two, was

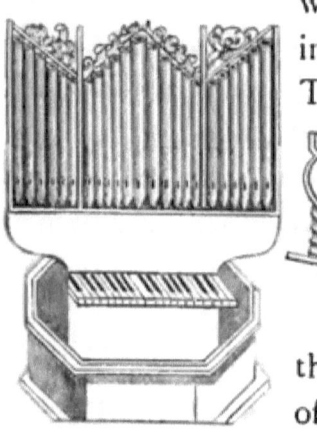

PORTATIVE, OR PORTABLE,
ORGANS.

coloured; or six letters would be painted red, another
six blue, the next six green, and so on. The letter
at the beginning of every piece always received the
greatest attention from these patient monks, and
some of these initial letters are marvellous specimens
of taste and talent. Not only are colours of great
richness and rare blending employed, but frequently
gold and precious stones are worked into these
illuminations with vast effect. The initial T was a
much-favoured letter, and in some religious books

this extends, like a great tree, over the top and sides of the page, storing all that is written under it.

The skill and materials for this workmanship would almost seem to have perished with the workers. The beautiful colours were mostly produced, however, with pigments made of gums, cinnabar, pyrites, juices of herbs, varnish, indigo and ochre. The beautiful black notes and lettering—superior to our common black ink concoctions—was made of soot or ivory black mixed with water.

The accounts and inventories of churches and private establishments abound with entries relating to the care or repairs of organs during the thirteenth, fourteenth, and fifteenth centuries.

Gervase, the monk of Canterbury, referring to the burning of the cathedral in 1174, tells of the destruction of its organ, and there is no doubt that at this date primitive instruments were general in the abbeys and churches of the country. At St. Alban's and Croyland it is recorded that there were 'organa solemnia in introita ecclesiæ superius situata,' and smaller organs were in the choir, hence the term 'choir-organ.' Chaucer's references—

Organs.

> ' His vois was merrier than the merry organ
> On masse days that in the churches gon.
>
> ' And while that organs maden melodie
> To God alone thus in her heart sung she '

—imply that they were common enough when he

wrote. Sometimes two organs, one large, the other small, were placed in the church. Such was the case in the fourteenth century at Uley Church, Gloucestershire, where a monk or clerk, not a lay organist, accompanied the Plainsong.

Frequent entries in parish records supply incontrovertible proof of the wide use of the organ throughout England. An interesting entry is that in the accounts of Ely Cathedral for the year 1407, wherein the Precentor accounts for items employed in making the organ. These particulars supply a clue to the calibre of these early organs: but quantities and money values differed so much from ours, and the details were often so slight, that we must not draw hasty conclusions as to results therefrom :

	£	s.	d.
20 stones of lead	0	16	9
4 white horses' hides for 4 pairs of bellows	0	7	8
Ashen hoops for the bellows ...	0	0	4
10 pairs of hinges	0	1	10
The carpenter 8 days making the bellows	0	2	8
12 springs	0	0	3
1 pound of glue	0	0	1
1 pound of tin	0	0	3
6 calf skins	0	2	6
12 sheep skins	0	2	4
2 pounds of quicksilver	0	2	0
Wire, nails, cloth, hoops, and staples	0	1	0
Fetching the organ-builder and his board, 13 weeks	0	40	0
Total	...£3	17	8

From these memoranda it is more likely that they were for repairs, and that it was the 'expense of making *good* an organ' rather than the building of a new instrument for which the materials were required. They are manifestly insufficient for an average fourteenth-century instrument, especially such a one as would be required in a cathedral.

A curious custom appears to have prevailed in these early times, which, while it redounds to the good nature and feeling prevailing among neighbouring ecclesiastics, also throws light upon the construction and portable character of fourteenth and fifteenth century organs. One church used to lend its organ to another church. Thus, in the accounts of St. Margaret's, Westminster, for the year 1508, we find an item 'For bringing the Organs of the Abbey' (evidently the portable instruments of the Westminster foundation) 'into the church, and beryng them home agayne ij*d*.' Not an extravagant expenditure, it is true, but it must be remembered that money values in those days were different from what they are now, and twopence may have been, after all, only a porter's 'tip.' Another entry is :

'1485. To John Hewe,* for repairing the organ at the altar of B.V.M. in the Cathedral Church, and for carrying the same to the House of the Minorite Brethren, and for

* John Hewe, organ-builder, was born at York in 1485, and was probably a son of the above. William Wotton was another organ-builder.

bringing back the same to the Cathedral Church, 13s. 9d.'

Such instrumental aid indicates that the organs were placed in close proximity to the singers—a natural and desirable arrangement, which should not have been departed from even nowadays, and from which we, no doubt, get the term ' choir' organ.

Matthew Paris, the English historian, who died in 1259, speaks of a species of musical instrument called ' bourdons' which were in use in the church of St. Alban's in his day ; and probably other churches of importance were similarly supplied.

The bellows in the early instruments appear to have been a perpetual trouble to the clergy, for entry after entry occurs of disbursements for repairs. The rodent tribe, not less active in those days than now, and with considerably more freedom for their proclivities and antics, played even greater havoc with the leather joints than they do now, necessitating constant patching and mending. Consequently there are repeated entries in the old books like the following :

' 1419. For constructing two pair of bellows for the organ, 46s. 8d.'

' For constructing the ribs of the bellows of the same organ, by John Cowper, 12d.'

' 1457. To John Roose [the first authenticated English organ-builder], brother of the Order of Preaching Friars, who repaired and restored the organ at the altar of the B.V.M. in the Cathedral Church of the City of York, and one pair of bellows for the same, 36s. 8d.'

‘ 1469. To brother John for constructing two pair of bellows for
the great organ, and repairing of the same, 15*s*. 2*d*.’

An excellent example was set in these early times
of bequeathing gifts of organs and money for their
repair to churches. Sometimes the choristers were
not forgotten. One such bequest appears in the
accounts of St. Mary’s Church, Sandwich, as early
as 1444 :

‘ 1444. Ress^d the bequeath of Thomas Boryner unto a payre of
orgonys, iiij*li*.’

Another item is :

‘ 1463. I wille y eche man y^t syngyit prykked songe on ye daye of
my enterment at our ladyes messe had ij*d*., and y^e
players at ye organys ij*d*., and eche childe j*d*., and y^t
yei preyid to dyner the same day.’

In 1475 Lord John Beauchamp willed

‘ xx marks to be bestowed in vestments and stuff, besides an
organ of my own.’

About the year 1450 Abbot Whethamstede, of
St. Albans, gave what must have been a princely
sum in those days, namely, £50, for an organ
for the Abbey. Similar instances of liberality on
the part of pious clergy and churchmen abound in
the fourteenth and fifteenth centuries, benefactions
which reflect the cultured tastes not less than the
piety and goodness of the large-hearted donors.
Well-known London and country churches whose
archives hold some of these interesting particulars are : Westminster Abbey ; St. Mary-at-Hill,
London ; St. Andrew’s, Eastcheap ; St. Helen’s,

Bishopsgate ; Allhallows, Barking ; St. Margaret's, Westminster ; St. Andrew's, Holborn ; Magdalen College, Oxford ; York Cathedral ; Trinity College, Cambridge ; Winchester Cathedral ; Holbeach Church, Lincolnshire ; Ely Cathedral ; Worcester Cathedral ; and many others.

Among wind instruments besides the organ were the horn, trumpet, bagpipes, and flageolet. The drum and tabor were popular, as was also that peculiar instrument the hurdy-gurdy. Bells were employed both for sacred and secular musical purposes. They were generally in chimes of five small bells, which were suspended from a frame and played by means of hammers. Cymbals were, no doubt, common enough, although representations of them do not appear in the early MSS. Of stringed instruments there were several. The old crwth, identified with England's musical history from the first, was very popular at this

AN ANGEL PLAYING UPON A THREE-STRINGED GIGUE (THIRTEENTH CENTURY).

period. It was generally a three-stringed instrument, played with a bow, and therefore a sort of primitive violin. With the English minstrels it was a favourite, just as its equivalent, the rota, was with the wandering musicians of France and Germany. In addition to the crwth and the harp, already referred to, there were the viol, the gigue or fiddle, the psaltery or shawm, which was a dulcimer played with one or two plectrums or with the fingers, and, lastly, the rote or zither, sometimes called the cittern. Our poet, John Gower [1320—1402], contemporary with Chaucer, mentions the 'giterne,' which was probably the guitar. Another instrument to which he makes reference is the cytolen or citole—*i.e.*, the zithern or cither—an instrument that is chiefly popular in Switzerland at the present day, though of late years it has been brought again into England. Such was mainly the instrumental material which gladdened the hearts of music-lovers in England, and helped to make life brighter and better here in far-off days of five hundred years ago.

PRINCIPAL AUTHORITIES.

'History of Music'	Burney.
'Dictionary of Music and Musicians'	Brown.
'English Songs'	Ritson.
'Popular Music of the Olden Time'	Chappell.
'Social England'	Cassell.
'History of Music'	Naumann and Ouseley.
'Anecdotes of Music'	Burgh.
'History of England'	Hume.
'Musical Instruments'	Engel.
'History of Music'	Hawkins.
'Songs and Ballads of the West'	{ Baring-Gould and Sheppard.
'County Songs'	{ Broadwood and Fuller-Maitland.
The Musical Times	Novello.

CHAPTER IX.

SECOND PERIOD—ENGLISH SCHOOL TO TUDOR TIMES.

Historians and the Grammatical Development of Music—The Nature of Early Musical Materials—England's Share in formulating Music—The Unshaped Natural Music—First Grammar and Polyphonous Music—The Borderland of Descriptive Music—Raw Material—Chaucer—The 'Canterbury Tales'—Chaucer's Musical References—The 'Angelus ad Virginem' Song—Davy and Longland's References—Native Reasoning Musicians—Dunstable—Tinctoris on Dunstable—Hamboys—The Supposed First English ' Doctor of Music '—Saintwix—Abyngdon—His Several Appointments—Abyngdon the First Cambridge 'Bachelor of Music'—Hothby—His Treatises—Wydow or Wydewe—Music at the Accession of Henry V.—King Henry's Objection to Street-music—The Agincourt Victory Song—Its Words and Music—Edward IV. founds the Chapel Royal and King's Band—Edward IV. and his Minstrels—Minstrels in Private Families—Dress and Pay of the Last Minstrels—Dr. Bull's Epitaph on the Wandering Musicians—Reaction in Secular Music—A Thirteenth-century Dance Tune—Sparseness of Early Secular Music—The Explanation—The Invention of Printing—Its Influence upon Music—Caxton and Wynken de Worde's First Music Types—' Sumer is icumen in ' to Dunstable hiatus.

Historians invariably, but erroneously, credit the Netherlanders with the honour of giving musical

art its grammatical foundation and early development in the rising Middle Age years which preceded
that Renaissance period following the fifteenth and sixteenth centuries.   Music,
youngest of the arts, was just beginning
to assert itself at the close of the Mediæval period,
and we have to state that England played a great
and worthy part in that movement.

Musical Grammar and Theory.

It will often have occurred to inquiring minds how
music came to be so far behind other arts in its rise
and development as a science and art at this time.
Yet the explanation is not far off.   Unlike the art
of the poet, sculptor, painter, and preacher, there
were no materials at hand upon which to base a
tangible musical record and argument until learning
and science had made great headway.   Music had
to find its materials out of other arts, sound not
being tangible in form and materialistic in the sense
that wood or stone is.

Then, again, being a mathematical and theoretical art, no foundations could be laid, nor a
structural form given to music, until a vast
amount of speculation and calculation had been
propounded, worked out, tested, and reduced to rule.
The deductions drawn and approved became the
first base of a formulated theoretical system.   It is
manifest that such an elementary musical grammar
could only come when learning and education
generally had made some headway here, which was

long after some of the most brilliant periods in the history of other arts and sciences.

With musical material and the means of its expression once formed, the art took eagle's pinions, never stopping in its great upward, onward course. All that the Eastern nations, the Greek philosophers, or the improvisatores had done for music was but little compared with the great art which it almost immediately became as soon as it was once a book-study. The Greek scales and Gregorian tones, with their bare monodic character, were as nothing compared to the idea of formulating, regulating, and interweaving the same. This notion supplied the grand starting-point of the glorious structure of musical art of to-day, and in generating and developing this conception England played a

HUNTING WITH HOUND AND HORN.
(*From carving under a seat in the choir of Sherborne Minster, time of Edward III.*)

greater part than did any other country. Secular music —the folk-song, the ballad, the traditional tunes, dance tunes, indoor and outdoor music of all kinds—existed here in abundance ; but this, with the hymns and tunes of the Church, lacked one great aid—it could not be perpetuated, accurately recorded, and, beyond all, logically expressed. Whatever had been the case with the original Britons and Welsh in the matter of musical systems, nothing of the kind existed in England at the period which we are considering—that time when music, especially secular music, was an unregulated, ill-ordered, shapeless art throughout the country. There were instruments, tunes, and dance rhythms without number, but there was no method of husbanding all this, of making it the vehicle of a reasonable art, or of using it in combination and in order, according as varying circumstances and conditions required. This vocal and instrumental material might be to-day where it was four hundred odd years ago save for the happy thought that overtook men's minds of moulding the art into a shape which, while it would be understandable to all musicians, would permit of development at the hands of those who applied themselves particularly to theory and composition.

Theoretical art needed the early labours of native theorists like Dunstable and others to effect a vast change in the region of music. What the English and subsequently the Netherlands theorists accomplished meant the first opening up of that vast mine of polyphonous realism in musical art which has yielded the priceless tone-treasures which we possess to-day. From such fourteenth and fifteenth century speculations and deductions came the general accep-

tance of music as a science. 'Sumer is icumen in'
had been written long before, but it was an excep-
tional native mind among a small band of native
composers that produced this fine piece of part-music,
—a sample of polyphonous art that is unequalled by
any Continental work of the period, and which proves
that there was in England, as early as the thirteenth
century, a school of musicians which was in advance
of anything possessed by the Netherlands at the
same period. With the labours of Dunstable and
other early contrapuntists, theoretical music became
a worthy subject for study, and men with the highest
reasoning instincts devoted their attention to it—one
gradually, but surely, improving upon another, until
the grammar of harmony and science of counterpoint
and fugue was evolved and gathered within the
prescribed limits of text-books, each one of which
did but serve as the basis for another.

Yet it was not the formulating of theories and the
perfecting of a musical science merely which made the
labours of the English and Netherlands theorists of
this period so valuable. The growth of mensural
music, the controlling of melodic outline, and then
the laws by which four-part music could be constructed, gave us the empty habitation—the structural edifice, with its walls and rooms. But the
whole wanted furnishing—making comfortable, enjoyable.

This bare art state was what our early theorists

remedied. We were not to have merely a language wherewith music could be expressed according to approved law and rule, but this systematized art was to assume its chief quality, that character which gives it the power of fullest poetical expression. A severe mathematical music system, evolved from rules classified and arranged, was by no means to be despised; yet it was immeasurably more valuable and satisfactory for musicians of such early times to find themselves upon the borderland of descriptive, illustrative music. All the colouring element of secular musical resource—vocal and instrumental—was at the will of the composer. With part-writing enjoined and practised, composers could begin to give colour and effect to their compositions, not only by an extension of the voice parts, but by drawing upon the instrumental resources at hand, which were plentiful and varied enough, especially in secular musical walks.

It is true that our early theorists did not avail themselves greatly of this material, so that the growth in musical colour and tone-painting was slow indeed; but this is attributable to sacred music almost solely occupying their attention. Here colour and effect were proscribed rather than encouraged, and the introduction of orchestral aid, other than the droning organ, was unallowable. Largely as secular music was practised by the people, and numerous as the popular instruments were, some time elapsed between the fixing of our musical grammar and the labours of our first contrapuntists ere they entered the domain of secular art to give rein to their ingenuity and fancy. For very many years secular art went along independent of Church music, prescribed rule, method or order. It still remained the improvised art of the travelling musician, the inborn accomplishment of the lad and lass of the village. Only here and there in England was there an inquiring mind, a cultured man of letters and philosophy, willing to devote himself to the labour of divining and investigating the possibilities of this wondrous science—music. We shall see presently who were these reasoning musical minds.

Fittingly enough, England's first great poet, Geoffrey Chaucer (1328-1400), supplies us with some of the most valuable of the scanty material **Chaucer.** that we possess relating to music in England. This 'father' of English poetry— superior to Gower or other contemporaries, and unsurpassed until Shakespeare arrived, for his language, perspicuity, and versification—never tires in his reference to music, musicians, and musical instruments. If he was not a practical musician himself, he was the next best thing to it, since he was a close observer of, and great enthusiast in, all that related to the art and its bearing upon the national life and character. The candid Caxton declared that 'for his swate wrytyng in our tongue he may well have the name of a laureat poete,' which the musical author of to-day, indebted as he is to Chaucer for much light upon an interesting period in the national musical history, will do more than endorse. If we may judge of the estimation in which music was held by our countrymen during the fourteenth century from the writings of Chaucer, it must have been at least equal to that of any other epoch of their history ; for throughout his works he never loses an opportunity of describing, or alluding to its general use, and of bestowing it as an accomplishment upon the pilgrims, heroes and heroines of his several tales and poems, whenever he can do so with propriety.

Chaucer for his powers of observation and knowledge of mankind has seldom been surpassed in any age, and the uncontrolled imaginative mind of the poet might readily lay him open to draw upon a vast accumulation of knowledge not necessarily always indigenous to the soil concerned. Thus, Dr. Burney very properly observes that 'as this venerable bard was frequently an imitator and translator of French and Italian writers, whose works have already been shown to abound with passages relative to music, both vocal and instrumental, some deduction should perhaps be made for what he says of it in stories not of his own invention, and where the scene is laid in foreign countries.*

* ' History of Music ' (Burney), vol. ii., p. 372.

This precautionary mood need not be extended
to his 'Canterbury Tales,' wherein all the characters
he so nicely delineates and discriminates are English. We may safely regard as national, and take
to ourselves, all the virtues,
vices, defects, and accomplishments, whatever they may be,
with which he has invested
them. Few readers are un-
acquainted with the Muse.
Twenty - nine
persons of
both sexes, of
professions
and employ-
ments as dif-
ferent as in-
vention could
suggest, to-
gether with
Chaucer him-

GEOFFREY CHAUCER.
(*From Harleian MS.*)

self, making in all thirty, are supposed to set
out from the Tabard Inn, in Southwark,* on a

* Formerly the lodging of the Abbot of Hyde, near Winchester.
The sign *tabarde* signified a short jacket, or sleeveless coat, open
on both sides, with a square collar, and 'hanging sleeves.' The
tabarde was the proper habit of a servant, and all the knaves in a
pack of cards are so dressed. The host in Chaucer's time was
Henry Bailie, a merry fellow, who was blessed with a shrew for
his wife. This circumstance, however, did not stifle all his
humour, judging by the quantity Chaucer drew from him.

pilgrimage to the shrine of St. Thomas-à-Becket, in the Cathedral Church of Canterbury. This motley company consisted of a knight, a 'squire—his son, and his yeoman—or servant ; a prioress, a nun, and three priests—her attendants ; a monk, a friar, a merchant, a clerk of Oxford, a serjeant-at-law, a franklin—or gentleman, a haberdasher, a carpenter, a weaver, a dyer, a tapiser—or maker of tapestry, a cook, a ship-man—or master of a trading vessel, a doctor of physic, the wife of a weaver of Bath, a parson, a ploughman—or farmer, a miller, a manciple, a reeve, a summoner, a pardoner, and Chaucer himself—who was a courtier, a scholar, and a poet. Quite a bright lot to go a-tramping !

Most of these were, after the manner of the times, endowed with some musical ability, or, if not, Chaucer at least credits them with it. Thus, the 'squire, besides possessing every courtly qualification necessary in those days—

> 'Singing he was or floyting* all the day.'

In addition to which

> ' He andè songès make, and well endite
> Justet and eke dance, and wel pourtraie and write.'

Then the dainty, cynical, 'mincing' prioress does not escape. Of her and her chanting we learn :

* Fluting.　　　　† Fence.

> ' And she was clepèd Madame Eglantine ;
> Full wel she sangè the service divine
> Entuned in hir nose ful swetely,'

the last two lines being generally true respecting
a nun's singing.

The monk was a jolly fellow and sportsman to
boot, whose music began and ended with the
sounds of hoofs, hounds, and the clanging of bits
and spurs :

> ' And whan he rode, men mighte his bridel here
> Gingéling in a whistling wind as clere
> And eke as loud as doth the chapel belle.'

The mendicant friar, called also a *limitour* (*i.c.*,
a friar licensed to beg within a certain district),
possessed qualities which rendered him a universal
favourite :

> ' And certainly he hadde a mery note
> Wel coude he singe, and plaien on the rote—
> In his harping, when that he had songe,
> His eyes twinkeled in his head aright,
> As dou the starrès in a frosty night.'

The Oxford clerk was a model :

> ' Sonning in moral virtue was his speech
> And gladly would he learn, and gladly teach.'

So fond was he of books and study, that he loved
Aristotle better

> ' Than robès riche, or fidel, or sautrie,'

and every parson might do worse than emulate him.

The miller, too, was a musician :

> ' A baggèpipe wel couthe he blowe, and soun
> And therewithal he brought us out of town.'

The summoner and pardoner both sang. To the one Chaucer gives a coarse bass voice, while the other, just arrived from Rome, without a beard, sings as a soprano :

> ' A vois he had as small as hath a gote.'

After telling us that he sung, ' Come hither, love, to me,' which was probably the beginning of a favourite song at that time, the poet adds :

> ' This sompnour* bare to him a stiff burdoun,†
> Was never trump of half so great a soun.'

It would seem that the pardoner himself put no small estimate upon his powers, since he thus jovially announces his own style in the pulpit :

> ' Lordings, quoth he, in church when I preach,
> I paine me to have a hautain speech.
> And ring it out as round as goeth a bell,
> For I can all by rote that I tell.'

The pardoner's singing in church did not escape Chaucer's observation :

> ' He was in church a noble ecclesiast :
> Well could he read a lesson or a story,
> But alderbest he sang an offertory ;

---

* Summoner or apparitor.   † *I.e.*, sings the bass.

> For well he knew when that song was sung
> He must preach and well afile his tongue
> To win silver, as he right well could,
> Therefore he sang the merrier and loud.'

In the pardoner's tale is the earliest mention by any English author of the lute :

> 'In flanders whilom was a campagnie
> Of yongè folk, that haunteden folie,
> As hazard, riot, stewès, and tavèrnes ;
> Whereas with harpès, lutes, and gitèrnes
> They dance and play,' etc.

The parish clerk's instruments in the miller's tale are adapted to his profession. On the whole, he must have been a merry fellow, for

> 'In tunsty manir culth he trip and daunce,
> After the scole of Oxenford (Oxford) tho',
> And with his legges casten to and fro,
> Could playen songès on a small ribible ;*
> Thereto he song sometime a loud quinible,†
> And as well could he play on a giterne.'

Of the same individual's singing we learn :

> ' He singeth brokking,‡ as a nightingale.'

The poor scholar, Nicholas, is a performer on the psaltry. Among his other talents was that of being able to sing well :

> '.And all above there lay a gay psaltry,
> On which he made on nightès melody

---

* The diminutive of rebec, a small viol with three strings.
† A *cantabile*.   ‡ Quavering.

So sweetly, that all the chamber rung,
And *Angelus ad Virginem** he sung ;
And after that he sung the kingès note : †
Full often blessed was his merry throet.'

Not less happy is Chaucer in his serious descriptions of singing. Of a pious young Christian boy, passing daily through the Jewry, he says :

' This little child, as he came to and
   fro,
  Full merrily then would he
     sing and crie
  O *Alma Redemptoris !*
     ever mo [more].
  The sweetness hath his
     hearte pierced so
  Of Christe's Mother, that
     to her to pray,
  He cannot stint of sing-
     ing by the way.'

CHAUCER AS A CANTERBURY PILGRIM.

And he has a still more beautiful passage upon a holy woman singing devoutly :

' And while that the organs maden melody,
   To God alone thus in her heart sung she.'

Chaucer speaks of the muse, Polyhymnia, as

* The angels' salutation to the Virgin (Luke ii. 28), of which more anon.
† ' King's Note,' or Chant Royal, was an appellation given to poems on lofty subjects.

> ' Singing with voice memorial in the shade,
>   Under the laurels, which that may not fade.'

Elsewhere he says :

> ' And as I sat the birdes hearkening thus,
>   Methought that I heard voices suddenly,
>   The most sweetest and most delicious
>   That ever wight I trow truely
>   Hearden in their life ; for the harmony
>   And sweet accord was in so good music,
>   That the voices to angels most were like.'

Even the singing of the birds did not slip his
attentive ear :

> ' I was waked
>   With smallè fowlès a great heap,
>   That had affray'd me out of my sleep
>   Through noise and sweetness of their song ;
>   And as me met* they sat among
>   Upon my chamber roof without,
>   Upon the tiles o'er all about,
>   And ever each sungè in his wise
>   The most sweet and solemn service
>   By note that ever man I trow
>   Had heard, for some of them sang low,
>   Some high, and all of one accord ;
>   To tellen shortly, at one word.'

Poet-musician that he was, he heard and felt music
in all around him :

> ' There heard I playing on a harp
>   That ysounded both well and sharp,
>   Him Orpheus full craftily ;

---

* Dreamed.

And on this other side fast by
Ysat the harper Orion,
And Gacides Chirion,
And other harpers many one,
And the Briton Glaskirion,
And smallè harpers with their glees,
Sat under them in divers sees ;*
And gone on them upward to gape,
And counterfeited them as an ape,
Or as Craft counterfeiteth Kind.'

The father of English poesy, in his own quaint
fashion, has noted the wearisomeness of monotony
in music—of playing perpetually the same thing :

' For though that the best harper upon live
    Would on the bestè sounded jolly harp
That ever was, with all his fingers five
    Touch aye one string, or aye one warble harp,
    Were his nailès pointed never so sharp,
It shouldè maken every wight to dull
To hear his glee, and of his strokès full.'

Chaucer has multiplied mentions of Minstrelsy :

' Before them stood such instruments of soun'
That Orpheus, nor of Thebes, Amphioun,
Ne maden never such a melody :
At every course in came loud minstrelsy,
That never Joab trumped for to hear,
Nor he, Theodomas, yet half so clear
At Thebes when the city was in doubt.'

' And before them went minstrels many one,
As harpès, pipès, lutès, and psalt'ry,
Allè in green ; and on their headès bare,
Of divers flowerès made full craftily,

* Seats.

All in a suit, goodly chaplets they wear,
And so, dancing, into the mead they fare ;
In mid the which they found a tuft that was
All overspread with flowerès in compas,
Whereto they inclined every one
With great reverence, and that full humbly ;
And at the last there began anon
A lady for to sing right womanly
A bargaret* in praising the daisy :
For (as methought) among her notès sweet
She said "Si douce est la Marguerite !"
Then they all answered her in fere,†
So passing well and so pleasantly,
'That it was a most blissful noise to hear.'

Golden singer of a far-off age! What need have
we of further quotation from him to show either the
artist mind of this fourteenth-century lyrist, or to
prove the wide reach of the harmonious art and its
general acceptance and appreciation by all ranks of
Englishmen in an age when this country, if we judge
wholly from the estimate of foreign historians, was
supposed to be without a shred of musical worth or
status ?

Chaucer's evidence is invaluable for this epoch,
furnishing as it does so much information upon the
internal musical life of the country. His references
to the instruments and musical methods are all
thoroughly English, not the borrowed colourings of
other countries' art. From them we learn that in
the convents the nuns sang the service to musical

---

* A pastoral ditty.   † Together.

notes, and that the lute, the rote, the fiddle, the
sautre, the bagpipe, the cittern, the ribible, the
trumpet, the clarion, and the flute, were instruments
in common
use. Other
instruments of
the time were
the shalm or
shawm, the
citole, the
hautboy or
wayte (from
which comes
the present-
day term 'the
waits'), the
horn, shep-
herd's pipe,
sackbut, dul-

THE HUNT IS UP.
(From bas-reliefs under seats of the choir in Ely Cathedral.)

cimer, etc. The organ, as we have seen, was
introduced into the churches many centuries before
the time of Chaucer. The terms 'treble,' 'counter-
tenor,' 'tenor,' and 'bass,' which he uses, show us
that four-part singing was common enough ; besides
which, that excellent habit of meeting together
for mutual vocal harmony also prevailed. This
was especially the case with the students at the
Inns of Court, where, we are informed, besides
studying jurisprudence, 'there they learnt to sing

and to exercise themselves in all kinds of harmony.'[*]

It is on record, too, in the statutes of New College, Oxford, drawn up by the founder, William of Wykeham, in 1380, that the scholars shall 'amuse themselves by singing in the hall after dinner, on festival days'; and, doubtless, this greatly tended to the advancement of music, and specially of part-singing, at the University.

Dr. Burney, passing over the famous Round, 'Sumer is icumen in,' and ignorant, probably, of the Anglo-Saxon Latin hymn of the Annunciation, *Angelus ad Virginem*, states that 'no English music in parts is preserved so ancient as the time of Chaucer,'[†] yet leans to the opinion, by the manner in which Chaucer describes a concert of birds,[‡] that full—that is, part—music-services in churches were common enough in Chaucer's time. Here is his authority:

> 'And everiche song in his wise
> The most swete, and solempne servise
> By note, that evir man I trowe
> Had herde, for some of hem songe lowe,
> Some highe, and all of one accorde.'

Coupling such evidence as these MSS. supply with Chaucer's references, it is more than probable that the worthy, industrious Doctor was correct in

* *De Laudibus Legum Angliæ*, cap. 49.
† 'History of Music,' vol. ii., p. 380.
‡ 'Dream of Chaucer,' v. 301.

surmising that vocal harmony was in vogue, at any rate, in the Church services in Chaucer's day. It is highly improbable that composers would write harmony—and such exists in two and three parts in the *Angelus ad Virginem*—if it was not intended to be sung, and since the construction of the organs would produce this, there is good ground for accepting the opinion of the famous historian on this point.

The reference which Chaucer* makes in his description of the poor Oxford scholar, Nicholas—who to soften the loneliness of his chamber turned betimes to music's consoling power

—introduces us to a valuable piece of documentary musical evidence which appears to have long escaped the notice of the historian and antiquary. The lofty subject —which he sang so noticeably, and doubtless accompanied on the psaltery—the *Angelus ad Virginem*, was an Anglo-Saxon Latin hymn, setting out the story of the Annunciation of the Virgin Mary. It supplies one further link in the

PERFORMER ON A PSALTERY OF THE FOURTEENTH CENTURY.

chain of English musical history—a much dislocated and disjointed record, towards the establishing of which each piece of indubitable proof becomes of . priceless value. Wonderful to relate, too, it takes us

* 'Canterbury Tales.'

22

back to the earliest days of England's school of composition—the First School Period of the thirteenth
century, when 'Sumer is icumen in' was composed,
and when this country indisputably owned creative
musical talent of the highest order, although so little
of it has survived by name or example. On this
account, then, and because it supports what has been
adduced respecting 'Sumer is icumen in'—with all
its early ingenuity and learning—this composition
will appeal to all lovers of ancient music, particularly
the champions of the English school.

When the Oxford scholar, in his loneliness, sits
beguiling the hours by chanting the *Angelus ad
Virginem*, he is sounding a melody that was written
more than a hundred years before—a tune which,
like many an *Ave Maria*, had perhaps become
familiar enough in the churches. The date of the
MS. has been approximately fixed at 1250 to
1260, or within twenty years of the famous Northumbrian Round, or 'Reading Rota,' as it is called.

Sir John Hawkins makes no mention of this composition in his 'History of Music,' nor does Dr.
Burney in his voluminous work, for the very good
reason that they did not know of its existence. It was
a treasure of the Norfolk family, one of the Howards
presenting it, together with other valuable MSS., to
the Royal Society, who a hundred years or so ago
transferred it to the British Museum, where it was
numbered 248 in the Arundel MSS. Collection.

There it attracted the attention of Mr. Henry Bradshaw, F.S.A., librarian of the University of Cambridge, and subsequently the Chaucer Society had the hymn photographed.

There are five stanzas in the Latin and five in the English version of the words appended to the MS. The following is a fair sample of the whole :

'Gabriel fram [h]evene['s] king
   sent to the maid[en] swete,
brou[gh]te hir blisful tiding
   and faire he 'gan hir grete :
Heil be thu, ful of grace ari[gh]t !
for Godes sone this [h]evenè light
    for mannes loven
    wil man bicomen,
and taken fles[h] of the maiden bri[gh]t,
   mank[ind] fre for to make
   of sinne and devil's mi[gh]t.'

The following gives the melody of the hymn, which, considering its antiquity, can scarcely be said to be crude, or to sound altogether foreign to modern ears. On the contrary, there is, here and there, a particular home flavour about the tune—one recalling the true Church spirit and character so strongly present in the Elizabethan age composers :

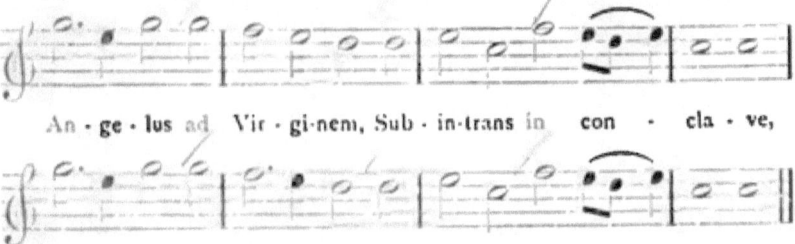

An · ge · lus ad Vir · gi·nem, Sub · in·trans in   con · cla · ve,

Vir · gi · nis for · mi · di·nem De · mul · cens in · quit....... A · ve.

A - ve, Re - gi - na vir - gi - num, Cœ - li ter - re - que Do - mi - num Con - ci - pi - es, et pa - ri - es in - tac - ta Sa - lu - tem, ho - mi - num, tu por - ta cœ - li fac - ta, Me - de - la cri - mi - num.

It remains to be added that the music is written in timeless notes, but so exactly over the words that there is no difficulty in barring the notes by the metre of the verse. This was the course universally adopted before music had notes of definite duration in proportion to others. One peculiarity of the writing should be noted—that where the accent falls upon a long vowel, two notes are placed close together, as if the singer were to iterate the note.

The book containing this piece has also three Latin motets and a beautiful English hymn, 'Quen of euene for ye blisse' (Queen of Heaven for the Bliss). The MSS. are in the thirteenth-century handwriting, beautifully penned. This volume and the Reading book are the sole records remaining to us of the existence of the First English School of Music that flourished about 1200-1250.

Chaucer is not, however, the only author-witness to musical names and customs of the day. Adam Davy of Stratford-by-London, who flourished *circa* 1312, writes :

> ' Mery it is in halle to here the harpè,
> The mynstrall synge, the jogelour carpe.'

Another author, Langland (*circa* 1300-1370), the reputed author of the ' Vision of Pieres Plowman,' reproaches himself for not being better qualified in the art, thus showing that it was still somewhat of a disgrace not to be musically educated and disposed in these early days :

> ' Ich can nat tabre, ne trompe, ne telle faire gestes,
> Ne fithelyn, at festes, ne harpen ;
> Japen ne jagelyr, ne gentilleche pipe ;
> Nother sailen, ne sautrien, ne singe with the giterne.'

Yet there was music in the soul of Longland, or he could not have written such alliterative, descriptive verse as that quoted.

During the fourteenth century all the rhymes and narratory poems were still sung to the accompaniment of the harp. The habit of reciting ballads or historical poems even crept into the public ceremonies. Bishop Adam de Orleton, on visiting the Priory church of St. Swithin, Winchester, was forced to listen to a Danish giant story, and a trial by fire narrative, accompanied on the harp by one Herbert, as a part of the festivities of the occasion.

But to return to reasoning musical art. John

Dunstable* (*i.e.*, John born at Dunstable) is a notable name in Early English musical annals. **Dunstable.** With him we meet the founder of the Second School of English Music. 'The father of English contrapuntists,' as he has been called, was born about the year 1400, and died in 1458. Both a composer and writer, his chief work was the '*De Mensurabiles Musica*,' which Thomas Ravenscroft, Mus. Bac., and other writers of the succeeding century, quoted and referred to as a standard work on music. This tract is, however, lost. Until quite recently the examples extant of Dunstable's music were the quotations made by Gafforius and Morley. A specimen of his work, a three-part song, *O Rosa Bella*, is to be found in MS. at the Vatican Library, and the British Museum possesses two examples from his pen. One is an enigma,† filling up a page (folio 18), and signed, 'Qd Dunstable.' The other is a three-part composition in a volume which once belonged to Henry VIII.‡ Four of this master's compositions are also to be found in the Liceo Filarmonico di Bologno Collection.

Dunstable was not only a musician, but a mathematician and eminent astronomer, while a tract in the Bodleian Library proves him to have been also

---

* Also named Dunstaple, 'John of Dunstaple,' and erroneously confounded by Marpurg and other writers with St. Dunstan.

† Treatises on Music, Add. MSS. 10,336.

‡ Add. MSS. 31,922.

an authority upon geography. He was buried in
the Church of St. Stephen, Walbrook, London, in
1458. The following epitaph, written by John of
Whethamstede, Abbot of St. Albans, and placed on
record by Weaver, is one of two which have long
preserved the fame of this musician :

> 'Musicus hic Michalus alter ; novus et Ptholomeus,
> Junior ac Atlas supportans robore cælos,
> Pausat sub cinere ; melior vir de muliere
> Nunquàm natus erat ; vicii quia labe carebat :
> Et virtutibus opes possedit vincus omnes.
> Cur exoptetur, sic optandoque precetur
> Perpetuis annis celebretur fama Johannis
> Dunstapil ; in pace requiescat, et hic sine fine.'*

The other, Stowe says, was inscribed on 'two
faire plated stones in the Chancele, each by other.'
It runs :

> 'Claudit hoc tumulo, qui Cœlum pectore clausit
> Dunstaple I., juris, astrorum conscius illo
> Judice novit hiramis abscondite pandere cœli
> Hic vir erat tua laus, tua lux, tua musica princeps
> Quique tuas dulces per mundum sperserat onus,
> Anno Mil. Equater, semel L trias jungito Christi.
> Pridie natale sidus transmigrat ad astra
> Suscipiant proprium civem cœli sibi cives.'

All trace of Dunstable's tomb disappeared with
the Great Fire of London.

Kiesewetter, in his history,† makes no mention of
Dunstable when treating the Dufay epoch (1380-

---

* 'Funeral Monuments' (Weaver), 1631 edition, p. 577.
† 'History of the Modern Music of Western Europe.'

1450) of musical art; but it must not be forgotten
that while this first or ancient Netherlands school was
growing up, forming and cementing the principles of
contrapuntal art, England was, both before and con-
temporaneously, helping in the work. If there was
a Dufay, a Binchois, and an Ockenheim improving
counterpoint, and otherwise raising the low state of
theoretical music, there was also a Dunstable—an
Englishman occupied with quite as valuable labours
in the department of mensural and figural music. The
credit of this has not been given to England by
historians generally ; but, happily, we have not only
Dunstable's writings, but also the evidence of a contemporary musician, to prove this.

The reader will know that early in the fifteenth
century the Abbé Baini, of the Pontifical Chapel,
sent to Belgium for some Netherlands musicians to
perform at Rome a Mass written in their particular
style. Among these musicians was Johannes Tinctoris (1434-1520), who became a celebrated teacher
in Italy, and it was he who bore testimony to Dunstable's labours at the renaissance, or revival, of
learning period in the following terms : ' Cujus, ut
ita dicam, novæ artis fons et origo apud Anglicos,
quorum caput Dunstaple exstitit, fuisse exhibetur, et
huic contemporanei fuerunt in Galliâ Dufai et Binchois.' (The source and origin of this new [form of
musical] art, if I may so speak, is to be found among
the English, of whom the chief musician was Dun-

stable, with whom Dufay and Binchois were contemporaries in France.)*

Dunstable could not have *invented* counterpoint however, inasmuch as several works upon it were written before he was born.

Many writers, Gafforius, Morley, and Ravenscroft, among other of Dunstable's immediate successors, quote from his writings, and make reference to his compositions, so that he must have been highly regarded both as a theoretical writer and composer. He rendered valuable services to theoretical art in ridding it of the obnoxious successions of fifths, perfect and imperfect, and octaves, with which all early music abounded ; in simplifying the voice parts, and in encouraging a steadier and more effective flow of the music generally.

Morley later on charged Dunstable with the great offence in the composer's art of separating the syllables of the same word by rests, but Burney easily refutes this. He is of opinion that Morley was so eager to make a pun on the name of Duns-table that he did not sufficiently consider the passages which he censured. Nothing can now shake the deserved reputation of Dunstable. There is no doubt that he was a distinguished Englishman at the head of a Second Period in that school of music in England which preceded the Netherlanders and Burgundians. The most recent Dunstable researches have

* *Proportionale* (Tinctoris).

been made by Mr. Barclay Squire, of the British Museum, who has lately discovered a large collection of Dunstable MSS. in the Modena Library. Here, in what was the library of Hercules II., Duke of Modena in 1471, have been found no less than thirty-one motets by Dunstable and seventeen by other English composers, copies of all of which have been made by Mr. Squire and deposited at the British Museum.

Another Dunstable discovery was made somewhat earlier than this. By a lucky accident Dr. Haberl, of Ratisbon, came across these Dunstable MSS. when searching for materials for his Dufay biography. In the capitular archives of Trent, in Austrian Tyrol, he found six large volumes of fifteenth-century music—a complete anthology of the best music of the day. No sooner was this known than Mr. Squire went to Trent (1889), and copied fourteen motets and a French chanson of undoubted Dunstable music. The Austrian Government placed an embargo on the copies, urging that their publication would diminish the pecuniary value of the originals, a restriction which it is hoped will some day be removed. This was the music that constituted the 'new art' which, a contemporary authority declared, originated in England. No wonder that Dunstable's name became one of more than local celebrity.

Following upon Dunstable was John Hamboys,* whose exact birth and death dates are unrecorded, although Holinshed refers to him as flourish-

Hamboys. ing in the reign of Edward IV. (1461-1483). Other authors—Pits and Bale—fix him under the year 1470, which, however, would be towards the end of his life.

He is generally believed to have been the first English musician on whom the degree of Doctor of Music was conferred—1463. This point it will always be difficult to determine, however, inasmuch as that at this time there also lived Thomas Saintwix —born about the year 1430. He was a Doctor of Music of Cambridge, and was appointed Provost of King's College in that University, a record which, being quite in order, gives some weight to his right to be considered the first English 'Mus. Doc.'

Possibly Hamboys may have graduated at Oxford —this does not appear—when it would have been possible for him to take precedence of Saintwix in the possession of this coveted academical degree. The names of no Oxford musical graduates are recorded before the sixteenth century, which is strange indeed, if such degrees were conferred ; but Holinshed, in enumerating the most eminent men of learning in the reign of Edward IV., includes ' John Hamboys—an excellent musician, who, for his notable cunning therein, was made a Doctor of Music.'†

* Spelt also Hambois and Hanboys.
† 'Chronicle,' vol. ii., p. 1355.

Whether he was musician enough to compose a song in six or eight parts and publicly perform the same 'tam Vocibus quam Instrumentis etiam Musicis'—the qualifying test in Dr. Burney's day—or whether he passed *honoris causâ*, is not known; but it is certain that he was the author of two tracts in Latin: 'Summum Artis Musices' and 'Cantionum Artificialum diversi Generis.'[*]

Abyngdon[†] (Henry) belongs also to this famous period in our national musical history. He was an

Abyngdon. English ecclesiastic and musician who became Sub-Cantor of Wells Cathedral, on November 24, 1447, which post he filled until his death, September 1, 1497.

In 1465 Abyngdon was appointed 'Master of the Song' at the Chapel Royal, London, which he held conjointly with the Succentorship of Wells, from which we may conclude that his services as a musician were much appreciated. This latter appointment brought him in an annual salary of forty marks—a sufficiently weighty matter to occupy the attention of Parliament in those days (1473-74). In the year 1478 the Mastership of St. Catharine's Hospital, Bristol, became vacant, and Abyngdon

---

[*] The exact period at which the distinction of 'Doctor of Music' was instituted in England is a debated point. One authority, Wood, in his 'History of Oxford,' says that the 'Mus. Doc.' degree was first conferred by Henry II. Spelman believes it to belong to the reign of King John, *circa* 1207.

[†] Spelt also Abingdon, Habengton, and Habingdon.

was elected thereto, thus adding another to his plu-
rality of appointments. His duties at this latter
institution have not transpired, but doubtless they
were of a similar nature to those occupying the
attention of the Foundling Hospital organist to-day.

Nothing is known of the works of this musician,
but he is believed to have composed Church
rather than secular music. He is credited with
being the first musician admitted to the degree of
Bachelor of Music at Cambridge. This was in 1463,
when Abyngdon's name is traced as proceeding to
that faculty. From the fact that so little is known
of his compositions, it is possible that he gave but
sparse time to composition; indeed, his widely
separated duties, unless exceptionally light, would
have precluded much writing. But there is another
explanation. Abyngdon's *forte* was singing and
organ-playing :

> ' Millibus in mille cantor fuit optimus ille,
>   Præter et hæc ista fuit optimus orgaquenista ;'

so that we may conclude that he occupied his time
largely with these branches of music.

Abyngdon shared the goodwill of Sir Thomas
More, who, as a young man, knew the musician.
The association does honour to both, and shows that
Abyngdon must have had points as a man as well as a
musician, especially as the Prelate styled him 'nobilis.'*

* 'Life of More' (Cayley), vol. i., p. 317.

Sir Thomas More wrote two epitaphs on Abyngdon. Hamboys, Saintwix and Abyngdon represent the Third Period English School, the archives of which are unfortunately lost.

Hothby* (John), whose precise birth and death dates are unknown, although it is conjectured that he died at Florence in 1500, was another fifteenth-

Hothby. century musician, whom it has been attempted by some to locate a century earlier. An English Carmelite monk, he long lived in a monastery at Ferrara, but settled eventually at Florence *circa* 1440. There is no doubt that he was a clever scientific musician, who, in search of information concerning his art, left England to travel in Italy, France, Germany and Spain, in the monasteries of which countries many scarce musical manuscripts were to be seen.

Hothby would seem to have been indebted to Muris for some of his erudition, for in a manuscript copy of a work by that learned and earlier theorist the copyist attests to having transcribed it for Hothby, adding the date 1471, and eulogizing Hothby. This, by the way, is ample proof that Hothby was no fourteenth-century worker.

He wrote several treatises on music, two of which Coussemaker has published in his collection of writings on music of the Middle Ages.†

---

* Also written Ottebi, Otteby, and Hothbus.
† '*Scriptorum de Musica Medii Ævi*,' iii. 328.

Hothby's chief work was on the 'Proportions of Music,' and copies of treatises on this subject are to be found in the British Museum and in the libraries of Paris, Bologna, and Ferrara. The latest researches warn us, however, that the treatise beginning 'Quid est Proportio,' dated 1500, of which there are copies at the British Museum and Lambeth Palace, is not identical with the 'Regulæ super Proportionem' of the foreign libraries. In the Florence Library is a Hothby MS., which, besides being a quotation from Dunstable, contains an interesting account of musical notation and the transition from neumes to square note characters.

It has not transpired whether Hothby was an executive musician besides being a composer; but there is little doubt that all these early theorists whose names have come down to us as composers only, were also organists, and in some cases singers in the royal chapels. The Paris MS. styles Hothby a Doctor of Music, but his name cannot be traced among the musical graduates of either Oxford or Cambridge.

To maintain as far as possible a chronological order at this disturbed period, we have next to speak of Robert Wydewe, who was sub-cantor of Wells **Wydewe.** Cathedral in 1447. In this same year John Bernard was Cantor of Wells, but unfortunately little more is known of him. Wydow*

* Spelt also Wedow, Widows, Wydewe, and Viduus.

flourished in the reign of Edward IV. (1461-1483).
The son of an Essex schoolmaster, he was sent to
Oxford, where he took the Bachelor of Music degree.
He also took holy orders, and was appointed Vicar
of Thaxted in 1481.   He held successively the appointment of ' Penitentarius' in St. Paul's Cathedral ;
Rector of Chalfont St. Giles ; Canon and Succentor
of Wells ; deputy between the Pope and the Chapter
of Wells ; and finally Vicar of Buckland Newton.
Among the poets of his day he was *facile princeps*,
but no musical composition of his has survived his
fame.   He died October 4, 1505.

Henry V. (1413-1432) was a monarch who would
seem to have entertained peculiar notions respecting
music, although we do not find that he used any
Henry V. severity in inter-
and Music. dicting its use in
any way.   At his corona-
tion in Westminster Hall
in 1413, for instance, we
hear of no other instru-
ments than harps being
used, although numerous
other instruments were in
every-day use.   Of harps
in the hall, however, there
was a prodigious number,

HENRY V.

if we are to believe one of his historians. 'The
number of harpers,' we are told, 'was exceedingly

great, and,' goes on the narrator, ' the sweet strings of their harps soothed the souls of the guests by their soft melody.' Possibly the Prince had an aversion to noisy music, prefer-ring what some people to-day describe as ' soft ' music. If so, we can but admire his taste, for nothing perhaps in the range of music is more disturbing than that blasting and blowing of trumpets which has to be en-dured upon important public occasions, even when these are enacted indoors nowadays, when a sweep of harp music would be infinitely more affect-

JONGLEUR PLAYING A VIELLE (FIFTEENTH CENTURY).

(From a MS. in the Arsenal Library at Paris.)

ing and less barbarous. Why the high personages mostly concerned in these functions, and whose minds are expected to be centred on what is going on, do not move for an abatement of this fanfare nuisance passes our comprehension. That music was much in vogue among the soldiers of those days—probably more than it is now—has come down to us as a historical fact. The night before the battle of Agincourt the English camp resounded with national songs and music.

Public expressions of applause were particularly distasteful to this King, who was more disgusted than gratified with praise for his valiant deeds.

23

When he entered the City of London after the battle of Agincourt, the gates and streets were hung

The Agincourt Song. with tapestry, representing the history of ancient heroes; and children were placed at temporary turrets to sing verses. Such arrangements, however, were of little avail. Henry, by a formal edict, forbade his subjects for the future to extol this Agincourt victory, 'for that he woulde have the wholle praise and thanks given to God.' In spite of edicts, however, one song got so firm a hold upon the people, either before or after the order, that it has been kept to this day. It is preserved in the Pepysian Collection at Cambridge. This copy is written upon vellum in Gregorian notes, and Dr. Burney was of opinion that it was 'little less ancient than the event which it recorded.'* Appended is a copy of this remarkable song, which is not less notable as a venerable historic relic than it is as a sample of native musical composition:

AGINCOURT VICTORY SONG (1415).

De - o gra - ti - as An - gli - - - - a red - de pio vic - - to - ri - a.

* 'History of Music,' vol. ii., p. 384.

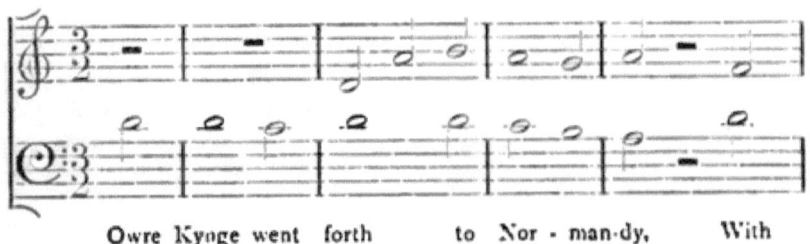

Owre Kynge went forth to Nor - man-dy, With

grace and myght of Chy - val - ry; The God for

hym wrought marv - 'lus - ly, Where-fore Englonde may

calle, and cry: De - o - - gra - - ti - as.

CHORUS.

The remainder of the narrative runs as follows:

'He sette a sege, the sothe to say,
To Harflue town, with royal array,
That toune he wan, and made a fray,
That Fraunce shall rywe tyl domes-day.
Deo gratias, etc.

'Than for sothe that knyght comely,
In Agincourt feld faught manly,
Thorow grace of God most myghty,
He had bothe felde, and victory.
     Deo gratias, etc.

'Then went owre kynge, with all his oste,
Throwe Fraunce for all the Frensshe boste;
He spared for drede of leste, ne most
Till he come to Agincourt coste.
     Deo gratias, etc.

'There dukys, and earlys, lorde and baron
Were take, and slayne, and that wel sone,
And some were ledde into Lundone
With joye, and merthe, and grete renone.
     Deo gratias, etc.

'Now gracious God he save owre kynge,
His people, and all his well wyllinge;
Gef him gode lyfe, and gode endynge,
That we with merth may safely synge
     Deo gratias Anglia redde pro victoria.'

We are indebted to Dr. Burney and his contemporary, John Stafford Smith—whose 'Musica Antiqua' collection renders him an authority upon ancient vocal music—for deciphering and disentangling the notation, etc., of this song. From the marked 'churchy' character of the music, and the fact that it is written in the Dorian, or first authentic mode, it would seem to have been composed by an ecclesiastic whose name has not come down to us. The thoughtful *Deo Gratias* somewhat confirms this view. At the same time, all the music of this period is steeped with a religious flavour—especially the scientific music—as if it was mainly the work of monks, or others, brought much into contact with ecclesiastical life and influence. The melody of this 'Agincourt' song is fairly regular and agreeable to the ear, but it well illustrates the fluctuating character of the composer's art in England in being far inferior to 'Sumer is icumen in,' both in melody and harmony, as well as in secular, local colour.

Henry V. was not wholly opposed to music, for when preparing for his eventful journey to France in 1415, an express order was given for his minstrels to attend him. Again, at the Feast of Pentecost in 1416, when he entertained the Emperor and the Duke of Holland, he ordered rich gowns for sixteen of his minstrels. At his death his son (Henry VI.) paid out of the Royal Exchequer a grant of one hundred shillings to each of the late King's minstrels, an annuity which the late King ordered orally just before his death, but was not able to endorse.

HENRY VI.

Little is heard of music in England during Henry VI.'s reign (1422-1461). It has been gleaned from records, however, that for the year 1430, and for some time both before and after, the minstrels were better paid than the clergy. In the reign of Henry VI. it was the custom to hold an annual feast of the fraternity of the Holy Cross. This took place at Abingdon, in Berkshire, and the disbursements show that while twelve priests each received 4d. for singing a dirge, the minstrels, of whom there were twelve, each received 2s. 4d., in addition to food for himself and fodder for his horse. Nor was this extra payment because they travelled far, since most of them hailed from the neighbouring town of Maidenhead.

That this King enjoyed and supported music, however, is clear, inasmuch as several of the musicians whom he paid for their solace and amusement went over, at his death, to the service of Edward IV.

The next reign was an auspicious one for music. Edward IV. (1461-1483) was minded to advance the art, and amid many demands which the continuation

Chapels Royal Founded.

of civil war made upon him, he found time and attention to accomplish not a little in the cause of music. Edward's name, indeed, deserves to be honourably remembered for what he did for the art at a particularly troubled period, especially as some of our most cherished musical institutions of to-day owe their origin to this King. Edward built the Chapel Royal at Windsor, and from his desire to have suitable musical services thereat came the foundation of those establishments — the Chapels

EDWARD IV.

Royal—with which so many of the foremost native musicians of to-day are, or have been, actively associated. In a work* containing an account of the household establishment of Edward IV., we meet with data which furnish us with the origin of the institutions—the Chapel Royal choir and the Royal Band—the King's or Queen's, as the case may be.

The particulars detailed concern the several musicians retained in the King's employment for his private amusement as well as for the carrying out of the chapel services. Thus there were : 'Minstrelles thirteene, whereof one is Virger, which directeth them all festyvall dayes in their statyones of blowings and pypyngs to such offyces as the offyceres might be warned to prepare for the King's meats and soupers ; to be more redyere in all services and due tyme ; and all these sytying in the hall together, whereof some be trompets, some with the shalmes

King's Court Musicians.

* '*Liber Niger Domus Regis.*'

and smalle pypes, and some are strange mene coming
to this Court at fyve feastes of the year, and then
take their wages of
Household, after iiij*d.*
ob. by daye, after as
they have byne pre-
sente in Courte, and
then to avoyd after
the next morrowe
aftere the feaste, be-
sydes theire other re-
wards yearly in the
King's Exchequer,
and clothinge with
the Household, wintere
and somere for eiche of
them xx*s.* And they
take nightelye amongeste
them all iiij galanes ale ;
and for wintere Seasone
thre candles waxe, vj
candles pich, iiij tale
sheids (billets of fire-
wood) ; lodging suffy-
tyente by the Herben-
gere for them and theire
horses nighteley to the
Courte. Aulso hauing into Courte ij servants to bear
their trompets, pypes, and other instruments, and

MINSTRELS OF THE FIFTEENTH
CENTURY.

torche for wintere nightes, whilst they blow to suppore
of the chaundry ; and alway two of thes persones to
contynewe stylle in Courte at wages by the cheque
rolle whiles they be presente iiij ob. dayly, to warne
the King's ridynge household when he goeth to
horsbacke as oft as it shall require, and that his
household meny may followe the more redyere aftere
by the blowinge of their trompets.   Yf any of thes
two Minstrelles be lete bloode in Courte, he taketh
two loves, ij messe of greate meate, one galone ale.
They part not at no tyme with the rewards given to
the Household.   Also when it pleasethe the King
to have ij Minstrelles continuinge at Courte, they
will not in no wise that thes Minstrelles be so
famylliere to aske rewards.'

Another entry runs : ' A Wayte that nightelye
from Mychelmas to Shreve Thorsdaye pipethe
watche withen this Courte fower tymes ; in the
somere nightes iij tymes, and makethe Bon Gayte
(good watch) at every chambere doare and offyce,
as well for feare of pyckeres and pillers.   He eateth
in the halle with mynstrielles, and takethe yverey
nighte a loffe, a galone of alle, and for somere
nightes ij candles pich, a bushel of coles ; and for
wintere nights halfe a loafe of bread, a gallon of ale,
iiij candles piche, a bushel coles ; daylye whilste he
is presente in Courte for his wages in cheque roale
allowed iiij*d*. ob. or else iij*d*. by the discreshon of the
steuarde and tressorere, and that, after his cominge

and diserninge : also cloathinge with the houshold yeoman or mynstrelles lyke to the wages that he takethe ; and he be syke he takyth twoe loves, ij messe of greate meate, one gallon ale. Also he partethe with the housholde of general gyfts, and hathe his beddinge carried by the comptroller's assygment ; and under this yeoman to be a groome watere. Yf he can excuse the yeoman in his absence, then he takethe rewarde, clotheinge, meat and all other things lyke to other Grooms of Houshold. Also this Yeoman-Waighte, at the making of Knightes of the Bathe, for his attendance upon them by nighte-tyme, in watchinge in the chappelle, hathe to his fee all the watchinge-clothing that the knight shall weare uppon him.'

The next entry concerns the 'Cildren of the Chapelle.' Of these there were 'viij founded by the King's priuie cofferes for all that longeth to their apperelle by the hands and oversyghte of the Deane, or by the Master of Songe assigned to teache them, which Mastere is appointed by the Deane, chosen one of the nomber of the felowshipe of chappelle after rehearsed, and to drawe them to other schooles after the form of Gacotte, as well as in Songe in Organies and other. Thes Children eate in the Hall dayly at the Chappele board, nexte the Yeomane of Uestery : taking amongst them for lyverye daylye for brekefaste and all nighte, two loves, one messe of greate meate, ij galones ale ;

and for wintere seasone iiij candles piche, iij talfheids,
and lyttere for their pallets of the Serjante-Usher
and carryadge of the King's coste for the competente
beddynge by the oversyghte of the Comptrollere.
And amongeste them all to have one servante into
the court to trusse and bear their harnesse and
lyverye in Court.   And that day the King's Chappelle
remoueth every of thes children then present re-
ceauth iiij*d.* at the Grene Clothe of the Comptying-
house for horshire dayly, as long as they be jurneinge.
And when any of these children comene to xviij
years of age, and their uoyces change, ne cannot be
preferred in this Chapelle, the nombere being full,
then yf they will assente the King assynethe them
to a College of Oxeford or Cambridge of his founda-
tione, there to be at fyndyng and studye bothe
suffytyently, tylle the King may otherwise aduance
them.'

Thus if Edward IV. somewhat curtailed the
liberty and audacity of the wandering minstrel he
accomplished a greater work in establishing musical
institutions which have survived to this day, and
which we hope, and believe, will remain for many a
long year to come.   The royal chapels and the
private bands of the Sovereign have ever since provided lucrative and coveted posts for a proportion of
our best native talent, and when all other musical
machinery has stopped and disappeared, these
establishments—and occasionally others like them

in wealthy private families—have been the means of preserving and keeping together the musical tradition and practice. But a greater value attached to Edward IV.'s action. The appointments in the King's service gave their holders a leisure free from concern as to 'ways and means.' They had time to think, and their thoughts naturally reverted to their beautiful art. As a consequence, these musicians took to writing music—music that was adapted to, and would meet with performance at, the chapel services. One vied with another in producing a beautiful anthem, motet, or *Ave* setting. Such was the genesis of that great glorious school

MINSTRELS OF THE FIFTEENTH CENTURY.

of English Church composers which has made the Elizabethan era for ever famous in the annals of music. The matter emanated entirely from among ourselves, and it is a wilful perversion of the facts to attribute the movement to any other—particularly any foreign—source or influence.

In a previous chapter we left the minstrels fast declining. A few more remarks need to be made respecting them before they disappear wholly, as an accepted element, from the story of English musical history.

Edward IV. (1461-1483) was the last monarch who recognized the minstrels. In 1469 he granted a Royal charter, dated April 24, to Walter Halliday,

Edward IV. and Minstrelsy. and seven others, whose duty it was to appoint officers from among themselves and to control and regulate the minstrel profession. Halliday became 'Marshal,' and Carlile 'Serjeant,' and the latter it was who, as the King lay one day on his bed, came to him in great haste, and 'badde hym aryse, for he hadde enemyes cumming for to take him, the which were within six or seven miles.'

Edward paid his musicians as a King should— right royally—and depended upon them not a little for assistance upon occasions of importance, whether in the Church or outside it. Thus when Elizabeth, his Queen, went to Westminster Abbey to be churched (1466), she was preceded by processions of choristers, chanting hymns, and to these succeeded long lines of the noblest and fairest women of London, attended by bands of musicians and trumpeters, and forty-two royal singers. Truly a reasonable, impressive pageantry—one which might, to some extent at least, be imitated nowadays, for surely the music from such a procession of Church musicians would be in every sense more appropriate upon many of our state occasions than is the nerve-tearing military music which so wholly and entirely obtains upon such opportunities to-day.

Every private family of note had its own musical staff in Edward IV.'s reign—those who could not afford a band of performers contenting themselves **Private** with a harper only. An Abbot or Bishop **Families'** —upon the score of expense, or, perhaps, **Musicians.** scruples of conscience—was sometimes reduced to this extreme. The household book of the Howard family abounds in entries relating to music and musicians. We find a payment of a 'new year's gift' to Lady Howard's grand-mother's harper 'that dwellyth in Chestre.' Singers' names—Nicholas Stapylton, William Lyndsey, and 'little Richard'—appear, besides entries referring to four, five, and six 'children of the chapel,' thus showing that private chapels were maintained upon a large scale even thus early.

From an item set down to 'Thomas, the harperd' for a 'lyard,' or gray 'gown,' it is clear that patrons robed their musicians in those days. Lord Howard did not scour the country for his musicians, but adopted the sensible plan of having promising young talent trained for the post of family musician.

Thus we find from an agreement that was made, the 14th day of October, 1481, that one William Wastell, harper of London, was engaged so that he should teach the son of John Colet, of Colchester, harper, for a year, in order probably to render him competent afterwards to fill the post of one of the house musicians. A 'gown' was to be presented to Wastell at the end of the year.

On the whole Wastell's appearance was picturesque enough. This 'squire minstrel of Middlesex, who travelled the country in the summer seasons unto worshipful men's houses,' had a long gown of Kendal green, gathered at the neck with a narrow gorget, and fastened before with a white clasp. The long sleeves falling down to mid-leg were slit from the shoulders to the hand, and lined with white. His harp hung 'in good grace dependent before him,' and his 'wrest,' or tuning-key, was tied to 'green lace hanging by.' He wore a red Cadiz girdle, and the corner of his handkerchief, edged with blue lace, hung from his bosom. Under the gorget of his gown hung a chain, 'resplendent upon his breast, of the ancient arms of Islington.'

Unfortunately for Wastell and his art, such fine appearances and considerate patrons had to give way before a more prosaic state of things—those inevitable changes and improvements which were to lead up to the machinery of music as a nineteenth-century business and profession. The vast musical life and work of to-day had to be opened up, and before this could be accomplished there were many processes, and many prejudices, which had to be broken through.

The short reign of Edward V.—whose unhappy fate with his brother Richard, Duke of York, is one of the most pathetic pictures in our national history —furnishes little further musical clue. With Richard III. (1483-1485), however, we meet with a monarch who was well disposed towards music and its professors. His chief aim was to maintain the excellence of the Chapel Royal choir which his brother had inaugu-

RICHARD III.

rated. To this end he empowered John Melynek, one of the gentlemen of the chapel, 'to take and seize for the King all such singing men, expert in the science of music, as he could find and think able to do the King's service, within all places of the realm, as well cathedral churches, colleges, chapels, houses of religion, and all other franchised or exempt places, or elsewhere.' Children were not excluded from this order, which was, indeed, an illustration of the robbing of Peter to pay Paul!

24

One of the last of the minstrels was Richard Sheale (*circa* 1548), who preserved 'Chevy Chase'

The Last of the Minstrels. for us, and who had the misfortune to be robbed on Dunsmore Heath. His loss was £60, an occurrence which he describes sorrowfully :

' After my robbery my memory was so decay'd
 That I could neither sing, nor talk, my wits were so dismay'd.

' Some said I was not robb'd, I was but a lying knave,
 It was not possible for a minstrel so much money to have.

' Because my carriage should be light I put my money into gold,
 And without company I rode alone—thus was I foolish bold ;
 I thought by reason of my harp no man would me suspect,
 For minstrels oft with money, they be not much infect.'

A salutary measure passed in the thirty· ninth year of Queen Elizabeth's reign put an end to the minstrels for ever. 'Minstrels wandering abroad were rogues, vagabonds, and sturdy beggars,' and were to be punished as such. The result of this was that there were no more orders of minstrels. They descended to street musicians, and roamed about singly, or in twos and threes very much in the same way as itinerant musicians do now.

When the minstrels died out, Dr. Bull wrote the

Bull's Minstrels' Epitaph. following lines, which might truly be called the 'Minstrels' Epitaph,' for minstrels never rose again to any importance in this country :

' When Jesus went to Jairus' house
(Whose daughter was about to die),
He turned the minstrels out of doors,
Among the rascal company :
Beggars they are with one consent,
And rogues, by Act of Parliament.'

It is a universal law that when one element dis-
appears it is but to make room for another.   Thus,
when minstrelsy declined in England, its place was

THE MUSICIANS.

*(Carvings representing the humours of a popular festival (a Whitsun Ale) on the
entablature under the parapet of the nave of St. John's Church, Cirencester.
Nave rebuilt in 1504.)*

soon filled by a substitute which the people made for
themselves.   Minstrelsy—the true minstrelsy which
for so many years had stood in place of any better
art—declined appreciably before the Reformation.

Caxton's great labours affected it as they affected
all else in England. 'The invention of printing,'
remarks Mr. Chappell, 'coupled with the increased cultivation of poetry and music by men
of genius and learning, accelerated the downfall of
the minstrels. They could not long withstand the
superior standard of excellence in the sister arts, on
the one hand, and the competition of the ballad-
singer (who sang without asking remuneration, and
sold his songs for a penny), on the other. In little
more than fifty years from this time they seem to
have fallen into utter contempt.'[*]

Secular music was greatly in advance of that of
the Church in the twelfth and thirteenth centuries,
but although such was the case very little secular
music has been handed down. There was nothing
to prevent the free and unembarrassed development
of secular music. The people liked it, and there
were plenty of wandering musicians—gifted enough
although unscientific—ready to make music for the
people. Folk-songs, refrains, roundelays, love-ditties,
ballads, and serenades'—all this was a perfectly
natural music-growth which filled the air with its
perfume. The people, and wandering musicians
between them, made the secular music, leaving that
less natural art—sacred music—in the hands of the
trained theorists, and rigid musical purists of the
monastery and cloister.

The last important secular composition referred to

[*] 'Popular Music of the Olden Time' (Chappell).

was that First Period School composition ' Sumer is icumen in.' Secular music did not begin and end with this example. Confining ourselves to early songs with music—songs without music are frequent enough—there is one of the thirteenth century, with music in two parts, to the words :

' Foweles in the frith, the fisses in the flod.'

This MS. is preserved in the Bodleian Library.

Another very early English song, with music, is the ' Song of a Prisoner,' to be found in the *Liber de Antiquis Legibus* in the London Guildhall archives.

In proof that secular music was considerably in advance of that of the Church in the twelfth and thirteenth centuries, we quote a specimen printed in John Stafford Smith's ' Musica Antiqua,' of an old English dance tune, taken from an ancient manuscript now in the Bodleian Library. Its notation is of the

ENGLISH CROWD.

(From a bas-relief on the under part of the seats in Worcester Cathedral choir. Date, twelfth or thirteenth century.)

same period as that of the Reading *Rota*—a First Period School composition—' Sumer is icumen in,' *i.e.*, about 1250. The bass is a modern addition :

Of the original of this tune and MS. Dr. Crotch observes : ' The abundance of appoggiaturas in so ancient a melody, and the number of bars in the phrases, four in one and five in another, nine in each part, are its most striking peculiarities. It is formed on an excellent design, similar to that of several fine airs of different nations. It consists of three parts, resembling each other excepting in the commencement of their phrases, in which they tower above each other with increasing energy, and is altogether a curious and very favourable specimen of the state of music at this very early period.'

' It is also a fact worthy of remark,' writes Sir F. A. Gore Ouseley, ' that this piece, like " Sumer is icumen in," is in the key of F major, and not in any of the Church modes, and is in strict conformity with the rules of modern music in its closes, which are uniformly composed of a leading note rising to its proper resolution. This goes a long way towards proving that our modern tonality was natural and spontaneous among our ancestors, although strictly excluded from the music of the Church, and ignored by all the theoretical writers on harmony for three centuries after that date.'*

This soil or land music became the later folk-music, and we have only to become acquainted with the rude beauty and warm sentiment of some of the oldest folk-songs, to gauge the attractive nature of

* ' History of Music ' (Naumann-Ouseley), vol. i., p. 555.

the early English secular music, and to account for its hold upon the people.

That practically all the secular music of England prior to the thirteenth century should be lost is greatly to be deplored, yet with the elegiac grace and beauty of that splendid remaining example—'Sumer is icumen in'—before us, it goes far to persuade us that this unrestrained, natural art of the people was characterized by a flavour and character that must have made it particularly attractive and enjoyable.

It is easy to understand how so little is known concerning the early secular music. The only learned people were the monks and religious teachers, and they devoted their attention mainly to sacred music—especially such as could be sung in churches. Sometimes, perhaps, weary with the everlasting plain-song, a venturesome spirit might hazard an original setting of a *canto fermo* to harmony; but the Gregorian tunes were ill adapted to harmonical treatment, and the result could only have been music in parts, with most stilted harmony.

The popular music—the secular art—was not so restricted. Those who could write, and who understood musical notation, had no restrictions in the invention of tunes and ballad airs, and there is no doubt that most of what they wrote was composed in those natural major and minor modes which we use to-day. Such popular music as was written down, however, must have been ill-proportioned indeed to that which was carried along by the ears of the people. Yet scarcely a vestige of all this has escaped the untoward conditions of age after age. Unfavoured by the clergy, secular music would not be protected by them. As all books and MSS. found their way eventually to the monasteries and religious houses, it is pretty certain that not a little secular music was confiscated in these establishments. Unfortunately, however, there was mischief beyond clerical resistance, scarcity of copyists, transcript-makers, etc. Before long there came the dissolution of the monasteries—with all the devastating processes and losses to literature and art which followed —when musical MSS. and books, whether sacred or secular, were dispersed, destroyed, or lost. In this way England lost untold musical material— creative, didactic, and historic, which it is hopeless to expect can, or will, ever be restored. We can only deplore its destruction, and admire the spirit of the Elizabethan masters which led them to repair the mischief as far as it lay in their power to do so.

When in 1437 Gutenberg gave the world his wonderful invention which was to change the face of the world, music, as well as literature, was immediately affected. Caxton set up his press at Westminster about 1471—*i.e*, in Edward IV.'s reign (1461-1483)—not long after which time music began to be printed instead of being transcribed and duplicated with the pen.

The first work printed in England having musical notation was the *Polychronicon*, written in Latin by Ralph Higden—one of our own countrymen—which,

CAXTON.

being translated by Trevisa in 1482, was subsequently printed. Apart from its printed musical example, this work is of interest from the quaint account which it contains of the discovery of the harmonic consonances by Pythagoras : ' Here wyse men I telle that Pieagoras passed symetyme by a smythes hous and herde a swete soune and accordynge in the smytyng of four hamers upon an anult, and therefore he lette way the hamers, and founde that one 'of the hamers weyed six pōnds, the seconde of twelve, the thyrde of eight, the fourth of ix. as this fygure sheweth.' In the first English edition, printed by Caxton, a space is here left for the insertion by hand of the following noting of the consonances of the diapason.

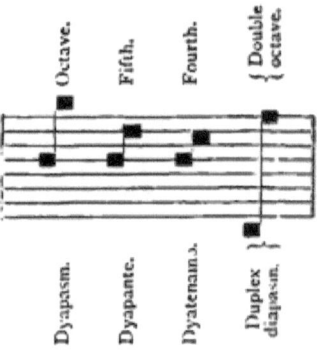

The second English edition was printed by Wynkyn de Worde, at Westminster, in 1495, and therein the solitary musical example is printed roughly in types for the first time.

Considering all things, the growth of works on music, after the invention of printing, was remarkable. It was obviously a slow process to print any books, whatever their nature ; but it is encouraging to know that by the year 1599 the number of works on music, printed in England, amounted to 250, which number had grown to 420 by the year 1650, . and to 750 by 1700.

It need hardly be pointed out that a boon like printing was soon seized hold of in connection with musical works, and it is, of course, to it that we are to-day indebted for our cheap editions in music, as well as in literature generally. As Sir John Hawkins observes : ' It proved an effectual remedy for all the evils arising from the instability of musical notation ; and besides easing the public in the article of expense, it introduced such a steady and regular practice as rendered the musical an universal character.'

With the invention of printing, and the facilities thus afforded of making ideas known, the expression of views and theories respecting music seem to have followed in a perfectly natural sequence. The close of the fifteenth century is marked by several disquisitions, learned and otherwise, upon music. Thus, about 1480 was published an English translation which John Trevisa had made in 1398 of Bartholomæus' *De Proprietatibus Rerum*, written in Latin about 1366, and one of the earliest books printed in England bearing upon the art and

science of music. Another work 'Hymage or
Myrrour of the Worlde,' 'emprysed and fynyssed
in the xxi year of the reign of the most crysten
Kyng, Kynge Edward the fourth'—*i.e.*, in 1481
—was printed by Caxton. Its twelfth chapter is
headed 'After of Music,' wherein the writer shows
that music is an art, because it ministers to the soul.
One of the two illustrations which it contains is a
man playing on a pipe. Another published work
was the oldest English-printed missal—the *Missale
secundum usum insignio Ecclesiæ Sarum*. The manuscript was compiled for the cathedral church of
Salisbury, in the eleventh century, by St. Osmund,
Bishop of the diocese. The earlier missals, according to the different uses of Sarum, Hereford and
York, were printed for English use at Rouen. For
the musical notation necessary for these first English
printed music-books various processes were employed. In some issues the notes were printed
from wooden blocks; in others the stave-lines only
were printed, for the notes to be added by hand; in
others the stave-lines and the notes were produced
by two separate printings; and early in the sixteenth
century the stave-lines and notes were printed at
once from musical type. This Salisbury missal was
printed and published at Westminster through the
Wynkyn de Worde press.

Reviewing the situation, Dunstable forms the
strong link between that remarkable epoch of the

early English School—the First English School it
should be called—when the *Rota*, or Round, 'Sumer
is icumen in,' was composed by one of its disciples,
and that later period early in the sixteenth century
when musicians like Fairfax, and Cornyshe, begin to
appear to form the Fourth English Period School.
Between these come the Third English School, with
such names as Hamboys, Saintwix and Abyngdon,
of whom and their compositions so little is unhappily
known.

How music fared during the 150 years which
separate that famous composition (1250) and Dunstable (1400) is a mystery. No names have come
down to us, and history is silent upon the point. It
can only be surmised that, amid the stormy, troublous
times music 'went to the dogs,' and that there was
no time and no disposition to follow it up; or there
was every prospect of such a small band, as these
musicians were, being stamped out, or that they would
die naturally without successors. The times were
ill suited to sustained regulated study such as the
art of composition demanded, and only here and
there could be found a patron willing to lend an ear
to constructional music, or to open his purse to the
man who made it. Church music would be going
on as usual, yet only to the extent that the Roman
service needed it in the Mass and other portions of
the ritual. This, too, would be restricted to the
Gregorian system, probably, for the age of service

and anthem music was not yet.   Unwritten secular
music—music of the people—would seem to be all
that the country had for years prior to the time of
Dunstable ; yet varied and plentiful as such music
was, it was necessarily transitional, and no attempt
appears to have been made to put it upon parchment,
or otherwise to record it.   The extent to which it
served musical progress was consequently but little,
if we except the bearing it had in keeping people
interested in music until those better days when it
was to become a scientific art.

As an instance of the fitful conditions surrounding
music in its early stages in England, and as some
evidence bearing upon its seemingly slow development in a country where it had attained to such
excellence as early as the thirteenth century, it is
only necessary to watch the course of events when
Dunstable died.   This took place just as the Wars
of the Roses broke out—when civil war ran rife here
for thirty years.   After Dunstable we hear little
more of the English musician for half a century and
more, until Christopher Tye was born.   Here and
there a sovereign, Edward IV. to wit, encouraged
music ; but the creative musician was sadly missing.
Not only was the musician silenced, but when, in
course of time, his voice was heard again, it was of a
much less exalted quality.   Dunstable—reputed as
excellent a musician as his contemporary, Dufay—
was far superior to the native composers of the

early sixteenth century. Both in the generation before and after Dunstable, therefore, the excellence of the thirteenth-century music was far from maintained.

It will be noted, however, that we do not need to wait until the Elizabethan period—that Augustan age of music in this country—before realizing that England possessed at odd intervals notabilities in music second to none, and often surpassing, those of other European countries. Nor is there the slightest room for doubt respecting our pre-eminence and supremacy in musical art during the early period which we have been considering. England led the way with a school of music and musicians—a school reflecting the true British style of harmony and melody—before any other country possessed a corresponding institution. This early English School fluctuated both in its measure of excellence and succession of masters, but this was due solely to the disturbed conditions of the times. The English musical spirit was always there, and could not be exterminated, whatever happened. No other country possessed so much dormant, slumbering musical vitality, even when national matters here were at their worst. Yet all that we have had has been ignored by foreign, as well as by several English, musical historians!

Here we must break our story—one which is perforce a long one, yet the gradual recounting of which will not, it is hoped, have been wearying to the reader. It must be allowed that the period of English musical history which this volume covers is not the most interesting one ; but we hope to make amends for this in the next volume. Though so much ground has been covered, much of it has proved barren and sterile from sheer force of political influences, which were bound to operate in the making of the country and its people. Some of these processes were particularly unfavourable to music, yet they had to go on. In some of these fitful years music is seldom traceable, so that a connected story respecting it becomes almost impossible. Then, when the art or one of its workers is descried, the glimpse is so slight as to be almost past recording. Nevertheless, we have seen enough to convince us of the sure and solid foundation upon which English musical art is based—a basis which easily disposes of that oft-put query as to whether there is, or ever was, a national English musical school or style. We may rest contentedly enough about this point from the evidence already before us. Much more relating to English musical lineage is to follow, and when the whole story has been told, it will be found that no country—neither France, Germany, nor Italy—has so ancient an origin in music, or a more glorious record than has England. In its far-off days England was really a more distinctive musical nation than any other, and more musically characteristic than it is to-day.

We have seen what this country was doing musically while the England of to-day was being formed fourteen and fifteen centuries back ; we have watched the rise of musical notation and the invention of materials for expressing music, and have noted how greedily our ancestors seized hold of these, and with quill and parchment left us splendid proofs of a pure First Period School ; our libraries have a few treatises and manuscripts which place this country in the front rank for her musical disputationists and writers upon the theoretical and speculative aspects of music ; secular music and that greater art, sacred harmony, have blossomed and grown under our eyes ; musical establishments and systems existing to-day have been founded and put upon workable footings—all this we have seen take place in this country of ours prior to the rise of the Tudors, before the close of the fifteenth century.

Yet with all this our story may be said to have hardly begun. We have, as it were, only just entered upon the threshold of our subject. Hitherto the times have been stormy and the soil comparatively unfavourable. The most interesting part of our narrative has yet to be told. Minstrelsy can scarcely be left until we have shown how music was long recognised by provincial cities and boroughs as a proper subject on which money should be spent. The records of such corporations as Lincoln, Leicester, etc., abound in interesting details of the encouragement of music and of the retaining of civic minstrels at regular salaries.

With Henry VII.'s reign a vast force of musical energy bursts forth—England rises to her fullest musical strength, and native musicians whose names will ever adorn an age particularly dear to Englishmen follow one another with great frequency. We have a glorious period before us in the Elizabethan age, when musicians rose up who were as great in their way as were Shakespeare, Bacon, Halley and Frobisher in theirs. And what shall we say of the Victorian era! We must never forget the men, however, who shared in the struggles of England's first musical supremacy—the men who made the First, Second and Third English Schools of Music.

PRINCIPAL AUTHORITIES.

'History of the Modern Music of Western Europe'	Kiesewetter.
'History of Music' - - - - -	Naumann-Ouseley.
'History of Music' - - - - -	Burney.
'Survey of London' - - - - -	Stowe.
'Dictionary of Music and Musicians' - -	Grove.
'Chronicle' - - - - - -	Holinshed.
'Biographical Dictionary of Musicians' -	Brown.
'History of Music' - - - - -	Stafford.
'English Songs' - - - - -	Ritson.
'Social England' - - - - -	Cassell.
'Popular Music of the Olden Time' - -	Chappell.
'The Organ: Its History and Construction'	Hopkins-Rimbault.
The Musical Times - - - - -	Novello.

INDEX.

THE END.

BILLING AND SONS, GUILDFORD, SURREY.
J. D. & Co.

MUSICAL BOOKS BY F. J. CROWEST.

THE GREAT TONE POETS.
EIGHTH EDITION.

'The subjects are well chosen; the memoirs bristle with piquant anecdotes. From Bach to Schumann he keeps our admiration at fever heat.'—*Academy.*

ADVICE TO SINGERS.
TWELFTH THOUSAND.

'Mr. Crowest is an accepted authority on the voice and voice production, and even the most cursory examination of these pages confirms that opinion.'—*Court Circular.*

'I cannot do better, I think, than draw this to a conclusion by quoting a great authority on the voice—namely, Mr. Frederick J. Crowest.'—*The Lady.*

CHERUBINI. 'Great Musicians' Series.

'Mr. Crowest has made musical biography his study, and his "Great Tone Poets" is one of the most popular books of its kind. He treats his present subject with care and judgment, and neither his statements nor his opinions are likely to be found fault with.'—*Globe.*

MUSICAL HISTORY AND BIOGRAPHY.

'An excellent little book—contains an immense amount of information, historical, biographical, and critical, in a very small compass.—*Musical Education.*

A BOOK OF MUSICAL ANECDOTE.
TWO VOLS.

'Mr. Crowest's volumes are readable and amusing. There is this difference in his books from previous publications, that he accompanies the anecdotes with a running commentary.'—*Athenæum.*

PHASES OF MUSICAL ENGLAND.

'What Mr. Crowest says of the acquirements necessary to a right exercise of the critical function is undoubtedly just. . . . He gives various examples in support of his charges, which we are bound to acknowledge he fully proves.'—*Saturday Review.*

MUSICAL GROUNDWORK.

'There is an excellent system throughout the book of imparting the instruction in such a way that it can be readily grasped and recollected. It is really a triumph to succeed as the writer of this little work has done, when we remember that nothing in the whole educational curriculum is more difficult to successfully convey to the student's mind, through the medium of a manual, than an all-round knowledge of the groundwork of music.'—*School Board Chronicle.*

THE DICTIONARY OF BRITISH MUSICIANS.

'We have no hesitation in saying that it is the most complete list of British musicians yet published. So far as we have been able to test the volume it is accuracy itself.'—*Musical Standard.*

WORKS ON MUSICAL SUBJECTS.

EDITED BY DR. JENSEN.

THE LIFE OF ROBERT SCHUMANN, told in his Letters.

Translated by MAY SIMPSON.   2 vols., crown 8vo., 21s.

'These volumes afford a revelation of the inner self of the composer, such as no biography (or even autobiography, if we had one) could furnish, seeing that they place before us, in all their vivid freshness and piquancy, the thoughts of Schumann written to his most intimate friends. The translation is admirably done, and these handsome volumes are a credit to translator and publisher alike.'—*Musical Standard.*

EDITED BY FREDERICK SCHÖNE AND FERDINAND HILLER.

THE LETTERS OF A LEIPZIG CANTOR, MORITZ HAUPTMANN, to Franz Hauser, Ludwig Spohr, and other Musicians.

Translated and arranged by ARTHUR DUKE COLERIDGE, Author of 'Eton in the Forties,' etc.   2 vols., demy 8vo., 21s.

'Moritz Hauptmann has a special claim on the sympathies of English readers, not merely as the intimate friend of Spohr and Mendelssohn, but as the teacher of some of the most eminent native composers and musicians, amongst others the late Walter Bache, J. F. Barnett, F. H. Cowen, and Arthur Sullivan. For a quarter of a century he enjoyed the reputation of being the greatest theorist and teacher of counterpoint and harmony. Those who knew him personally learnt to appreciate his singular courtesy, independence, and moral worth, and the kindly humour of the man reveals itself in his letters.'—*Graphic.*

'Mr. Coleridge has done good service by this judicious selection of the familiar, but always critical, letters of Moritz Hauptmann, and he has translated them in a manner which brings out the charm of the original.'—*Standard.*

By THE LATE MR. BEALE.

THE LIGHT OF OTHER DAYS: Musical Reminiscences of Half a Century.

By WILLERT BEALE (formerly of Cramer and Co.), 2 vols., demy 8vo., with portrait, 28s.

> 'Mr. Willert Beale has in his Reminiscences given us a greater romance of real life than will be found in twenty volumes of novels by the most eminent authors. Yet all so naturally and so simply told.'—*The Baron de Bookworms in 'Punch.'*

By THE LATE MISS WALKER.

MY MUSICAL EXPERIENCES.

By BETTINA WALKER. With Reminiscences of Sir Sterndale Bennett, Tausig, Sgambati, Liszt, Deppe, Scharwencka, and Henselt. One vol., crown 8vo., 6s.

> 'A book which will delight students of the piano. They will revel in the details given of the "little ways" of various "masters" named. Miss Walker writes very frankly and ingenuously, and those who have ever engaged in the same sort of study will follow her narrative with abounding interest.'—*Globe.*

By MR. ROWBOTHAM.

THE HISTORY OF MUSIC.

A New Edition, by J. F. ROWBOTHAM. One vol., crown 8vo., 7s. 6d.

> 'Mr. Rowbotham's work appears interesting, not only to all lovers of music—the most popular of the arts—but to every student of human history and progress. The book deserves to be earnestly recommended to all who care for that entrancing study—the study of human evolution of man slowly opening from the bud into the blossom of civilization.'—*Daily News.*

LONDON

RICHARD BENTLEY & SON, NEW BURLINGTON STREET

Publishers in Ordinary to Her Majesty the Queen

AND AT ALL LIBRARIES AND BOOKSELLERS'.

www.ingramcontent.com/pod-product-compliance
Lightning Source LLC
Chambersburg PA
CBHW051517100726

47898CB00005B/1489